GRACE AND JUDGMENT

Based on the
Basic Bible Studies Course
Series 2

By
Roger D.G. Price

"Let the word of Christ dwell in you richly"
(Colossians 3:16a)

ISBN 0 9527633 1 1

Published by Chichester Christian Fellowship Tapes (CCF Tapes)
Registered Charity No. 276242

Further copies of this book can be obtained from:
CCF Tapes, 30 Crescent Road, Bognor Regis,
West Sussex, PO21 1QG (England)
Tel/Fax: 01243 862621; Email: sales@ccftapes.co.uk

A full list of Bible studies by Roger Price on audio cassette is given at the back of this book (available from the same address).

Unless otherwise stated, Scripture quotations are from:

The Holy Bible—New King James Version (British usage text), first published as the Revised Authorized Version (RAV) by Samuel Bagster and Sons Ltd., London, in 1982. Copyright subsequently reverted to Thomas Nelson, Inc., USA.
New Testament & Psalms ©Thomas Nelson, Inc., 1979, 1980.
Old and New Testament complete ©Thomas Nelson, Inc., 1982.

The following versions are also quoted occasionally where indicated:

The Authorized Version (AV), also known as the King James Version.

New American Standard Bible (NASB), Copyright ©The Lockman Foundation, USA, 1960, 1962, 1963, 1968, 1971, 1975, 1977.

Written by Alan Manchester, based on tapes by Roger D.G. Price
(Basic Bible Studies 15-28 of the Basic Bible Studies course).

Page make-up assisted by Paul Shearing, Software Development Services, Caterham, UK.

Cover make-up assisted by Mike Levett and Neill Blume.
Cover picture from a painting by Nigel Purchase.

Printed in England by Stanley L. Hunt (Printers) Ltd., Rushden.

Copyright of this edited version only, but not any original tapes or other source materials ©Alan D. Manchester, 1999.

All rights reserved. No part of this publication may be reproduced, stored in a retrieval system or transmitted, in any form or by any means, electronic, mechanical, photocopying or otherwise, without the prior permission of the publisher or editor.

Introductory Verses

Jesus said:
"Most assuredly, I say to you, he who hears My word and believes in Him who sent Me has everlasting life, and shall not come into judgment, but has passed from death into life."
(John 5:24)

The apostle Paul said to the religious men of Athens:
"We ought not to think that the divine nature is like gold or silver or stone, something shaped by art and man's devising. Truly, these times of ignorance God overlooked, but now He commands all men everywhere to repent, because He has appointed a day on which He will judge the world in righteousness by the Man whom He has ordained. He has given assurance of this to all, by raising Him from the dead."
(Acts 17:29b-31)

"And as it is appointed for men to die once, but after this the judgment, so Christ was offered once to bear the sins of many. To those who eagerly wait for Him He will appear a second time, apart from sin, for salvation."
(Hebrews 9:27-28)

Acknowledgments

Roger Price read widely and drew from a number sources for these studies. He gave no detailed bibliography for his tapes, on the basis that it would have to be extremely long and that truth ultimately belongs to and originates from God Himself. However, a short bibliography is given at the back of this book which names works referred to regularly during the compilation of this book, or from which information has been drawn, for inclusion in the footnotes in particular.

A number of people helped in the production of this book in various ways. The contributors all share a high regard for Roger Price's teaching and the conviction that its publication in written form will be of benefit to the Church as a whole. The following helped with research or proof-reading, made useful suggestions, or assisted with the cover: Martin Emerson, Ros Price, Malcolm Coulson, Zul Kahan, Nigel Purchase, Mike Levett, Neill Blume.

Paul Shearing assisted with page design and software configuration to enable the production of pages to be completed successfully.

Alan Manchester (Compiler and Editor)

CONTENTS — MAIN CHAPTER HEADINGS

INTRODUCTORY VERSES	I
ACKNOWLEDGMENTS	II
TABLE OF CONTENTS—IN DETAIL	V
NOTES ON STYLE	X
PREFACE	XI
SYNOPSIS OF THE BOOK	XIII
OPENING REMARKS BY ROGER PRICE —*THE UNCHANGING WORD OF GOD*	XV

INTRODUCTION: GRACE AND JUDGMENT

1. JESUS IS THE JUDGE — BBS 15&16 — 1
2. GRACE BEFORE JUDGMENT — BBS 15 — 17

GRACE BEFORE JUDGMENT ILLUSTRATED

3. THE AGE OF METHUSELAH — BBS 16 — 27
    —*GRACE BEFORE JUDGMENT SEEN AT THE FLOOD*
4. JAMES & JOHN, AND JONAH — BBS 17 — 41
    —*HOW GOD TAUGHT LESSONS ABOUT GRACE*

THE JUDGMENT OF SATAN

5. THE THREE FALLS OF SATAN — BBS 18 — 61

THE JUDGMENT OF JESUS

6. CROOKED COUNSEL — BBS 19 — 81
    —*THE UNJUST, IRREGULAR AND ILLEGAL JUDGMENT OF JESUS BY MEN AND SATAN*
7. WHEN CALVARY BLOSSOMED — BBS 20 — 101
    —*THE RIGHTEOUS JUDGMENT OF JESUS IN OUR PLACE BY GOD*

THE JUDGMENT OF BELIEVERS

8. SELF-JUDGMENT OR CHASTENING? — BBS 21 — 117
    —*THE IMPORTANCE OF SELF-JUDGMENT FOR THE BELIEVER*
9. REASONS FOR DISCIPLINE — BBS 22 — 133
    —*CHASTENING: GOD'S JUDGMENT OF SIN IN HIS CHILDREN*

THE JUDGMENT OF BELIEVERS' WORKS

10. PALACES OR MUD-HUTS? — BBS 23 — 151
    —*THE JUDGMENT OF BELIEVERS' WORKS*

THE JUDGMENT OF ISRAEL AND THE NATIONS

11. THE FIVE CYCLES OF DISCIPLINE — BBS 24 — 167
    —*GOD'S CHASTENING OF ISRAEL*
12. THE HORNS AND HORN-CUTTERS — BBS 25 — 189
    —*THE JUDGMENT OF NATIONS*
13. THE BAPTISM WITH FIRE — BBS 26 — 209
    —*THE JUDGMENT OF ISRAEL AT THE SECOND COMING OF CHRIST (BACKGROUND)*

14. THE WISE AND FOOLISH VIRGINS   BBS 27   227
  —*THE JUDGMENT OF ISRAEL AT THE SECOND COMING OF CHRIST*

THE JUDGMENT OF UNBELIEVERS

15. THE GREAT WHITE THRONE   BBS 28   243
  —*THE JUDGMENT OF UNBELIEVERS*

APPENDIX: EXAMPLES OF VISIBLE DEMONSTRATIONS
THAT GOD USED IN THE OLD TESTAMENT   261

BIBLIOGRAPHY   265

OTHER BOOKS BY ROGER PRICE (IN PRINT)   266

BIBLE STUDY TAPES BY ROGER PRICE   267

TABLE OF CONTENTS — IN DETAIL

1. JESUS IS THE JUDGE — 1
JESUS IS THE JUDGE—John chapter 5...1
   Jesus claims to be God 2
   The Love within the Godhead 3
   Jesus Christ is the One appointed to Judge 5
      1. Equal Honour...6
         The Inconsistency of the religious Jews 6
      2. Jesus is the only Mediator between God and Man............................8
         What is a Mediator? 9
   Conclusion: Jesus will Judge Righteously 11
      Other implications of Jesus identifying Himself with us 13
         Jesus the Lamb and the Shepherd 13
         Jesus our compassionate High Priest 14
         The Throne of Grace 14

2. GRACE BEFORE JUDGMENT — 17
   Judgment is alien to God..17
   Nations must not take God's grace for granted 18
   Examples of Grace before Judgment in the Bible 19
      Adam and Eve 20
      The Flood 21
      Sodom and Gomorrah..21
   The Cross: the greatest grace 26

3. THE AGE OF METHUSELAH — 27
GRACE BEFORE JUDGMENT AT THE FLOOD...27
The Reasons for the Flood..28
   1. The Building of the Ark 29
   2. Noah himself was a sign..31
   3. Methuselah was a sign...35
      The Sign of the Rainbow 37
Grace before the Coming Judgment..37
   Noah's Ark: a Picture of Christ 38
   Conclusion 39

4. JAMES & JOHN, AND JONAH — 41
JAMES & JOHN: Transformed by God's grace..41
   The Prophets 45
JONAH: Wonderful Lessons about Grace...46
   Jonah chapter 1 47
   Jonah chapter 2 51
   Jonah chapter 3 53
   Jonah chapter 4 56
   The Object Lesson...58
   Lessons for Us...60

v

5. THE THREE FALLS OF SATAN — 61

- Understanding our Enemy — 61
  - The Names of Satan — 62
  - The Character of Satan — 63
  - The First Fall of Satan: the Sin of Lucifer — 64
    - Isaiah chapter 14: The five "I wills" of Satan — 66
      1. "I will ascend into heaven" — 66
      2. "I will exalt my throne above the stars of God" — 68
      3. "I will also sit on the mount of the congregation, on the farthest sides of the north" — 69
      4. "I will ascend above the heights of the clouds" — 70
      5. "I will be like the Most High" — 71
    - God's Judgment on Lucifer — 72
  - Satan's Second Fall: his fall from heaven — 73
  - Satan's Third Fall: into the lake of fire forever — 75
  - Timetable of Future Events — 75
  - Ezekiel chapter 28 — 76
  - Conclusion — 79

6. CROOKED COUNSEL — 81

- Those Responsible for the Judgment of Jesus — 81
- Jesus was Sinless throughout His Whole Life—including on the Cross — 84
- The Irregular and Illegal Trials of Jesus — 85
  1. The first two trials were held at night — 85
  2. The sentence should not have been passed on the same day that evidence was given in the trial — 86
  3. The court was biased: the judges acted as the prosecution and extracted false testimony — 86
  4. No one argued on behalf of Jesus — 87
  5. All the witnesses were false — 88
  6. There was violence in the courtroom — 88
  - The Thirty Pieces of Silver — 88
- The Trial before Caiaphas — 89
- Jesus' Final Trial before Pontius Pilate — 95
- Conclusion — 100

7. WHEN CALVARY BLOSSOMED — 101

- Jesus had to Die by Crucifixion — 101
- The 'miracle' of Jesus reaching the Cross — 102
  - The role of Simon of Cyrene — 103
- How God was Responsible for the Judgment of Jesus on the Cross — 105
  - The Son of God's role — 105
  - The Father in heaven's role — 107
  - The Holy Spirit's role — 108
  - God willed it — 108
- The Uniqueness of the Cross of Christ — 109
- The Timetable of the Cross — 109
  - Jesus became the Sin Offering for us All — 111
  - "It is finished!" — 113
  - The Centurion by the Cross — 114

Sin has been Paid for Once and for all... 115
When Calvary Blossomed 116

8. SELF-JUDGMENT OR CHASTENING? — 117

Kindred Relationship... 117
Fellowship with God our Father... 118
Fellowship needs Continual Refreshing.. 119
No judgment for believers in relation to the kindred relationship 122
Judgment in Relation to our Fellowship with God 123
The Importance of Self-Judgment 123
The need to Confess our Sins to God 124
The Purpose of Chastening by the Father.. 126
Chastening is a Family Matter—Zechariah chapter 3 127
God gives Grace, then Disciplines Appropriately 130
The Corinthians' Sin.. 130
Conclusions 131

9. REASONS FOR DISCIPLINE — 133

The Importance of Confessing Sin 133
Beware of the Deceitfulness of our own Hearts 134
The Sins of the Corinthians 136
The Scriptures Teach us to Recognize and Avoid Sins 138
GOD'S DISCIPLINE—Hebrews chapter 12..141
Lay aside Weights and Sin 141
Looking unto Jesus 143
God Chastens His Sons... 144
The Corinthians got back into Fellowship with God 147
Conclusion.. 149

10 PALACES OR MUD-HUTS? — 151

The Believer: Sinner, Son and Servant... 151
  1. The Believer as a Sinner 151
  2. The Believer as a Son.. 152
  3. The Believer as a Servant... 152
THE JUDGMENT OF BELIEVERS' WORKS..153
The Parable of the Sower... 153
What determines the Quality of our Works?... 154
When is this Judgment of our Works?.. 155
Judgment at the 'Bema' seat of Christ 157
Palaces or Mud-Huts? (1 Corinthians 3:11-16) 158
How to Produce Enduring Works 162
The Matter of Rewards 163
Conclusion.. 165

11. THE FIVE CYCLES OF DISCIPLINE — 167

The Uniqueness of Israel 167
THE FIVE CYCLES OF DISCIPLINE...169
Blessings and Judgments: Leviticus chapter 26 170
  The First Cycle of Discipline.. 172
  The Second Cycle of Discipline... 173

VII

    The Third Cycle of Discipline 173
    The Fourth Cycle of Discipline 174
    The Fifth Cycle of Discipline 175
 Grace is always available 176
 The Fourth and Fifth Cycles in Deuteronomy 177
 Examples from Israel's History 181
    1. Israel taken away by the Assyrians (c. 721 BC) 181
    2. The Assyrians withdraw from Jerusalem at the time of
       Hezekiah (c. 701 BC) 182
    3. Judah taken away to Babylon by Nebuchadnezzar (c. 606 to 586 BC) 184
    4. Worldwide Dispersion after AD 135 186
 Lessons for the Gentiles 187

12. HORNS AND CRAFTSMEN   189

 The Importance of Blessing Israel 189
THE HORNS AND THE CRAFTSMEN 190
 The meaning of Horns 191
THE FOUR HORNS 192
    1. The First Horn: the Assyrian Empire (c. 750 BC to 612 BC) 193
    2. The Second Horn: the Babylonian Empire (c. 612 BC to 539 BC) 194
    3. The Third Horn: the Greek Empire (c. 331 BC to 146 BC) 195
    4. The Fourth Horn: the Romans (2nd Century BC to AD 476) 196
    God's Judgment on the Four Horns 197
THE FOUR CRAFTSMEN 197
    1. The First Horn-cutter: Babylon (Nabopolassar the Chaldean) 198
    2. The Second Horn-cutter: Medo-Persia (Cyrus the Great) 200
       Belshazzar's Feast 201
    3. The Third Horn-cutter: The Romans 205
    4. The Fourth Horn-cutter: Barbarian Tribes (the chieftain Odoacer) 206
 Lessons we should learn 207

13. THE BAPTISM WITH FIRE   209

 The Mystery of the Church 209
 Jesus came Principally to Israel 214
 God's Timetable of History 216
 Rightly Dividing the Word of God: What the Baptism of Fire is not 217
The Baptism with Fire 218
 Examples of the Baptism with Fire in the Old Testament 219
    Ezekiel 20:33-38 219
    Zechariah 13:8-9 220
    Malachi 3:2-6 221
 After the Baptism with Fire 222
 The Parallel of Pentecost 222
 John the Baptist's Message 223
 Jesus referred to the Parallel Event in the Church 226

14. THE WISE AND FOOLISH VIRGINS   227

 How to Interpret a Parable 227
 The Picture of Christ and the Church as a Bridegroom and Bride 229
 The future Wedding and Wedding Feast of Christ and the Church 230

    The Context of the Parable 232
    The Format of a Wedding 235
    The Characters involved in the Parable 236
    The Parable of the Ten Virgins (Matthew 25:1-13) 237
    Conclusion 241

15. THE GREAT WHITE THRONE   243

    All will be Resurrected: Believers *and* Unbelievers 245
    The Timing of the Two Resurrections 247
    "Each one in his own order" 248
        A Company 248
        B Company 248
        C Company 249
        D Company 249
    Death is Finally Defeated 250
    The Events described in the Book of Revelation 251
    The Millennium (Revelation 20:1-6) 252
        The First Resurrection 253
    Satan is Loosed at the End of the Millennium (Revelation 20:7-10) 254
    Final Judgment at the Great White Throne (Revelation 20:11-15) 254
        The Second Resurrection 255
    Conclusion: the Urgency of Trusting in Christ 258

APPENDIX: EXAMPLES OF VISIBLE DEMONSTRATIONS THAT GOD USED IN THE OLD TESTAMENT   261

        1. Zechariah 261
        2. Ezekiel 261
        3. Jeremiah and Hananiah 262
        4. Jeremiah and Seraiah 263

BIBLIOGRAPHY   265

OTHER BOOKS BY ROGER PRICE (IN PRINT)   266

BIBLE STUDY TAPES BY ROGER PRICE   267

NOTES ON STYLE

This book was first compiled using transcripts of the audio tapes of Basic Bible Studies 15 to 28. The resulting text was then edited extensively, with much research being carried out to verify the material.

Footnotes are indicated by superior numbers in the text. Some contain information on the tapes that constitutes a diversion from the main logic. Others have been included to help clarify a point, to explain terminology or to provide additional information or cross-references.

The Appendix, containing information from BBS 16, provides additional examples as background to Chapter 3.

Roger Price used the Authorized (King James) Version of the Bible (AV) in all his studies. Scripture quotations in this book are from the British usage edition of the New King James Version (NKJV), formerly published as the Revised Authorized Version. This modern version is based on the AV and is closest to it. The translators of both used the Greek Received Text (*Textus Receptus*) for the New Testament. The AV is sometimes quoted or given as a helpful alternative rendering. The New American Standard Bible (NASB) is also quoted occasionally.

All Scripture quotations are shown in bold type. Lower case letters have very occasionally been changed to upper case, or vice-versa, to fit in with the sentence structure in this book. Quotations have sometimes been slightly extended or shortened compared with the tapes. Square brackets are used around a name, phrase or alternative translation when it has been inserted to make a biblical quotation more easily understood. Italics and special layout of poetic passages have been omitted in biblical quotations. In some places where a verse was quoted or alluded to on the tapes, but the Bible reference was not given, the reference has been included. Many additional Scripture references are also given.

Throughout the text and within biblical quotations, personal pronouns and nouns have been capitalized when they refer to God, as in the NKJV. The personal covenant Name of God in the Old Testament, YHWH (which is sometimes transliterated as 'Yahweh' or 'Jehovah' with added vowels) is rendered as LORD or GOD.

PREFACE

Roger Price was a gifted Bible teacher, who dedicated his life to being a channel for discovering and communicating the truths and principles of the Word of God. He died in January 1987, aged 39. During his ministry, he travelled widely, teaching and encouraging God's people to love the Lord and to study the Word of God for themselves. He inspired many by his own enthusastic love for the Lord and for His Word.

Between 1974 and 1986 he recorded approximately 280 Bible studies on audio cassette tape, in the context of providing teaching for his own local church fellowship and for those he visited during the course of his ministry. These comprised a course of 100 Basic Bible Studies, about 150 Special Topic Studies, studies relating to church life and instruction for local church elders, etc. He always maintained that the teaching of the principles of God's Word provided a 'springboard' for people to search out more truth for themselves. It was his desire that the Basic Bible Studies course should be made available in written form so that the material might become more accessible.

The first book, "Salvation", covering Series 1 in the Basic Bible Studies course (BBS 1 to 14) was published in 1996.

Most of the chapters in this second book represent one of the 14 studies in Series 2 of the course (tapes BBS 15 to 28). However, BBS 15 and 16 have been split and reordered slightly to form the first three chapters in this book, since introductory material was contained in both. The first chapter in this book is therefore designated BBS 15&16.

The studies are called "Basic", not because they deal with topics superficially or require no thought or effort, but rather because they cover topics which are *foundational* and which are essential for Christians to understand. The truths and principles covered in this book are foundational for a sound and balanced understanding of God's grace and His judgments, and provide a firm basis for further study of the Scriptures.

This book has been produced to provide a useful reference for those already familiar with the tapes, as well as to make the teaching available to a wider audience, both in English and through translation. It is envisaged that further volumes might be produced to cover all the material in the course.

These studies were recorded early in Roger's ministry, in 1975-76. It has been necessary to modify or update some of the material by making minor additions and amendments. The purpose of any changes has been to eliminate any ambiguity or inaccuracies, to make this book consistent with Roger's later, more detailed teaching on certain subjects, and to improve clarity. Extra information has been included in a few places, some material has been reordered to complete the logic, and repetition has been avoided where possible.

It is the purpose of these studies, now in written form, to provide a clear understanding of how God's wonderful grace always precedes His righteous judgments. The aim of those involved in the production of this volume has been faithfully to represent Roger's teaching, and his gift of communicating the truth with liveliness and clarity.

SYNOPSIS OF THE BOOK

This book provides an overview of the subject of Judgment, as well as an examination of major instances of God's judgments throughout the Bible. It quickly becomes clear that God is actively involved in the affairs of this world as a merciful and gracious Judge. He is intimately involved in the affairs of Israel, His chosen people, as well as in the nations of this world. As a Father, He disciplines those He loves, so He chastens and draws to Himself both Israel and Christian believers, for their good.

In the early chapters, two key principles are given. The first is that Jesus is the One appointed as Judge of all—because the Father wants His Son to have equal honour with Himself, and because Jesus is the only Mediator between God and man. The second principle, which can be seen throughout the whole Bible, is that God always gives grace and offers opportunity to repent before sending judgment. The greatest example of this Grace before Judgment principle yet seen took place at the Flood.

To bring the subject down to a personal level, the lives of James & John, and the prophet Jonah, are examined in Chapter 4. They illustrate how God has always patiently taught and disciplined His individual children, so that they might come to understand His merciful and gracious nature.

In Chapter 5, the history of Satan is traced throughout the Bible to show that God's enemy, who is also our enemy, has been under the progressive judgment of God ever since he led a 'universe-shattering' rebellion against God. Despite being a beautiful and mighty creature who beheld the glory of the Lord, he chose to challenge the very authority of God. His sentence has been pronounced and his judgment is now being worked out. The days are numbered before he will be chained up for 1000 years and finally cast into the lake of fire prepared for him and his angels.

Chapters 6 and 7 are pivotal, since they focus on the Cross of Jesus Christ, the central event of history. This judgment of the Son of God is discussed in the light of those who caused it. It is shown that, although Satan and men, including us, were responsible for Christ's unjust suffering, God's righteous judgment of His Son in our place had been planned from the foundation of the world. The death and resurrection of Jesus was in fact the greatest victory ever. It was a complete triumph over Satan, and Christ purchased, once and for all time, forgiveness, freedom and exclusion from future judgment for all that will believe in Him.

Aspects of judgment in the lives of believers are then discussed in Chapters 8 to 10. Although we have been judged for our sins in the past, in Christ, we are still chastened by the Lord as His beloved children. This is because He requires holiness in our lives now and has predestined us to be conformed to the image of His Son. We have the privilege of being able to serve the Lord—to build on the foundation that God has laid, namely Christ, through our works. The choice of building materials that we use is up to us, but we should remember that, one day, all our works will be judged. By God's grace we have the opportunity to receive rewards for our works and to play a part in how Christ's glorious bride, the Church, will be adorned.

In Chapters 11 to 14, the scope is broadened to look at national and international judgments. Understanding the significance of Israel is a key to understanding history and the Bible; therefore how God disciplines His beloved people, the Jews, is outlined first. God has always graciously chastened them, according to "Five Cycles of Discipline". God's discipline has at times been very severe, but the Jews have always been given warnings and opportunities to repent.

How nations treat Israel plays a major part in determining their own destiny, as prophets such as Daniel, Jeremiah and Isaiah understood. Therefore, the history of world empires that have affected the Jews is discussed in Chapter 12, in the light of Zechariah's famous prophecy of the horns and craftsmen. The remarkable end and disappearance of the greatest empires that this world has ever seen are summarized from biblical and world history.

Jesus Christ will come again to implement the final stages of God's judgment on this world. The fact that He will return to Israel as a Bridegroom with His bride is a challenge to be ready, both for those in the Church, but in particular for Israel. In discussing these events, important principles of biblical exposition are established, that enable some 'difficult' prophetic passages to be understood. Terms such as the Kingdom and the Baptism with Fire become clear, illustrating that some popular teachings in the Church are not strictly biblical. This background facilitates an exposition of the Parable of the Ten Virgins—a story Jesus told to lay alongside truths about His Second Coming.

The final chapter, Chapter 15, describes the Last Judgment, before God's great white throne. First, the fact that every single person will be resurrected, resulting in a complete defeat of death, is emphasized. The culmination of human history after the Second Coming is then surveyed, giving a panorama of the various resurrections, the Millennial Kingdom, Satan's final rebellion and the final judgment of unbelievers. This judgment day should hold no fear for Christians, but its reality should spur us on in our role as ambassadors of Christ. The urgency for unbelievers to trust in Christ is plain, since eternal resurrection makes the destiny of believers so glorious, yet the destiny of unbelievers so horrific.

OPENING REMARKS by Roger Price —THE UNCHANGING WORD OF GOD

I once heard the radio commentator Brian Redhead say that, in these days, it is a brave man indeed who speaks seriously about Sin, about Heaven and Hell, or about Judgment. It used to be quite acceptable to talk about these things, but our society has changed. The Word of God, however, has not changed and is still talking about them today. Therefore, whether the world accepts these things or not, we need to take note of them, because they are revealed in the Word of truth.

1 Peter 1:23 talks about the permanence of God's Word: "**[You have] been born again, not of corruptible seed but incorruptible, through the word of God which lives and abides forever.**" Long after all of today's radio commentators have disappeared, and long after radio itself may have been replaced, the Word of God will still be thundering out the same truth, and there will be people like myself thundering out exactly the same truth!

I love the Word of God. I was so challenged when I read in *National Geographic* magazine about an orthodox Jewish teacher who was so thrilled with the first five books of the Bible that he danced for joy. He hugged the Book; and in front of hundreds of people he rejoiced and had tears streaming down his cheeks. I found it so challenging, and had to ask, "Lord, why don't I love your fuller Word as much as that?"

The Law came through Moses; and Moses' face glowed when he received the Law of God. But what came through Jesus Christ? "**Grace and truth came through Jesus Christ**" (John 1:17). This should be enough to set our feet dancing, as we're filled with love for the Lord and rejoice in His Word.

Jeremiah knew such a joy, didn't he? After Hilkiah the high priest had found the Book of the Law during the reign of King Josiah (2 Chronicles 34:14), Jeremiah recalled, "**Your words were found, and I ate them...**" (Jeremiah 15:16a). God's words were good enough to eat! "**And Your word was to me the joy and rejoicing of my heart**" (verse 16b). I imagine that Jeremiah danced round his home, wherever he lived! He began dancing for joy just because a dusty old scroll had been discovered in the Temple!

It is the same Word that we have today, and more, which so thrilled Jeremiah. And if Jeremiah was here today, I believe he'd still be dancing for joy, because he'd be so thrilled with the complete Word of God.

Thus it is with joy and rejoicing that we can come to consider the subject of Judgment—because it is truth revealed in the Word of God. It is a serious and fearsome subject. But gone should be the sober faces, because there is good news. There is judgment indeed, but there is mercy and grace with it. Praise the name of Jesus!

Roger Price

(from his introductory talk given at the start of BBS 15)

1. JESUS IS THE JUDGE

In this book we will discover some important truths about judgment—and specifically God's judgment. We begin, in the first two chapters, by looking at two fundamental principles. The first is that Jesus Christ is the One appointed as Judge. The second is the principle of Grace before Judgment.

JESUS IS THE JUDGE—JOHN CHAPTER 5

John chapter 5 recounts a conversation between Jesus and a group of religious unbelieving Jews in Jerusalem. Before we look at it in detail, however, I want to point out something: in our Bible translations, different words are often used to translate the same Greek or Hebrew word; and this can sometimes be misleading.

If we consider the three English words 'judgment', 'condemnation' and 'damnation', for example, most people would say that damnation is the worst. If we consider which is the least serious of the three, most of us would probably say condemnation, and judgment would be put in the middle. However, this is unfortunate because, in the New Testament, these three English words are usually all translations of the same Greek word, *krisis*! The word *krisis* actually means 'separation', and judgment is usually the best translation. It is therefore helpful, whenever you see the word "condemnation", to remember that it means 'judgment' and, every time you read the word "damnation", also to substitute 'judgment'.

In John chapter 5 the Greek word *krisis* appears five times (in verses 22, 24, 27, 29 and 30). In verse 22 Jesus said, **"For the Father judges no one, but has committed all judgment to the Son"**. Here *krisis* is translated as "judgment". In verse 24 Jesus said, **"Verily, verily, I say unto you, he that heareth My word, and believeth on Him that sent Me, hath everlasting life, and shall not come into condemnation..."**, using the AV, with *krisis* being translated as "condemnation". However, it could have been rendered 'judgment', as it is in the NKJV. In verse 29: **"...And shall come forth; they that have done good, unto the resurrection of life;**

and they that have done evil, unto the resurrection of damnation", *krisis* has been translated "damnation" in the AV, whilst the NKJV translates it as "condemnation". It is the same Greek word *krisis*, meaning judgment, in each case.[1]

JESUS CLAIMS TO BE GOD

In John 5:17 we find Jesus answering the religious Jews, who were persecuting Him and seeking to kill Him. They objected to Him healing a man on the Sabbath day and to His claims about who He was: **"But Jesus answered them, "My Father has been working until now, and I have been working." Therefore the Jews sought all the more to kill Him, because He not only broke the Sabbath, but also said that God was His Father, making Himself equal with God"** (verses 17-18).

Whether or not the Jehovah's Witnesses, the Mormons or any other sect admits it, Jesus *was* claiming to be divine. Clearly, these Jews understood Him perfectly, just as we should. He was claiming equality with God, His Father in heaven (whose name the Jews read out as "Adonai").[2] He was revealing His unique relationship with the Father, saying, "God is My Father. I do the same works that My Father—God Himself—is doing. Therefore, I am equal with God."

---

[1] *Krisis* literally means a 'separation' or 'discrimination'. It involves deciding, determining or judging. It can have degrees of meaning, depending on the context. In addition to the three translations used in John chapter 5 (AV), *krisis* is translated "accusation" in 2 Peter 2:11 and Jude 9. It could also mean 'vindication' in certain contexts.

[2] The personal name of God, which God revealed to Moses (Exodus 3:13-15; 34:5-7), consisted of the four Hebrew consonants which transliterate as YHWH. It is thus often called the "Tetragrammaton", meaning 'four-letter writing'. God commanded that His name should not be taken in vain (Exodus 20:7). However, the Jews gradually avoided using God's personal name at all, out of a sense of religious awe, and the correct pronunciation became lost to the people. By the time of Christ, no one ever spoke the name—except the High Priest when he entered the Holy of Holies on the Day of Atonement. When the Masoretes wrote down the vowel points for reading the Old Testament (the Hebrew Bible), they deliberately did not include the vowels for pronouncing YHWH. Instead, they always inserted the vowel points for "Adonai" under the four letters, because this was a term for God (meaning 'my/the Lord') found frequently in the Old Testament. The Jews had developed the habit of saying "Adonai" whenever they read YHWH in the Scriptures, as they still do today. Other euphemisms used by the religious Jews were "The Power" or "The Name" (Ha-Shem). The English 'Yahweh' and 'Jehovah' are representations of the name YHWH using the vowel sounds of Adonai. However, there is no reason to assume that either is the correct pronunciation of God's name. God's name is not a proper name in the conventional sense, but it evokes His immediate presence. It is derived from the verb 'to be' and implies "I am ever present". In Exodus 3:14, where God revealed His name in a verbal form to Moses, it could be translated "I am who I am" or "I will be who I will be" or, in other words, "I will be there howsoever I will be there".

JESUS IS THE JUDGE

The religious Jews hated it! They were so proud. "We are the only people who serve the living God, the one true God, the God of Israel," they thought. But here was Jesus, an itinerant teacher from Galilee, coming along and saying, "Yes, Adonai is the one true God; but I am equal with Him!" And they loathed Him for it.[3]

"Then Jesus answered and said to them, "Most assuredly, I say to you, the Son can do nothing of Himself, but what He sees the Father do..."' (verse 19a). This would have infuriated the Jews even more. The Scriptures said that no man could see God and live (Exodus 33:20, for example), yet Jesus was saying, "Not only do I do the works of God, My Father, but I do them because I see Him working. And what I see Him do, that's what I do." For the religious Jews this was contemptible. They simply could not accept what Jesus was saying. Nevertheless, it was true. Whatever Jesus saw His Father do, that was what He also did: **"...for whatever He** [the Father] **does, the Son also does in like manner"** (verse 19b).

THE LOVE WITHIN THE GODHEAD

Jesus' next statement introduces another wonderful topic: **"For the Father loves the Son, and shows Him all things that He Himself does..."** (John 5:20a). Has it ever struck you fully what the first phrase here means? It reveals to us how the Father and the Son are in a relationship based on love. They are overflowing with love for one another. They are 'burning' with an all-consuming love for one another. They just love and love and love.

I believe Jesus was consumed with love for His Father as He walked on the earth. He truly loved His Father—just as His Father loved Him. It must have been the most heart-rending day when the Son of God had to 'pack His bags', leave the glory of heaven, and come down to the earth. What must that have done to His Father's loving heart? The Father must have said, "I love You, Jesus, I love You so much! I'm sending You, but I can't bear for You to leave. I'm going to be with You every step of the way." (I have to speak in human terms since this is a mystery.) Jesus must have

---

[3] There are many passages in the Bible which show clearly that Jesus Christ is and always has been God (for example: Matthew 28:20; John 1:1, 14; 8:56, 59; 10:30; 18:1ff; Romans 9:5; Philippians 2:5; Colossians 1:15-19; 2:9; 1 Timothy 3:16; Titus 2:13; Hebrews 1:2-3, 8; 13:8). Many descriptions of God used in the Old Testament are also used of Jesus, particularly in the Book of Revelation. Jesus' divinity was particularly affirmed at His baptism and transfiguration in the gospels. Jesus also clearly accepted people's worship. Further details of the Bible's teaching on the divinity of Jesus Christ are given in Basic Bible Study 68, entitled "The Trinity (Part 3)".

said, "Father, I understand that it's necessary. I love You so much as well, Father, and I want to do Your will. The people of the world, whom We love so much, need Me to go to them; so I've got to go!" And the Father said, "Holy Spirit, go and be with Him. Be with Him always!" (see John 7:29; 8:29).

The Holy Spirit also loves the Father; the Father loves the Holy Spirit; the Son loves the Holy Spirit; and the Holy Spirit loves the Son. Jesus, the Son of God, loves the Father; and the Father loves Jesus. They all love one another fervently. What a truth this is! I believe that a revelation of this truth alone is enough to set the children of God free. We have three wonderful Lovers over us, who are consumed with the love they have for one another. Oh, hallelujah!

It is no wonder they are "three-in-one" and "one-in-three". Where there is love like that, how could three ever be separated? They act as one. They *are* one (John 17:22). They have the same nature, the same character and the same love for one another. They are in unity. They live for one another. They submit to one another. They prefer one another. Why?—Because they *love* one another.

Have you ever noticed how Jesus always wanted to glorify His Father? He rejoiced whenever His Father was glorified (John 17:1-4 and Luke 10:21, for example). The Holy Spirit, who was sent to testify of Jesus (John 15:26) and glorify Jesus (John 16:14), is likewise thrilled whenever Jesus or the Father is glorified. The Father is similarly thrilled whenever people recognize and honour His Son. They simply love one another. Praise God's wonderful name![4]

I would suggest that if they love one another so much and they love us so much, then we should love one another. I don't know of any other way we can live the Christian life. Our lives are supposed to be a walk of love (Ephesians 5:2): loving God and loving others—submitting to one another, preferring one another, rejoicing when others are blessed. I cannot see any other way; we have to be motivated by love.

Some Christians say, "It's so hard to love!" But how can it be hard if the Holy Spirit, who is a deeply involved Lover, is inside us? **"God has sent forth the Spirit of His Son into [our] hearts, crying out, "Abba,**

---

[4]Further details of how the Father, Son and Holy Spirit interrelate are given in Basic Bible Study 66, "The Trinity (Part 1)". The Father says, "This is My Beloved Son" and sends the Holy Spirit to do His work on earth. The Son says, "Father, glorify Yourself" and He did all His works on earth by the power of the Holy Spirit. The Holy Spirit speaks of Jesus Christ, the Son, and reveals the Father's plan.

Father!'" (Galatians 4:6). The Holy Spirit loves and yearns for the Father and the Son. He yearns to glorify the Father and the Son in me. It therefore is not difficult to love one another; it is not difficult to love God. The thing that is hard is to deny ourselves and live according to the Holy Spirit (Romans 8:5). However, God is able to help us. When we come into a revelation of *His* love, *then* we will begin to love one another. *Then* we will begin to prefer one another, submit to one another and rejoice when another brother or sister is exalted—even if he or she has just snubbed us.

The Holy Spirit dwells in us now and He teaches us how to love (1 Thessalonians 4:9). There is not one Christian who can say, "I can't love!" He can do it in you—*He* can. God's love is the *fruit of the Holy Spirit* in us. Therefore, allow the Holy Spirit to move in your life; and then love, joy, peace, long-suffering, kindness, goodness, faithfulness, gentleness, self-control—all of these things—will come pouring out (Galatians 5:22-23). Then it will not be you striving. All you will have done is presented yourself to God (Romans 6:13, 16) and said, "Father, I lay myself on the altar. Take me, Lord. I don't want *me* to show. I want *You* to show! I want Christ to live through me. I want the fruit of the Holy Spirit to be produced in me." Suddenly people will say, "What's happened to him? He's had a baptism of love!" We all need a 'baptism' with the love of God.

When the love of God starts flowing between believers, suddenly the Body of Christ starts functioning and growing (Ephesians 4:16). Souls are saved and miracles begin to happen. Why? Because the love of God is filling us, motivating us and moving through us.

Jesus went on: **"For the Father loves the Son, and shows Him all things that He Himself does; and He will show Him greater works than these, that you may marvel. For as the Father raises the dead and gives life to them, even so the Son gives life to whom He will"** (verses 20-21). The Father and Son always act as one.

JESUS CHRIST IS THE ONE APPOINTED TO JUDGE

Jesus continued: **"For the Father judges no one, but has committed all judgment to the Son"** (John 5:22). This is a very important verse. It tells us that the Father has given His right to carry out all judgment to His Son. It is therefore not the Father who is going to judge the world, but His Son, Jesus Christ.

The passage gives two important reasons why the Father has entrusted all judgment to His Son. The first is in verse 23 and the second is in verse 27.

1. Equal Honour

The first reason is: **"That all should honour the Son just as they honour the Father..."** (verse 23a). The Father has the supreme right to judge, but, because He loves Jesus so much, He has laid down the right due to Himself and said, "Jesus, You can be Judge." The Father thus wants to share His honour with Jesus. The Father is the author of all things, the One who designed the universe, but He wants Jesus to have equal honour with Himself. And with Jesus as Judge, all the people of this world will have to give Jesus completely equal honour with the Father. This shows the Father's love for His Son—He wants to share all things with Him (John 3:35).

Christians sometimes talk about the humility of John the Baptist and quote how he said, **"He [Jesus] must increase, but I must decrease"** (John 3:30). But the Father's attitude, in saying, "My Son, I want You to have equal honour with Myself," is on a completely different scale.[5]

Jesus emphasized how all must honour Him if they are to honour the Father: **"He who does not honour the Son does not honour the Father who sent Him"** (John 5:23b). We honour the Father, but we should honour the Son too; and we should also honour the Holy Spirit. The three are inseparable.

We should not be persuaded by those who say, "Jesus was merely a very good man," or, "We believe Jesus was a prophet sent by God." We should press home the point, "But was He <u>God</u>? Do you give Him equal honour with the Father?" If these people are honest, they have to admit, "No."

The Inconsistency of the religious Jews

Many of the religious Jews were very proud of how they loved and served God but, when they encountered Jesus and began to investigate Him and accuse Him, their hypocrisy was exposed.

John chapter 8 records how Jesus answered the accusation of some Pharisees that He bore witness of Himself: **"Then they said to Him, "Where is your Father?" Jesus answered, "You know neither Me nor My Father. If you had known Me, you would have known My Father also""** (John 8:19). Jesus was saying to them, "You can't love or know the Father without loving and knowing Me. We are inseparable. You can't profess to love God and yet hate Me."

---

[5] *I sometimes wonder what would happen in our churches or fellowships if we gave equal honour to every member? It would take real humility from us all, but it would transform us instantly.*

He reiterated this in verse 42: **"Jesus said to them, "If God were your Father, you would love Me, for I proceeded forth and came from God; nor have I come of Myself, but He sent Me.""** Then, in verse 44, He laid it on the line: **"You are of your father the devil, and the desires of your father you want to do..."**. The religious Jews thought that they loved God. In reality, however, many of them merely loved their rituals: they loved the Temple and the synagogue; they loved their ceremonies; they loved the prayers; and they loved the sacrifices. Many particularly loved the acclaim of men: being called "Father" as they walked along, or "Rabbi" (meaning 'my great one', thus 'Teacher'); and many loved money. Sadly, they did not truly love or honour God. For if they had loved the Father they would have loved the One He had sent—the Lord Jesus, their Messiah—because the Son of God and the Father are 'inseparable', always acting together.

In John 5:24 Jesus preached the gospel message to the Jews who were persecuting Him, just as He did on so many other occasions: **"Most assuredly, I say to you, he who hears My word and believes in Him who sent Me has everlasting life..."** (verse 24a).

Who had sent Jesus? The Father had. And the Father had already said and done several things to reveal who His Son was—as well as provided the Scriptures that pointed to Him.

The Father had raised up John the Baptist, who had come baptizing with water, announcing that One much greater was coming, on whom the people should believe (Matthew 3:11, Acts 19:4). At the Jordan, when Jesus was baptized, the Father's voice had come from heaven saying, **"This is My beloved Son, in whom I am well pleased"** (Matthew 3:17).[6] Then, when John saw Jesus coming towards him, he said, **"Behold! The Lamb of God who takes away the sin of the world! This is He..."** (John 1:29-30a).

The Father had therefore been announcing, "Here He is! This is My Son. This is My Anointed One, the Messiah.[7] I've sent Him. Believe on Him!" Now Jesus was saying to the Jews, "If you believe the Father who sent Me, you will accept Me and honour Me. Then you will have everlasting life." This was the gospel message.

---

[6]Later, at the Mount of Transfiguration, the Father's voice again boomed from heaven, saying, "This is My beloved Son, in whom I am well pleased. Hear Him!" (Matthew 17:5 and similarly Mark 9:7 and Luke 9:35).

[7]Note that the words Messiah (*mashiach* in Hebrew) and Christ (*christos* in Greek) both mean 'Anointed One'. In the Old Testament, God promised that salvation would come to the Jews and, through them to all peoples, through His Anointed One—the Messiah.

If you accept Jesus as the Christ, as Lord of your life, that is salvation. As Paul and Silas later told the Philippian jailer, **"Believe on the Lord Jesus Christ, and you will be saved"** (Acts 16:31b). It was the same gospel message that Jesus Himself preached to the Jews.

These Jews were without excuse. Their Scriptures said that two or three witnesses were needed to establish any matter (Deuteronomy 19:15). Jesus was not claiming to bear witness of Himself: **"If I bear witness of Myself, My witness is not true"** (John 5:31). Rather, His Father had witnessed of Him, John the Baptist had witnessed of Him, and the works that He did witnessed of Him (John 5:36; 14:11). The Jews had the writings of Moses and all the other Scriptures that testified of Jesus (John 5:39-47). Nevertheless, they still refused to come to Him to receive life.

In John 5:24 Jesus continued: **"...he who hears My word and believes in Him who sent Me has everlasting life, and shall not come into judgment, but has passed from death into life."** Paul later reiterated this truth in Romans 8:1, **"There is therefore now no condemnation to those who are in Christ Jesus"**. Whoever is in Christ—those who are believers—shall not be judged. (The word **"condemnation"** means 'judgment', as we saw earlier.)

Jesus then gave more detail: **"Most assuredly, I say to you, the hour is coming, and now is, when the dead will hear the voice of the Son of God; and those who hear will live"** (John 5:25). As Jesus went on to explain in verses 28-29, all the dead will hear His voice and be resurrected, either to everlasting life or to everlasting judgment.[8]

"For as the Father has life in Himself, so He has granted the Son to have life in Himself" (verse 26). Here is the same principle again, of the Father sharing all that He has with His Son. The first reason why the Son is going to be the Judge, therefore, is that He might receive equal honour with the Father.

2. Jesus is the only Mediator between God and Man

The second reason is given in verse 27: **"And [the Father] has given Him authority to execute judgment also, because He is the Son of Man."**

In verse 25 Jesus called Himself "the Son of God": **"...when the dead will hear the voice of the Son of God"**. However, here in verse 27 we find Him describing Himself as **"the Son of Man"**. He is both the Son of God and the Son of Man.

---

[8] *This passage on resurrection is explained in more detail in Chapter 15.*

Jesus has been given authority to judge because He is both divine and human.[9] As such, *He is the only Mediator there is between God and man.* We find this truth in 1 Timothy 2:5, "**For there is one God and one Mediator between God and men, the Man Christ Jesus.**" Here Paul was emphasizing that Jesus Christ is a man. The *only* mediator between the one God and men is the *Man* Christ Jesus.

We need to understand the characteristics and principles of a mediator and, as usual, the Bible itself provides us with the details. In this case, it is a most surprising book that we need to look at—the Book of Job.[10]

What is a Mediator?

Job had some friends who tried to encourage him in his suffering. They are often called "Job's Comforters". They were believers, and they knew a few things. But unfortunately the proverb, "**The fear of the LORD is the beginning of wisdom**" (Proverbs 9:10a) had not been written at the time, and Job's Comforters tended to quote ideas and teaching that did not comfort Job at all! Many of the things they said were true, although they made a few mistakes. Nevertheless, most of their words did not apply to Job and were a wrong diagnosis of his situation.

Can you imagine 'poor' Job? He had lived righteously before God, but suddenly he'd been smitten down. Then these 'friends' came along and basically told him, "You must have sinned! Do you think God would do this to you for nothing?" They were *partly* right, of course; God would not do such a thing for no reason at all. However, in Job's case, God had not afflicted him because of something *he* had done. Rather, God had allowed Satan to afflict Job to resolve an amazing conflict between Himself and

---

[9]The title "son of man" in the Old Testament was often an expression of lowliness and humility, or simply of humanity (see Psalm 8:4, for example). God used it frequently in addressing the prophet Ezekiel, in particular. However, it was used in Daniel 7:13-14 to describe the One to whom God will give His kingdom and His glory forever, whom all will serve. Jesus' regular use of the title "Son of Man" to describe Himself thus reflected the fact that He was fully and ideally human, but it was also a claim to be the ultimate head of the whole universe. It was thus an even more remarkable title than Son of God (see Matthew 26:63-65 and Special Topic Study 35).

The title "Son of God" was a title of the Messiah only hinted at in the Old Testament. It pointed to the virgin birth of Christ (Isaiah 9:6), revealed the relationship He would have with God as His Father and implied having the same character as God. It thus pointed to the fact that all the fulness of God's being would dwell in Christ. It was also a title of the King of Israel (2 Samuel 7:14) and pointed to God's Son being heir of all things (Hebrews 1:2).

[10]The Book of Job is probably the earliest book of the Bible. It was probably written before the Law was given, before the Exodus, because it contains no mention of the Law. It is an amusing book in parts, but it is also tragic in other parts.

Satan. The issues were much deeper than Job's so-called Comforters understood. Therefore, Job not only had to put up with his boils and his discomfort, but he had to endure these men preaching 'truths' at him that simply did not help.[11]

In Job chapter 9 we find Job replying to Bildad the Shuhite. Job agreed with him about God being just, but still he did not know what he had done to cause his own suffering. **"Then Job answered and said, "Truly I know it is so, but how can a man be righteous before God? If one wished to contend with Him, he could not answer Him one time out of a thousand. God is wise in heart and mighty in strength. Who has hardened himself against Him and prospered?""** (Job 9:1-4). Job knew that he could never be righteous enough to argue his own case before God.

In verse 32 Job continued: **"For He [God] is not a man, as I am, that I may answer Him, and that we should go to court together."**[12] Job wished that he could simply go to God and say, "Look, God, I haven't done anything!" But he feared God and realized he could not contend with Him. "God is not a man like me, so I can't just approach Him and protest my innocence. He is Almighty!"[13]

"Nor is there any mediator between us, who may lay his hand on us both" (verse 33). Job longed for a mediator, who could **"lay his hand on"** both himself and God. It is the last phrase here that is so informative, because it tells us the one essential characteristic of a mediator: *a mediator has to be able to represent both parties* in a dispute.

To 'lay one's hand upon someone' meant to *identify* with that person. For example, when a Jew took an animal for a sin offering, he would lay his hand on the head of the animal as a sign meaning, "I identify myself with this sacrifice." Then he would kill it, and the priest would carry out the Law's instructions relating to the blood and fat and would burn the animal (see Leviticus 4:27-31).

---

[11] Such people are still around in the Body of Christ today. They know something about God, but they think that they have all the answers; and the 'truths' they bring often do not touch others at a spiritual level at all. Instead, we need people who have the mind of the Lord for our situations, who do not make assumptions and then misapply inappropriate truths or simply regurgitate their own ideas as doctrine.

[12] The AV translates this last phrase as *"come together in judgment"*.

[13] Isaiah recorded God's words, *""Come now, and let us reason together," says the* LORD" (see Isaiah 1:18a). However, Job pre-dated Isaiah by many centuries; and this incident probably took place before Moses recorded the Law. Job only had his own personal knowledge of God to live by, and whatever wisdom had been passed down from generation to generation. Job feared God. Therefore, it is no surprise that he saw his predicament as an irresolvable dilemma.

If workers have a dispute with the management in some industry today, for example, a person (or team) has to be found who can represent both sides. They often call in an outside arbitrator. However, the union might complain that he's on the management's side and so not accept him. Similarly, the management might say, "Go on, he's a union supporter. He's not independent." The dispute thus remains unresolved without the help of a suitable mediator.

Job was saying, "There is no mediator who can identify with both me and God." He assumed there could never be such a person. But he was wrong—there was One. Hallelujah! The *Lord Jesus* is such a mediator—the *only* such mediator! He is God, so He can speak from God's side; yet He is fully human, so He can speak from man's point of view too. Jesus therefore represents God to us. The unseen, invisible God is revealed to us in Jesus Christ, the visible member of the Godhead for us. However, Jesus also represents man before God. He knows what it is to be human and to live on this earth. Therefore, He is able to represent us. He knows what it is to experience the worst human suffering.

If Jesus were not fully God, then we would have no mediator to represent God to us. But Jesus *is* God—which is why we focused on His divinity at the beginning of this chapter. Similarly, if Jesus were not fully human, then we would have no mediator to represent us. But Jesus *is* a man and He sits as a man in heaven today.[14]

Conclusion: Jesus will Judge Righteously

All judgment has therefore been committed to the Lord Jesus so that He should receive equal honour with the Father—that every knee should bow and every tongue confess that He is Lord (see Philippians 2:10-11). Also, Jesus has been appointed as Judge because He is the only One who can ever fully identify with both man and God. Praise His wonderful name!

---

[14] After Adam caused the downfall of the whole human race by his sin, all mankind was cut off from God. But when Jesus rose from the dead, He went, as a perfect man, back to heaven and presented Himself, saying, "Here I am, Father, a perfect Man!" The Father was able to say, "I can accept You, Jesus! Now the breach between Me and mankind has been healed." Jesus Christ then came back to the earth as a resurrected man for a time, to represent God again to us. He had more to teach His disciples (Acts 1:2-3), but then He ascended and sat down at the right hand of God, where He remains today. (This subject is covered in Special Topic Study 11, "The Glorified Man".)

The fact that Jesus ascended to His Father on His resurrection day, as a fulfilment of the Feast of Firstfruits, prior to His 40 days of appearances and His later 'permanent' ascension to heaven is explained in Special Topic Studies 49-50 (compare John 20 verses 16-17 and 24-27).

The fact that Jesus is Judge ensures that *not one person will be judged unfairly*, because Jesus understands man. **"He will judge the world in righteousness by the Man whom He has ordained. He has given assurance of this to all, by raising Him from the dead"** (Acts 17:31b).

Jesus Christ received worse treatment from mankind, and Satan, than anyone else ever has or ever will receive. Therefore, He is the perfect One to come and say, "You, O man, stand in condemnation. I know, because I also am a Man. I was tempted in the same ways as you." Yet to the Father He can say, "Father, I want to represent them. I'm their Advocate. I sympathize with their weaknesses." He'd probably say to us, "Don't say a word, lest you incriminate yourself!" And we would! We'd try to justify ourselves and put up every excuse for our failings. But Jesus comes before the Father and says, "Remember My blood, Father! I paid the price for all their sin."

Returning to John chapter 5, Jesus stressed the certainty of forthcoming judgment for all—which will result in a division of mankind. **"Do not marvel at this; for the hour is coming in which all who are in the graves will hear His voice…"** (John 5:28). All who are dead, both believers and unbelievers, are going to hear the voice of Jesus Christ, **"…and come forth—those who have done good, to the resurrection of life, and those who have done evil, to the resurrection of condemnation"** (verse 29). How do we do good? It is principally by believing on the Lord Jesus Christ (see John 6:28-29). This is the only truly good thing we can do, and it is the essential foundation of any other good works. But for those who have done evil—who do not believe on the Lord—there is the fearful prospect of judgment.[15]

"I can of Myself do nothing. As I hear, I judge; and My judgment is righteous, because I do not seek My own will but the will of the Father who sent Me" (John 5:30). Jesus was saying, "Yes, judgment is Mine; but I am going to judge by what I hear." In other words, Jesus *will* be the Judge, but He will rely on His Father.

In fact, Jesus went on to say later that He Himself will not judge those who refuse to believe, but His words will judge them in the last day, for He did not come to judge the world but to save it (John 5:45; 12:47-48). However, He only spoke the words that His Father gave Him (John 12:49-50). Jesus

---

[15] There are some that think that by living a 'good life' they will be saved. They sometimes quote the first part of John 5:29 and say that all who have done good shall come forth to the resurrection of life. However, they fail to discover what Jesus said was necessary for doing good. They are ignorant of the truth and do not really believe in judgment to come. As many people do, they take half a verse, misinterpret it, and conveniently ignore the other half.

was again revealing the total interdependence of the Father and Son—which is because they so love one another![16]

Other implications of Jesus identifying Himself with us

I am so thrilled when I think of how the Lord Jesus became the perfect mediator for us. He was not ashamed to identify Himself fully with every person. He is therefore not ashamed of me today. It doesn't matter how low we may have sunk to, He is still prepared to identify Himself fully with us. We may sometimes be afraid to come alongside someone who is in a mess; but Jesus is not. He loves the lovely and the unlovely just the same.

Jesus the Lamb and the Shepherd

Revelation 7:17 tells us: "**For the Lamb who is in the midst of the throne will shepherd them**".[17] It is the 'mastermind' of God that has devised this. He has chosen "**the Lamb**" to be the Shepherd of His flock! Jesus Christ is the Lamb of God, and now He has become the shepherd of God's sheep.[18] Therefore, if you are a Christian, the Lamb of God has become your Shepherd.

This is glorious! Jesus is the One who identified Himself fully with every member of the flock. He is the One who understands every path you are taking, because He's been there before. He is the One who has been through every trial, every tribulation and every fear in the night. Now He is the One whom God the Father has appointed Shepherd over the flock—to be personally in charge of you. What a Shepherd! Praise God—What a Shepherd!

That is why, as we look back at our lives, we can truly say, "He has never forsaken me. He has never let me down. He has always understood. He has always been there to provide a word of comfort just when I needed it!" Praise God! The wonderful Lamb of God has become Shepherd of the flock.

---

[16] The rest of this chapter is taken from the start of tape BBS 16.

[17] The AV says "**feed them**", but the word used means 'to shepherd'.

[18] A lamb signifies vulnerability. It is the weakest member of the flock, prone to wander into danger. It is the one so busy feeding that it doesn't notice that the rest of the flock has moved on; and suddenly it looks up and feels all alone. The lamb is the one that feels bogged down in the wet part of the field. It wakes in the middle of the night and is afraid of the dark; and all it can hear is the singing of the shepherd to keep it company. A lamb rushes up to a ewe, only to find that she isn't its mother, and the ewe pushes it away.

Jesus our compassionate High Priest

Hebrews 4:14-16 describes further Jesus' ministry today: "**Seeing then that we have a great High Priest who has passed through the heavens, Jesus the Son of God, let us hold fast our confession. For we do not have a High Priest who cannot sympathize with our weaknesses, but was in all points tempted as we are, yet without sin. Let us therefore come boldly to the throne of grace, that we may obtain mercy and find grace to help in time of need.**"

How marvellous! The Lord Jesus is in heaven today as our great High Priest. He has lived as a man on this earth and been through the same things we go through. Therefore, no matter what we are going through or what we are feeling, He understands perfectly. He was tempted in every way just as we are, yet He was without sin. He knew that His Father was with Him in everything He went through (John 8:29). There wasn't one time when He was faithless. There wasn't a time when He thought, "Father, You've let me down!"

The writer exhorts us, "**Let us therefore come boldly to the throne of grace**" (verse 16). Come boldly! He is not going to cast us out. He understands us fully. Therefore, we should not be afraid, but should turn to Him who loves us and approach Him with confidence!

For what purpose? First, "**that we may obtain mercy**". Sometimes, when sin has bogged us down, we think, "I can't come. My problems are too big!" or "Surely, He'll reject me?" But He understands. He understands completely—and His arms are held out! He says to us, "Come on, come to Me! I understand exactly what you're going through. Come and receive mercy from Me!" Second, we come to "**find grace to help in time of need**". Every Christian has times of need, times of trouble and anguish, and times of testing. These are the very times we need to draw near to our Shepherd, so we should come boldly before Him knowing that He sympathizes with all our weaknesses.

The Throne of Grace

Notice the expression "**the throne of grace**" in verse 16. It seems almost a 'contradiction' to me. A throne represents supreme authority: it represents great might; it represents rulership; and it represents a seat of judgment. Jesus is on God's throne in heaven, but there is grace available there. Praise God!

The idea of great authority is summed up for me by a famous incident in 168 BC which involved the powerful and notorious leader Antiochus IV Epiphanes of Greece. He had decided to attack Alexandria in Egypt (while the Romans were preoccupied fighting Macedonia), and he was on his way to join his army as it besieged the city.[19]

However, before he arrived at Alexandria, a man called Popillius Laenas came to meet him—who was an envoy from Rome. Unarmed, this man walked up to Antiochus, stood calmly in front of him and handed him a decree from the Roman Senate ordering him to leave Egypt at once. He also informed him that Rome had just triumphed over Macedonia. Then, with a stick, he drew a line in the sand around Antiochus and demanded his answer before he stepped out of the circle! He was saying, in so many words, "Thus far and no further! For, Antiochus Epiphanes, if you dare put one foot over this line without agreeing to leave Alexandria, then you are not at war with Egypt but with Rome!"

Antiochus Epiphanes knew what that meant. He knew that this man was speaking in the place of Rome. If he ignored this ultimatum and carried on, then all the might of Rome would be against him—and his forces would surely be annihilated.

History tells us that Antiochus Epiphanes agreed to submit. He was wise! He immediately retreated—a bitter man. Tragically, however, his forces then went on to commit many atrocities against the Jews in Israel.

This incident illustrates the meaning of a throne of authority. Popillius Laenas acted and spoke with all the power of Rome behind him. But what is grace? Grace is unmerited, undeserved favour. Grace originates from the love of God and doesn't force anyone or anything. Grace is that which woos—that which comes along and appeals and doesn't coerce. Grace is that which helps us but never tries to push us down.

Yet what do we find together? The throne of God and grace! **"Come boldly to the throne of grace"**! This is almost a contradiction; but the juxtaposition of these words tells us two marvellous things:

1. *God's grace is enthroned.*

The love of God has power behind it. Praise His wonderful Name! God's love is not the unhappy type of love that sees its children suffering and cannot do anything about it: that would be a weak type of grace. No! God's grace has unlimited power behind it!

---

[19] Antiochus IV "Epiphanes" was leader of the Seleucid Empire based in Syria, part of the former Greco-Macedonian (or "Greek") Empire which became divided after Alexander the Great died. Egypt was the other major remaining part of that empire, ruled by the Ptolemies. The two parts fought regularly for many years. Israel often became caught up in the contest, being situated between them.

How my heart has gone out to King Zedekiah, the last king of Judah. He was captured by the Babylonians and, in front of his very eyes, had to watch his children being put to death, powerless to do anything about it. The love of God for His children is not like that. Rather, it is enthroned. It has got 'teeth'. When God sees His children suffering—when He sees them almost at the point of death or destruction or despair— He is always able to come and meet their need.

2. *The Almighty God has a 'beating heart' of love.*

God does not preside over a tyranny. He is not ruling over a regime that seeks to kick everyone down. No! God has a Father's loving heart, beating for His children. When He disciplines and corrects us, it is because we need it; and He always disciplines us appropriately, for our good—not because He wants to suppress us or to cause us harm. Praise His name!

I could go on about these two glorious words that are used together—throne and grace. It is the throne indeed—of grace indeed. Hallelujah!

This has been an introduction to the series. We have considered the first great principle of judgment: Jesus is the One appointed as Judge. The Father has committed all judgment to His Son. We have ended the chapter with the love of God, and from this springs the next great principle of God's judgment.

2. GRACE BEFORE JUDGMENT

We now come to a magnificent principle that can be observed throughout the whole Bible: There is *always* grace before judgment with God. God never sends judgment without first giving grace. I call this the "Grace before Judgment" principle.[1]

JUDGMENT IS ALIEN TO GOD

To see this, I have chosen a little known verse in the Old Testament: "**For the LORD will rise up as at Mount Perazim, He will be angry as in the Valley of Gibeon—that He may do His work, His awesome work, and bring to pass His act, His unusual act**" (Isaiah 28:21).

Mount Perazim was where the judgment of God fell on the Philistines through King David. David organized the army, but it was actually *God* who judged the Philistines through him (see 2 Samuel 5:20, 1 Chronicles 14:11). The Valley of Gibeon was also a place of judgment, on two occasions. Joshua defeated the Amorites there (Joshua 10:10), and David again defeated the Philistines there (2 Samuel 5:24-25, 1 Chronicles 14:15-16). However, it was ultimately *God* again, through both of these men, who judged the enemies of His people.

Note how the verse ends: "**...that He may do His work, His awesome work, and bring to pass His act, His unusual act.**" The Hebrew words translated "**awesome**" and "**unusual**" both mean 'alien', 'foreign' or 'strange'. This verse therefore implies that it is an 'alien' work to God when He rises up in judgment and anger. It does not mean God won't ever rise up in judgment, but it suggests that He does not like judging—it is alien to Him. In other words, He would prefer not to judge.[2]

---

[1] It could also be described as the "Mercy before Judgment" principle. God shows both mercy and grace before He ever sends judgment. Mercy refers to God not giving us what we do deserve, whereas grace refers to God giving favour to those who do not deserve it.

[2] This wonderful truth is emphasized in Lamentations 3:33, where Jeremiah said, "For He does not afflict willingly, nor grieve the children of men."

If you have heard or read the first series of Basic Bible Studies, especially the study covering propitiation (BBS 7), you will understand why God has to judge human beings. It is because He is absolutely holy, righteous and just—these are unchanging facets of His character. Wherever there is sin, rebellion or wickedness, God has to punish these things. He *must* judge them, because He is perfectly just. Man's sin, rebellion and wickedness offend God's holiness and righteousness.[3] Therefore, He has to judge mankind. However, the good news is that God is a God of love. And, in the Cross of Jesus Christ, we can see how the love of God, the holiness and righteousness of God, and the justice of God were all manifested.

God's loving nature always leads Him to say, "I will give mercy and grace first, before I send judgment." He always gives a person, a group or a nation opportunity to repent—a chance to turn from what would lead to judgment—before His judgment comes. Nevertheless, if that person, group or nation repeatedly refuses to turn back to God, despising His grace, then judgment *will* come, as surely as God is in heaven and as surely as the Word of God stands true. This principle is so important.

Nations must not take God's grace for granted

I am thinking especially of Great Britain as I say this. I believe that, during the 19th Century, Britain was living under great blessing from God, not under the judgment of God. There were many tremendous believers then, and British missionaries were sent out to every corner of the world to proclaim the gospel message. This was one of the largest missionary efforts there has ever been (except, perhaps, for those from the USA, South Korea and Brazil in recent years). Many precious missionaries spilled their blood for the gospel of Christ, and this country was never worthy of them—although other nations were turned completely upside down by their work.

Yet Britain has now largely turned its back on God; there can be no doubt about this at all. This country is now a predominantly pagan, atheistic and humanistic society. It names the name of God, but it is just lip service. There are so few godly believers, relatively speaking. And the time has now come when God's judgment is beginning to come upon our nation. I believe we have been living in a period of God's grace for several decades now, in which God has been giving us opportunity to turn back to Him. But if we don't repent as a nation then, after grace, there will be judgment.

---

[3] In view of these things, God is cut off completely from every person and, apart from Jesus Christ's work on the Cross, fellowship between man and God would be utterly impossible. This is one aspect (the fourth brick) of the 'Barrier' described in the first series of Basic Bible Studies.

Interestingly, it is not just Christians who realize this shift; many non-Christians also recognize that forces have been coming into this country that are forces of judgment. The only answer is repentance from the whole nation. As Psalm 33 says, **"Blessed is the nation whose God is the LORD"** (verse 12a). We need to turn back to the institutions God has ordained: back to marriage, back to the family, back to discipline in the home situation. Above all, we need to turn back to God Himself, and acknowledge and worship Him.

The Grace before Judgment principle is being demonstrated here. God could have wiped Britain out because of our sin; but He has chosen not to do so. Instead, He is still giving us grace. He could have wiped out so many countries but, instead, He is giving them grace too. But after grace, as surely as God is God, judgment will come. This is a serious thing that we are talking about, because I believe Britain is on the verge of experiencing the judgment of God to a much greater extent unless there is repentance.[4]

We who are Christians may be living in a place that is under judgment, but *we* live under God's grace in days of grace. There is no condemnation (that is, judgment) for those in Christ Jesus (Romans 8:1). We need to allow the Holy Spirit to move through us so that many might hear the gospel and come to see that Jesus has provided salvation. And if many people turn to the Lord, God's judgment may yet be delayed or averted in our nations.

The whole world would have putrefied utterly if Christians had not preached the gospel. **"You are the salt of the earth"**, Jesus said (Matthew 5:13a). We thus help to provide, or make a way for, God's grace in the places where we live. Therefore, it is up to us in this country. All Christians, in all fellowships and churches should pray fervently for our nation. We must represent God and keep on preaching the gospel. And as we obey God, we will know His blessing in our own lives.

EXAMPLES OF GRACE BEFORE JUDGMENT IN THE BIBLE

The Bible is overflowing with examples of God's grace before judgment— some of which we will consider in this and subsequent chapters. It is a wonderfully fruitful subject on which to do your own Bible study. In Series 1, we looked at the account of Adam and Eve receiving grace in the Garden of Eden, but we will review it briefly here.

---

[4] This Bible study was given in 1975. These observations are still relevant to Great Britain, and even more so now. When the study was given, Roger Price specifically mentioned the Soviet Union at this point and said that God might soon wipe it out. Since that time, the Soviet Union has indeed collapsed.

Adam and Eve

Satan deceived Eve into eating the forbidden fruit. However, Adam then sinned deliberately and premeditatedly by eating it too. Genesis 3:6b-7 tells us, "**…she took its fruit and ate. She also gave to her husband with her, and he ate. Then the eyes of both of them were opened, and they knew that they were naked; and they sewed fig leaves together and made themselves coverings.**"

We need to understand what led to the Fall. I am convinced that the real reason Adam rebelled was that his first fervent love for the Lord had cooled. Otherwise, he would not have let anything come between him and God. He would have valued his fellowship with the Lord so much that he couldn't bear to disobey Him. He should have loved the Lord with all his heart. However, having forsaken his first love, his hardness of heart allowed rebellion to come in, leading to his actual sin.

We who are believers are warned of a similar thing in Scripture: we must not allow ourselves to become hardened through the deceitfulness of sin. If we allow ourselves to become hardened and unbelieving, we may depart from the living God (see Hebrews 3:12-13). God is *always* offering grace to us—but we can shut ourselves off from enjoying fellowship with Him through our sin.

God knew the suffering that was going to come into the world because of Adam and Eve's disobedience. He could have utterly destroyed them because of their sin; but He did not. Instead, He gave them grace: "**And they heard the sound of the LORD God walking in the garden in the cool of the day, and Adam and his wife hid themselves from the presence of the LORD God among the trees of the garden**" (verse 8). Adam and Eve were so fearful and ashamed that they went and hid. The Lord could have said, "I'm not going to go and find them or talk to them; they must come to Me now." But He didn't do that. Rather, it was grace before judgment.

"**Then the LORD God called to Adam and said to him, "Where are you?"**" (verse 9). Adam and Eve, in the 'wilderness' of sin, suddenly heard the voice of Jesus—the fruitful voice, the river-like voice of the Lord—calling out, "Where are you?" He was effectively saying, "I *want to* talk with you. I want to see you. I miss you. I love you!" This truly was grace.

Have you heard the voice of the Lord calling you sometimes? When we get up late and rush out of the door to work, and don't even have time to acknowledge the Lord, He calls to us and says, "I want to have time with you. I want to come and commune with you!" We might reply, "Oh, there's not time now, go away!" But He is still there when we come home that evening, longing for fellowship with us. He is so gracious. He is so lovely and loving. That is our God. Hallelujah!

The LORD God then made coverings for Adam and Eve after shedding the blood of an innocent animal. That again was an act of grace, as we have seen before.[5]

The Flood

The Flood is a great example of grace before judgment. We will consider it in some detail in the next chapter.

Sodom and Gomorrah

Genesis chapter 18 records the history of Sodom and Gomorrah, whose inhabitants had sinned greatly against the Lord. Their sin is described in Ezekiel 16:49-50a: **"Look, this was the iniquity of your sister Sodom: she and her daughter had pride, fullness of food, and abundance of idleness; neither did she strengthen the hand of the poor and needy. And they were haughty and committed abomination before Me..."**. This passage lists some of the sins of Sodom. Pride was the main cause; and that led to the other abominable sins.

In Genesis 18 we find two angels and the Lord Jesus discussing the situation in Sodom and Gomorrah.[6] The three came to visit Abraham as he was sitting in the door of his tent in Mamre. **"Then the men rose from there and looked toward Sodom, and Abraham went with them to send them on the way. And the LORD said, "Shall I hide from Abraham what I am doing, since Abraham shall surely become a great and mighty nation, and all the nations of the earth shall be blessed in him? For I have known him, in order that he may command his children and his household after him, that they keep the way of the LORD, to do righteousness and justice, that the LORD may bring to Abraham what He has spoken to him""** (Genesis 18:16-19). Note how

---

[5] This is described in Chapter 4 (BBS 4) of the book "Salvation" by Roger Price, which covers the first series of Basic Bible Studies (BBS 1 to 14).

[6] The account implies that the three men who visited Abraham were in fact two angels and the LORD God Himself. God appeared in visible form on a number of occasions in the Old Testament (these appearances are often called 'Christophanies' or 'theophanies'). The Son of God was the One whom people saw when God needed to be represented by Himself, even before His incarnation as Jesus Christ of Nazareth. He walked in the Garden of Eden, He led armies, He spoke prophetic words to some, and He came to comfort and encourage others. Here in Genesis 18 we find Him appearing with two angels to discuss the destruction of Sodom and Gomorrah with Abraham. (The doctrine of Christ appearing in the Old Testament is explained more fully in Appendix 3 of the book "Salvation" by Roger Price.)

the Lord said of Abraham, "**For I have known him**" (verse 19a). Could the Lord say that about you?

"**And the LORD said, "Because the outcry against Sodom and Gomorrah is great, and because their sin is very grievous, I will go down now and see whether they have done altogether according to the outcry against it that has come to Me; and if not, I will know"**" (verses 20-21). The LORD did not say, "Because their sin is so great, I will go down now and smash them to pieces." Instead, He said, "I will go down now and see." That was grace: He would go down into their very midst. He did not just appear fleetingly and then immediately leave again. Instead, He stayed and talked with Abraham for some time. And the two angels stayed all night in the city, where they didn't belong and where they certainly would not have liked being. It was grace.

"**Then the men turned away from there and went toward Sodom, but Abraham still stood before the LORD. And Abraham came near, and said, "Would You also destroy the righteous with the wicked?"**" (verses 22-23). Abraham knew that Sodom and Gomorrah deserved judgment, but he had a nephew called Lot who lived in Sodom. Abraham knew that if there were believers in that place, God would not judge it. He wondered how good Lot had been at leading people to the Lord, so he started speaking to the LORD. "There are believers there, Lord," he said, "You're surely not going to destroy them along with the wicked, are You? That would be contrary to the way You judge!" The LORD knew that, of course!

"**Suppose there were fifty righteous within the city; would You also destroy the place and not spare it for the fifty righteous that were in it?**" (verse 24). "Lord," Abraham was saying, "If my nephew Lot has managed to lead 49 people to You, will You destroy the city then?" "**Far be it from You to do such a thing as this, to slay the righteous with the wicked, so that the righteous should be as the wicked; far be it from You! Shall not the Judge of all the earth do right?**" (verse 25).

God *cannot* ever judge believers and unbelievers together. This principle is still true today. And that is why believers will be taken away before the judgment of this earth.[7] Even Abraham knew this principle. But isn't it

---

[7]God cannot judge believers with unbelievers. Therefore, all believers will be removed prior to the forthcoming severe judgment on the earth during the Tribulation (as explained in BBS 50, entitled "The Rapture of the Church"). There is *always* separation of believers and unbelievers prior to judgment. Similarly, at the Second Coming of Christ at the end of this age, unbelievers (the tares) will first be gathered and removed for judgment before the believers (wheat) are taken into the barn (see Matthew 13:24-30, 36-43).

amazing how many Christians have forgotten it in our day? Yet here it is stated clearly in Genesis. "**So the LORD said, "If I find in Sodom fifty righteous within the city, then I will spare all the place for their sakes"**" (verse 26).

Then Abraham remembered what Lot was like! "**Then Abraham answered and said, "Indeed now, I who am but dust and ashes have taken it upon myself to speak to the Lord: Suppose there were five less than the fifty righteous; would You destroy all of the city for lack of five?"**" (verses 27-28a). "What if Lot has missed by five?" Abraham asked, "Will you still destroy all the city?" "**And He said, "If I find there forty-five, I will not destroy it"**" (verse 28b).

Then Abraham remembered more clearly what Lot was like! "**Then he spoke to Him yet again and said, "Suppose there should be forty found there?" And He said, "I will not do it for the sake of forty." And he said, "Let not the Lord be angry, and I will speak: Suppose thirty should be found there?" And He said, "I will not do it if I find thirty there." Then he said, "Indeed now, I have taken it upon myself to speak to the Lord: Suppose twenty should be found there?" And He said, "I will not destroy it for the sake of twenty"**" (verses 29-31).

Abraham must have thought, "Oh dear, it's Lot we're talking about!" so he continued: "**And he said, "Let not the Lord be angry, and I will speak but once more: Suppose ten should be found there?" And He said, "I will not destroy it for the sake of ten."**" (verse 32). The LORD thus agreed, "If ten righteous people can be found in Sodom—just ten believers—then I won't destroy the city." "**So the LORD went His way as soon as He had finished speaking with Abraham; and Abraham returned to his place**" (verse 33).

Lot hadn't been a very successful evangelist. In fact, as far as we know, he led no more than two or three people to the Lord. *He* was a believer, and so were his two daughters; and there is a query about his wife—we cannot be sure about her. There were not ten righteous people in the city, so God was going to destroy Sodom. However, He could not destroy the righteous with the wicked. That is an unchanging principle of His judgment. Therefore, what had to happen? *Lot and the other believers (that is, his family) had to be taken out.*

Isn't that grace? Lot was a failure in many ways as a believer; yet still he could not be judged along with unbelievers. There is no condemnation for those who are believers (Romans 8:1). Therefore, before God could send judgment on Sodom, all the believers had to leave. Praise God!

This is wonderful. It tells us that, even if you are, or feel, a 'failure' as a believer, you will not be judged along with unbelievers. However, we should all aim to bear fruit for Jesus and to win souls for Him. And if we are successful in our gospel outreach in the place where we live, our town or city might be spared when judgment does finally come. This is a call for us all to heed.

Let's see the rest of the story of Lot in Genesis 19. "**When the morning dawned, the angels urged Lot to hurry, saying, "Arise, take your wife and your two daughters who are here, lest you be consumed in the punishment of the city." And while he lingered, the men took hold of his hand, his wife's hand, and the hands of his two daughters, the LORD being merciful to him, and they brought him out and set him outside the city**" (Genesis 19:15-16). Lot didn't want to go! But Lot *had to go*, because God would not judge the city with him still inside. A believer stood in the way of judgment, and the angels knew that. The city had to be judged, so they helped remove Lot and his wife and their two daughters. The LORD was merciful to Lot.[8]

"**So it came to pass, when they had brought them outside, that he said, "Escape for your life! Do not look behind you nor stay anywhere in the plain. Escape to the mountains, lest you be destroyed." Then Lot said to them, "Please no, my lords! Indeed now, your servant has found favour in you sight, and you have increased your mercy which you have shown me by saving my life; but I cannot escape to the mountains, lest some evil overtake me and I die"**" (verses 17-19). Look at 'faithless' Lot! He was saying, "Not to the mountains! Don't send me to the mountains!" Can you believe it? As if the angels would rescue him from death in the city just to leave him to die in the mountains!

Such a negative and fearful attitude shows us why Lot was so faithless and why he was so unsuccessful. Are you like that? We need to realize that God is quite able to take care of our lives and our circumstances and, if He has put us in a place, He is able to maintain us in that place. He is the One who is going to look after us; so we need not worry. We should not start complaining about the 'mountain' to which God sends us, but should just get on with obeying Him.

"**See now, this city is near enough to flee to, and it is a little one; please let me escape there (is it not a little one?) and my soul shall live." And he said to him, "See, I have favoured you concerning this thing also, in**

---

[8] Note that if Lot's wife was not a believer, she was sanctified and thus rescued in this temporal judgment because Lot was a believer. This principle is given in 1 Corinthians 7:14.

that I will not overthrow this city for which you have spoken. Hurry, escape there. For I cannot do anything until you arrive there" (verses 20-22a). Note the last phrase. God could not permit anything to be done until Lot and his family had escaped to this little city nearby. **"Therefore the name of the city was called Zoar"** (verse 22b). Zoar means 'little' or 'insignificant'; and it seems clear that Zoar was spared because of Lot's arrival there.

Geographical, geological and archaeological research has shown some extremely interesting things. The southern tip of the Dead Sea used to be land; and underneath the Sea there, and in the area around, are great deposits of salt, sulphur and bitumen, and evidence of destroyed cities.[9] The remains of Sodom and Gomorrah are now almost certainly under the Sea!

But where was Zoar? Zoar was near the mountains, now right on the edge of the shore! God preserved Zoar—because there were believers there! He allowed them to go there; therefore, He could not destroy Zoar.

The account of Lot's deliverance from Sodom tells us how God gave grace before judgment in several ways. First, the Lord went down to investigate the cities before He decided to judge and destroy them. Then, He allowed Abraham to intercede for them. Finally, Lot and his family were removed safely before the judgment came. Praise God for His wonderful grace!

---

[9] Genesis 14:3 implies that the Valley of Siddim, containing Sodom and Gomorrah, had been inundated by the "Salt Sea" by the time Moses wrote Genesis. It has been shown that there were five streams at the southern end of the Dead Sea in ancient times, possibly sources of water for the five cities in the Valley mentioned in Genesis 14:2. Writers around the time of Christ made reference to traces of cities being visible in their day at the southern edge of the Dead Sea.

Alongside the southern part of the Dead Sea is a mountain called "Jebel Usdum", Arabic for 'Mount Sodom'. The mountain shows evidences of a violent eruption, with strata welded together by intense heat. Salt, sulphur and bitumen may have been hurled into the air when an oil basin beneath the cities was disturbed, perhaps by an earthquake. Natural gases would have ignited once released into the atmosphere, and fire and bitumen would literally have rained from the sky. The word translated "brimstone" in Genesis 19:24 means 'bituminous (asphaltic) material'. Bitumen is plentiful in the area, just as Genesis 14:10 states clearly.

It is interesting that Genesis 19:28 tells us that Abraham looked towards the plain and saw the smoke of the land going up like the smoke of a furnace. From where Abraham was (close to Hebron), his view over several mountain ridges would have meant he could see the smoke rising several miles away, but he would not have been able to see the cities in the valley on fire!

(The information in this footnote is from the book "That Incredible Book the Bible" by Dr. Clifford A. Wilson, published by Pacific Christian Ministries, Australia.)

The Cross: the greatest grace

The Bible is full of examples of the Grace before Judgment principle so, in the next chapter, we will continue on this theme by looking at the Flood. However, I want to state one last but very important thing. The Lord Jesus has shown the greatest grace of all by dying for us on the Cross, that we might be reconciled to God. But if anyone will not receive the grace of God—by believing on Christ and accepting the salvation God has provided—then the fearful prospect of judgment remains. God is gracious and He is waiting for every person to repent and turn to Him. Nevertheless, His judgment will come.

Receiving salvation is simple. Paul and Barnabas explained it in Acts 16:31, when they told the jailer in Philippi, "**Believe on the Lord Jesus Christ, and you will be saved**". As Jesus Himself said, "**He who believes in Him is not condemned; but he who does not believe is condemned already, because he has not believed in the name of the only begotten Son of God**" (John 3:18).

3. THE AGE OF METHUSELAH
Grace before Judgment seen at the Flood

Judgment is always preceded by grace with God. Therefore, in this book we are staying true to this principle, by having several chapters on God's grace followed by several describing His judgment. In the previous chapter we began to look at the marvellous principle of Grace before Judgment, and saw how events in the lives of Adam and Eve, as well as Abraham and Lot, demonstrated it. Now we are going to look at a further major example, because it is so important for us to understand this principle. We are going to deal with Noah's Flood.

GRACE BEFORE JUDGMENT AT THE FLOOD

No one should be mistaken into thinking that the Flood was just a local deluge of water, covering just a few hundred square miles. The Flood truly was worldwide, just as the Bible tells us. It is the worst judgment from God that this earth has yet experienced. Make no mistake; God was prepared to annihilate every living creature on the surface of the *whole* earth and, if there had been no one who was righteous, every person would have died.

There has never been another judgment on that scale in the whole of history. There has never been a time when the wrath of God was so revealed. One more time is approaching when God's wrath will be revealed further still. However, in biblical history, Noah's flood is the greatest example of God's judgment that we have.

Romans 5:20b says something very important: "**But where sin abounded, grace abounded much more.**" The Flood followed a period of terrible rebellion and sin upon the earth. According to this principle, then, great grace must also have been revealed—more than at any other event in the Old Testament. Therefore, in this study, instead of simply looking at the wrath of God being poured out, we are going to consider the cataclysm of Noah's Flood from the aspect of God's grace in it all.

THE REASONS FOR THE FLOOD

The Flood account commences in Genesis chapter 6, and begins with a description of some of the wicked things taking place on the earth. It continues: "**Then the LORD saw that the wickedness of man was great in the earth, and that every intent of the thoughts of his heart was only evil continually. And the LORD was sorry that He had made man on the earth, and He was grieved in His heart. So the LORD said, "I will destroy man whom I have created from the face of the earth, both man and beast, creeping thing and birds of the air, for I am sorry that I have made them""** (verses 5-7).

If we go back to verse 3, this is the warning that God gave: "**And the LORD said, "My Spirit shall not strive with man forever, for he is indeed flesh; yet his days shall be one hundred and twenty years.""** God was saying, "You people living on the earth—I give you 120 years to repent! Decide whether you will go My way or your own way during that time! At the end, you will all perish in My judgment—unless you repent!"

Sometimes the phrase, "**My Spirit shall not strive with man forever**" is used out of context. I've heard it used wrongly in evangelistic sermons, when the preacher has said, "God's Spirit will not always strive with you! If you leave this place without having given your heart to the Lord there'll never be another opportunity. That's what the Bible says!" But this is off-base, because the Spirit of God so loves people that He never stops searching out those whom He may save.[1] This was a warning that was *only* given prior to the Flood: "You've got 120 years to repent before My Spirit will stop striving with you!"

The account then goes on: "**But Noah found grace in the eyes of the LORD. This is the genealogy of Noah. Noah was a just man, perfect in his generations. Noah walked with God. And Noah begot three sons: Shem, Ham, and Japheth. The earth also was corrupt before God, and the earth was filled with violence. So God looked upon the earth, and indeed it was corrupt; for all flesh had corrupted their way on the earth. And God said to Noah, "The end of all flesh has come before Me, for the earth is filled with violence through them; and behold, I**

---

[1] If someone is on his death-bed, having rejected God all of his life, the Holy Spirit is still there with him, saying, "Believe on the Lord Jesus Christ, and you will be saved!" Never does the Holy Spirit give up until someone has breathed his final breath. Of course, we don't know for certain what is going to happen to anybody. We could find that our days have actually been 'called' up in heaven today and that the time of our death has arrived. But never is it true to say to someone that the Spirit of God will stop striving with him.

will destroy them with the earth. Make yourself an ark of gopherwood...'" (verses 8-14a).

This was the situation prior to the Flood. God had promised terrible judgment. But where was His grace in all this? I can see three major areas of grace, which I'll deal with in turn.

1. THE BUILDING OF THE ARK

We need to remember that, at that time, the people probably could not read and write. Therefore, instead of having someone write and distribute leaflets,[2] God, being a good teacher, had Noah preach a message *and* give a clear visible sign of what he was talking about. God was so gracious to the people. This manner of communication can be seen time and time again in Scripture.

The tabernacle was a picture, for example. The priests used to teach about the LORD and about salvation, but the tabernacle *demonstrated* the truths they were talking about. For example, the candlestick represented Christ, the light of the world; and in the darkness light would shine out, lighting everything in the Holy Place. Whenever the tabernacle was dismantled and the Israelite camp was moving on, the people would see the covered items of furniture and utensils being carried by the Levites. And the priests would say, for example, "That candlestick represents the Messiah who will come soon. He's going to bring light to every single person."[3]

Such visible demonstrations were "visual aids".[4] And Noah's Ark was just such a demonstration. Noah, in the midst of the dry land, suddenly started building a boat!

---

[2] After King Nebuchadnezzar had been humbled by God, he wanted to declare the signs and wonders that God had worked for him. He was so thrilled with the LORD that he printed a tract and sent it out to all peoples, nations and languages that dwelt on the earth—even though most of the people probably couldn't read (see Daniel chapter 4)!

[3] Numbers chapter 4 explains how the priests were responsible for dismantling the tabernacle, covering the various items and preparing them for carrying. Then the descendants of Kohath, Gershon and Merari, the three sons of Levi, would come and carry them; but they were forbidden from touching any of the holy things, lest they die. The Gershonites and Merarites were given carts and oxen to help carry the large, structural items. However, the Kohathites had to carry the holy things on their shoulders, using poles or carrying beams, lest they die (see Numbers 7:1-9). These holy things included the ark, the table of shewbread, the lampstand and the golden altar, together with all their utensils.

[4] Further examples of how God used visible demonstrations in the Old Testament are given in the Appendix.

Prior to the Flood, not one drop of rain had fallen on the earth. Rain came only after the Flood.[5] We can therefore imagine the people's reaction when suddenly, in the middle of the land, Noah began building his boat. It was really a large ship. In fact, it was huge! It was about 450 feet (137 m) long, 75 feet (23 m) wide and 45 feet (14 m) tall—see Genesis 6:15. It was about half the size of the old *Queen Mary*—that is, about half the length and height of the *Titanic* and about three-quarters as wide. It was as high as a four-storey house.

The Ark would have had a cubic capacity of about 1.5 million cubic feet (43,000 m^3), and a displacement of about 20,000 tons. It certainly was not the type of boat that you could tow behind a car and take down to the sea! Once Noah's ship was built, it was going to stay exactly where it was.[6]

For 120 years, probably, the Ark was under construction. And I imagine that people came from miles around to see the spectacle of Noah building his ship. They would have flocked to the area to see this 'strange' man with his 'strange' family. You can imagine the taunts: "Hey, Noah, what are you going to use that for?"; "How are you going to get it to the sea, Noah?"; "What's all this about, Noah?" They would have mocked and mocked.

What was God's intention in this? This was grace! People came to see the ship, but they were going to get more than they came for. For they were going to hear about the grace of God, as well as the coming judgment of God. Every single day Noah would have had a new congregation! I imagine that trips were arranged especially, just to go and see the sight and, as the ship got bigger and bigger, it must have caused such a stir! I can imagine Noah and his sons painting the pitch on the huge sides of the Ark, 45 feet tall, with great care, surrounded by a large circle of people all the way round. To every taunt, I believe Noah and his family gave an answer.

That was grace! It was God arranging to bring a message to a people who did not want to hear the message. God had every right to say to the people,

---

[5] Genesis chapter 2 explains how the earth received water prior to the Flood: "**But a mist went up from the earth and watered the whole face of the ground**" (Genesis 2:6). Enough water came from this mist for everything to grow, making rain unnecessary.

[6] The figures given are based on 1 cubit = 18 inches (1.5 feet). However, it is possible that the cubit referred to in Genesis was significantly longer.

To compare, the *Titanic* was 882.5 feet long, 92.5 feet wide and 97 feet high (keel to boat deck). Its gross tonnage was 46,328 tons, and its displacement tonnage about 66,000 tons. In the book "The Genesis Flood" by John C. Whitcomb and Henry M. Morris (Baker Book House), based on 1 cubit = 17.5 inches, the authors estimate that Noah's ark would have had a volume of 1.396 million cubic feet, gross tonnage 13,960 tons and displacement tonnage 19,940 tons.

"You don't want to hear, so I'm not going to tell you!" But He didn't. Instead, He called one man and his family to be fools for Him. Praise God!

I believe that God is looking for such people in these days. There are so many of us, aren't there, who are quite content so long as no one thinks that we're odd, so long as no one thinks we're doing something strange, so long as everyone respects us? But God may tell you to 'build an ark' in the middle of your town. He may tell you to begin a 'strange' fellowship in some particular place—and other people might laugh and scorn. But when they come along to see, I trust they'll hear the gospel message. That's grace.

The Ark, standing there, black in all its beauty, must gradually have caused doubts in many people's minds. The growing ship must have spoken volumes to them, especially when Noah began to waterproof it so carefully. "Do you think it's true?"...."Is a flood really going to happen?" These must have been nagging questions in their minds.

God's grace was thus revealed in the form of a ship. What was the second way?

2. Noah himself was a sign

Noah himself was also a sign to the people (see Hebrews 11:7). Noah preached and he preached and he preached, year after year. That was grace. And what was his message? "Unless you repent, you're doomed! Unless you repent and live righteously, the judgment of God is coming upon you. You've got 120 years!…. But I'm building an Ark so that people might be saved!" As time went on, I imagine that Noah announced, "You've got 100 years left!", then, "You've got 80 years left!", then, "You've got 70 years!".... "You've got 50 years!".... "You've got 10 years!".... "Five years!".... Then he announced, "It's coming now—this year! The judgment is coming! Repent, repent, repent!"

The people would mock, saying, "Coming? How is this flood going to come, that you keep talking about?" And Noah would reply, "There's going to be rain. Water is going to pour down from the sky!" Then they'd laugh and laugh. "Oh really, Noah? You're mad!" Noah might have recited the history of Creation—Genesis chapter 1—which he'd been taught faithfully by Adam's descendants. (Noah's father may have learnt it personally from Adam.) He would have recounted the word of God, which probably had not yet been written down, and said, "The water is up there; but soon it's coming down!"

Let's have a look at this. Genesis 1:6-7 tells us, **"Then God said, "Let there be a firmament in the midst of the waters, and let it divide the waters from the waters." Thus God made the firmament, and divided the waters which were under the firmament from the waters which were above the firmament; and it was so."** At first, the earth was covered with water, but then God made a **"firmament"** in the midst of the waters. This is a word for 'expanse' or 'atmosphere'. **"And God called the firmament Heaven"** (verse 8a)—or the 'atmosphere'.

Therefore, on the surface of the earth, there was now one layer of water right the way round, the atmosphere above it and, then, above the earth and the atmosphere, another layer of water. The 'firmament' or 'atmosphere' was between the two layers of water.[7]

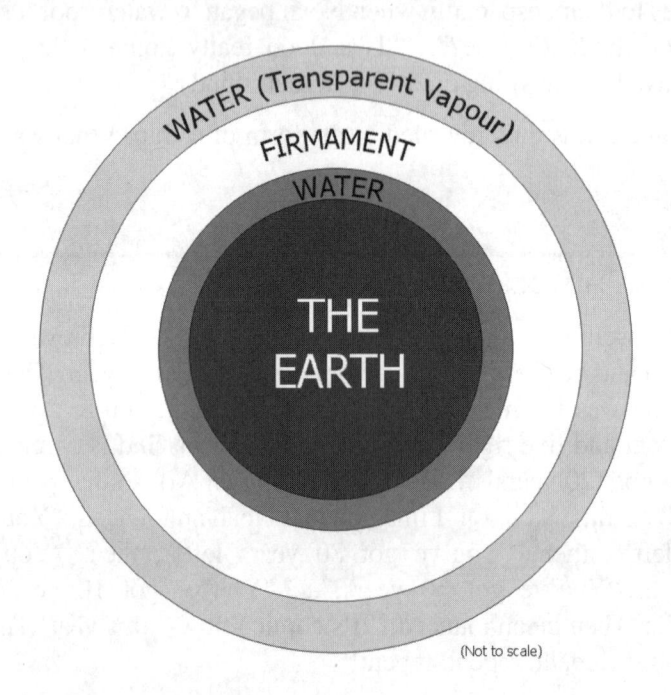

(Diagram: concentric circles labelled from outside to inside — WATER (Transparent Vapour), FIRMAMENT, WATER, THE EARTH. (Not to scale))

---

[7] This account of Creation helps to explain why three 'heavens' are mentioned in the Bible. The first is the atmosphere, the second is outer space, and the third is the throne room of God (see 2 Corinthians 12:2). When the Lord Jesus ascended, the Bible says He went **"through the heavens"** (Ephesians 4:10, Hebrews 4:14). He went right through the earth's atmosphere, right through the universe, and right into the presence of God the Father in the third heaven. We are going to do the same when we are raptured or raised from the dead! And it will not take years to get there. It's going to take just the **"twinkling of an eye"** (1 Corinthians 15: 51-52). Way out beyond Pluto, way out beyond the furthest galaxy—in the twinkling of an eye—because God made it all. And if He can ensure that we will travel millions of light years straight into His throne room, then our beloved Father can certainly look after us down here on this earth!

Incidentally, Genesis 1 tells us that God not only created the atmosphere, but later the birds, and the land creatures and man, in one day. These creatures breathe the atmosphere, so this suggests that God created the atmosphere essentially as it is today. There are scientists trying to simulate how life could 'spontaneously' have arisen out of methane or ammonia or gaseous atmospheres like that. No! God created the atmosphere basically as it is today, containing nitrogen, oxygen, carbon dioxide, neon, argon and all the other rare gases that we find in it. Then He created the living creatures. God made it in a moment of time, just as He did life.

The belt of water outside the atmosphere was probably in the form of water vapour (transparent, super-heated steam). I'm not going to say much about this but, if it was water vapour, then it is most interesting—because water vapour would have absorbed heat and radiated it uniformly all around the earth. The climate of the earth before the Flood would thus have been very different from the climate we find today. In fact, it is probable that every part of the earth had exactly the same climate.

This is rather an interesting thought. It has baffled scientists for a long time as to how, for example, frozen mammoths in Siberia happened to be eating tropical plants when they died. These mammoths are perfectly preserved in ice, yet they've got orchids and other tropical plants in their mouths! I think the answer is that, before the Flood, the earth's climate was uniform. Such a climate would have made it easy, of course, for Noah to have every type of animal inside the Ark, because all the animals would have been living near to each other. Polar bears would have been living in the same area as camels and every other creature! However, we haven't got time to go into this in detail.[8]

The day after God created the atmosphere, the water remaining on the surface of the earth was "**gathered together into one place**" (Genesis 1:9b) and dry land appeared. Some of this water was probably hidden away in vast underground caverns beneath the ocean floors at that time. There would thus have been water right around the earth above the atmosphere, water on the surface of the earth surrounding an area of dry land and water underneath the surface of the earth as well. The earth was ready for habitation—and it was also poised for judgment.

"**In the six hundredth year of Noah's life, in the second month, the seventeenth day of the month, on that day all the fountains of the great deep were broken up, and the windows of heaven were opened**"

---

[8]For more information see the book "In the Beginning" by Roger Price.

(Genesis 7:11). Look how accurate this date is. We shall see the significance of the timing later. The "**fountains of the great deep**" were the reservoirs of water under the surface of the earth. They were broken up.[9] And God caused the water vapour surrounding the atmosphere to condense. This did not happen all at once, or nothing at all would have withstood the volumes of water unleashed. Rather, for a period of 40 days and nights God controlled the flows as water came up from beneath the surface of the earth and as huge volumes of rain fell from above. "**And the rain was on the earth forty days and forty nights**" (verse 12).

Until this time Noah had been preaching, warning of the judgment to come. He had told the people what would happen, and probably had said to them, "Look, Adam told us that when the earth was created God put a belt of water right around. It's up there, and it's going to come down!"

Noah preached faithfully for 120 years. But how many converts did he get? Not one! Only the members of his own immediate family were saved. If we were asked to assess Noah on his ability as an evangelist, we'd probably reject him—we really would! But God was with Noah. It was the evil time in which he lived that explains the reason why so few were saved. It takes a true man of God to preach for 120 years, while being scorned and laughed at. Noah was faithful. Peter tells us he was a "**preacher of righteousness**" (2 Peter 2:5). Noah preached and he preached; and it was grace. God was prepared for one of His beloved children to be mocked and scorned for 120 years, so that the message of salvation might be spread and people could be saved. However, not one person chose to be saved apart from Noah's family. Then the Flood came.

Jesus Christ received similar scorn before He died on the Cross. And He was prepared to take all the scorn, every single part, because He loved us so much. He was faithful. For the joy set before Him, He "**endured the Cross, despising the shame**" (see Hebrews 12:2).

Noah was thus the second sign revealing God's grace. But what was the third sign? Where was the third great area of grace that preceded the flood? It wasn't through Noah this time; and it wasn't through Noah's father. Instead, it was through Noah's *grandfather* that it came—and his name was Methuselah.

---

[9] I think we can observe the remains of some of these today, near the West Indies and in the Pacific, for example, where there are very deep 'trenches'—some up to 35,000 feet (10.7 km) deep—that's about 6000 feet (1.8 km) more than the height of Mount Everest!

3. Methuselah was a sign

Methuselah represents the grace of God as few men have ever done. Methuselah really did live to be 969 years old, and he died at the very time God wanted him to die. His death could not have happened one year later or one year earlier. It was exactly on time. When I was a school teacher, I was asked, "Is it true that Methuselah lived to be 969 and, if so, why?" There's only one answer: it was the grace of God. What am I talking about?

Every name has a meaning in Hebrew. For example, Joshua (Hebrew *Y'hoshua*) means 'the LORD saves'—so if you met a man called Joshua, you should have felt very safe! Related names were *Hoshea*, meaning 'salvation', and *Yeshua*, also meaning 'the LORD saves' or 'salvation' (from which the Greek spelling *Iesous* and the English *Jesus* are derived). Similarly, the name Joel means 'the LORD is God' in Hebrew. I think my favourite name in the Old Testament is Hananiah. There was a false prophet called Hananiah, but there was also another Hananiah who was a friend of Daniel; and his name means 'the LORD is gracious'. It would certainly help in preaching the gospel if you had a name like that, wouldn't it! "What's your name?" you would be asked, and you could reply, "The LORD is gracious!" Everywhere you went you would have an immediate opening to preach the gospel.[10]

The name Methuselah had rather an odd meaning, because it was a short sentence. It meant 'When he is dead it shall be sent', or literally, 'His death shall bring'. What was this talking about? The implication was this: when this man dies, judgment is coming. When Methuselah died, the Flood would be on its way!

As Methuselah grew older and older, I believe God made sure that every wrinkle showed and every grey hair stood out, so that the people would know Methuselah was getting extremely old! Every wrinkle represented God's grace. Perhaps his back bent more and more as the years went by. Children would say, "Look, father, he's got another wrinkle," and the reply would come, "Oh, that's Methuselah—when he is dead it shall be sent." I imagine people pointing out Methuselah, saying, "There's that man called 'His death shall bring'," but many would mock, saying, "It's rubbish!

---

[10] The name 'Noah' was also significant. It means 'rest' or 'comfort'. Through Noah would come rest from mankind's hard toil because of the ground that had been cursed by God (see Genesis 5:29). This probably referred to Noah being God's deliverer of the whole world. In fact, a revelation of God's plan of salvation can be identified within the meaning of the 10 names in the genealogy from Adam to Noah (see Genesis 5).

Nothing is going to happen when he dies." And children would wonder whether anything *was* going to happen. To see the timing of what did happen, we need to examine Genesis chapter 5.

The genealogies found in the Bible are important and tell us a lot of interesting things. Genesis chapter 5 tells us: "**Methuselah lived one hundred and eighty-seven years, and begot Lamech**" (verse 25). Methuselah was 187 when Lamech was born. Then we are told "**Lamech lived one hundred and eighty-two years, and begot a son. And he called his name Noah...**" (verses 28-29a). Lamech, Noah's father, was 182 when Noah was born. Methuselah was Noah's grandfather. Therefore if we add these years together we find out how old Methuselah was when Noah was born; and he was 187 + 182 = 369 years old.

Methuselah lived to be 969 years old. So how old was Noah when Methuselah died? He was 969 − 369 = 600. Noah was *600 years old* when Methuselah died; and 'when he is dead it shall be sent'.

Let's turn back to Genesis 7:11. What did it say? "**In the six hundredth year of Noah's life....all the fountains of the great deep were broken up, and the windows of heaven were opened.**" Who wasn't there? Methuselah wasn't—praise God! He'd just died. Noah was 600, Methuselah died, and *then* the Flood came! These genealogies are so important. It was grace. It was the grace of God.

Notice how specific this verse is: "**In the six hundredth year of Noah's life, in the second month, the seventeenth day of the month, on that day...**". There were 30 days in the first month; then 17 days later it began to rain. That means it was 47 days into the 600th year of Noah's life when the Flood began. I think God probably planned it so that Methuselah died right at the beginning of the year. That would have given Noah 47 days[11] during which to preach, using Methuselah as his example. I expect Noah preached at Methuselah's funeral service as well! He wouldn't have said, "Love your neighbour and everything will be all right!" Rather, Noah would have declared, "When he is dead it shall be sent; and, folks, he's now dead—the judgment is coming any day now!" That was Noah's message—and it was still a message of grace, just days before the Flood came. There was still time for people to repent and be saved by entering

---

[11] It was 40 days into the year when Noah entered the Ark; then there were seven further days during which the animals came in before the Flood began. It is not clear whether Noah could preach during those last seven days. Perhaps he preached from the top window of the ship!

the Ark. The forgiveness of God was still available. Thus, Methuselah stands in our Bible as a wonderful testimony to grace before judgment.

The Sign of the Rainbow

We have seen three ways in which God reached out to the sinful people in the days prior to the Flood: (1) the Ark; (2) Noah himself; and (3) Methuselah. They all were important ways in which God's grace was revealed.

Directly after the Flood, God made a covenant with Noah and his descendants, and promised, **"Never again shall there be a flood to destroy the earth"** (Genesis 9:11b). And He gave a sign of that covenant—the rainbow (see Genesis 9:8-17). How is a rainbow formed? It is caused by light passing through *raindrops*! There could not have been a rainbow before the Flood, because there had been no rain; but following the Flood, rain has been falling regularly upon the earth. To me a rainbow always represents the grace of God and the faithfulness of God in keeping His promises. Doesn't it to every Christian? I have seen a rainbow so often and been encouraged. It reminds us of God's presence with us and of His covenant with man: "I'm never going to destroy the earth with water again."

The history of the Flood is indeed one of the greatest stories of God's grace in the whole of the Old Testament. God's grace was truly revealed before His judgment came in the form of water.

GRACE BEFORE THE COMING JUDGMENT

God's judgment will come with fire next time. Peter wrote, **"Beloved, I now write to you this second epistle (in both of which I stir up your pure minds by way of reminder), that you may be mindful of the words which were spoken before by the holy prophets, and of the commandment of us the apostles of the Lord and Saviour, knowing this first: that scoffers will come in the last days, walking according to their own lusts, and saying, "Where is the promise of His coming? For since the fathers fell asleep, all things continue as they were from the beginning of creation""** (2 Peter 3:1-4). We are now living in these very last days. Today, many people mock, saying, "Jesus isn't coming! Where is He, if He's coming?" They assume that the world has always carried on and will always carry on just as it is.

However, such mockers are forgetting what happened at the Flood. **"For this they wilfully forget: that by the word of God the heavens were of** old, and the earth standing out of water and in the water, by which the world that then existed perished, being flooded with water. But the heavens and the earth which now exist are kept in store by the same word, reserved for fire until the day of judgment and perdition of ungodly men. But, beloved, do not forget this one thing, that with the Lord one day is as a thousand years, and a thousand years as one day. The Lord is not slack concerning His promise, as some count slackness, but is long-suffering toward us, not willing that any should perish but that all should come to repentance**" (verses 5-9). This was the apostle Peter's view of the Flood and of the judgment to come, inspired by the Holy Spirit. As was the case during the years prior to the Flood, God is now patiently withholding His judgment, offering grace so that people might turn to Him before He sends judgment—because He does not want any to perish.

NOAH'S ARK: A PICTURE OF CHRIST

To complete our study of the Flood, I want to list six things that Noah's Ark typifies about Christ and about our salvation.

1. *The Ark was God's appointed means of saving the human race.* God was the One who designed the Ark. He knew how big to make it; He knew how strong it had to be. The analogy for us is that Christ is God's appointed means of salvation for man. He is the One appointed for the salvation of any person who will choose to come and take refuge in Him.

2. *The Ark was the only means of saving the human race.* Water cascaded down on the earth from above and water gushed up from beneath. No other boat or ship could have withstood the forces unleashed upon the earth at that time. The Ark was the *only* vessel that could survive the battering, because it was perfectly designed to do so. It was a unique ship; and it was the *only* means by which the people could be saved. Similarly, there is salvation in none other than the Lord Jesus Christ. As Peter declared in Acts 4:12, "**Nor is there salvation in any other, for there is no other name under heaven given among men by which we must be saved.**" Christ is the *only* means of salvation.

3. *The Ark took all the beating.* All of the water falling down and crashing around, all the water swirling up from beneath, all the rocks being picked up and thrown about, all the trees being hurled—the Ark took it all; and the people inside didn't take any of the violence of it. Similarly, Christ took all the beating for us. He was the One who was scourged when I deserved to be scourged. He was the One who came within an inch of His life through all the beatings, and then chose to give up His life on the Cross of Calvary. *I* should have been there; but *He* took the beating for me. Praise His wonderful name!

4. *Entrance into the Ark was voluntary.* Noah could not force anyone to get into the Ark. I'm sure he would have done so if he could; but neither he, nor his family, could force anyone. The people of the world had freewill; they had a choice whether or not to come on board. In the same way, we cannot force anyone to accept Christ. It is only when someone *willingly* repents, puts his trust in the Lord and chooses the salvation God has provided that he becomes a Christian and is saved.

5. *Entrance into the Ark was free.* No tickets were necessary to enter the Ark and no payment had to be made. Entrance was entirely free. Similarly, salvation is by grace and is free. You cannot pay for it, you cannot earn it and you can never deserve it. "**For by grace you have been saved through faith, and that not of yourselves; it is the gift of God, not of works, lest anyone should boast**" (see Ephesians 2:8-9).

6. *It was God who shut the door and it was God who looked after the Ark during the time that it was afloat.* It was *God* who shut Noah and his family inside the Ark and kept them safe. Noah couldn't shut the door once aboard. Only God could do it, so "**the LORD shut him in**" (Genesis 7:16b). Noah also could do nothing to help keep the Ark afloat. Thus Peter wrote that we are "**kept by the power of God**" (see 1 Peter 1:5). We who are in Christ are kept by God's power—because *He* has shut us in Christ.

CONCLUSION

"**Now to Him who is able to keep you from stumbling, and to present you faultless before the presence of His glory with exceeding joy, to God our Saviour, who alone is wise, be glory and majesty, dominion and power, both now and for ever. Amen**" (Jude 24-25). Our future is entrusted to God; and He cannot fail. Therefore, our future is certain and clear. We who are believers are going to be preserved. We will not be destroyed in the judgment to come, because we are kept by God's power! We are eternally secure, and will be kept safe through the wrath to come. Praise God!

I want to look at one last scripture to end, which is 2 Peter 2:4-9. "**For if God did not spare the angels who sinned, but cast them down to hell [Tartarus] and delivered them into chains of darkness, to be reserved for judgment; and did not spare the ancient world, but saved Noah,** one of eight people, a preacher of righteousness, bringing in the flood on the world of the ungodly; and turning the cities of Sodom and Gomorrah into ashes, condemned them to destruction, making them an example to those who afterwards would lead an ungodly life; and delivered righteous Lot, who was oppressed with the filthy conduct of the wicked (for that righteous man, dwelling among them, tormented his righteous soul from day to day by seeing and hearing their lawless deeds)—then the Lord knows how to deliver the godly out of temptations and to reserve the unjust under punishment for the day of judgment".

In Christ there is no judgment (Romans 8:1), but outside of Christ judgment remains (John 3:18, 36). Today is still a day of grace; but the day of judgment will follow directly afterwards. We live in a day of grace before judgment—a day of salvation. Therefore, receive Christ now in the day of grace! When the day of judgment comes it will be too late. May the Lord use His Word to bring many people to Him in this day of grace, and may they not harden their hearts as they did in the time of Noah. The 'Ark' of Christ remains open, and God still longs for people to come to Him, wretched sinners that we are. Though we deserve all the judgment that God will bring, the Holy Spirit *is* striving with man still. Praise His name!

4. JAMES & JOHN, AND JONAH
How God taught them Lessons about Grace

Grace before Judgment has become one of my favourite subjects. I have received so much grace myself, throughout the whole of my Christian life, that it is a sheer delight to talk about the grace of God. Grace cannot be earned; therefore, on the basis of grace, we are immediately all equal. I can testify, as all Christians can, that the grace of God *is* sufficient for every need. We thus have the privilege of representing the grace of God to everyone around us. Judgment *is* coming, but now grace is manifest through each one of us.

This is our final study on the Grace before Judgment principle, so to bring this vast subject down to a more personal level I have chosen to look at three men found in the Bible. These three characters did not at first understand the principle of Grace before Judgment, and certainly didn't apply it, yet God showed great grace to them and graciously taught them about His grace. The first two go together, for they were brothers.

JAMES & JOHN: Transformed by God's grace

Mark chapter 3 recounts: "**Then He [Jesus] appointed twelve, that they might be with Him and that He might send them out to preach, and to have power to heal sicknesses and to cast out demons: Simon, to whom He gave the name Peter; James the son of Zebedee and John the brother of James, to whom He gave the name Boanerges, that is, "Sons of Thunder"...**" (verses 14-17). Here are the two men: James and John. They were the sons of Zebedee; but Jesus called them "Sons of Thunder", in view of their thunderous natures.

Everyone knows that thunder can be very noisy, and may seem frightening, but not everyone knows how it is created. It is caused when an electrical spark goes through the air. The intense heat from that fork of electricity causes the air around it to expand and rush outwards. Then, as soon as the spark is gone, there is instantaneous cooling and a vacuum is formed. Air rushes into the vacuum causing a 'crash', and there is a loud rumble as this occurs. So what is thunder? It is *noise created by a lot of hot air and wind*! And I think that summarizes aptly the early lives of James and John: they caused lots of noise and ferment, but it was all 'hot air' and 'wind' inside!

There are Christians who are like this. However, God is leading us all to a place of solidity in our lives. Note that it was *Jesus* who named them 'Boanerges', which means 'Sons of Thunder'.[1] Let's have a brief look at their lives.

It was the mother of James and John who later went with them to Jesus and asked, **"Grant that these two sons of mine may sit, one on Your right hand and the other on the left, in Your kingdom"** (Matthew 20:21b). What a request! And whenever there was a dispute about who was going to be the greatest, always James and John were the ones most concerned about their position, full of selfish ambition.

Luke 9:46 says, **"Then a dispute arose among them as to which of them would be greatest."** Jesus responded by taking a child; and the answer He gave is recorded at the end of verse 48: **"For he who is least among you all will be great."**

James and John then both tried, with Jesus watching, to show how great they were going to be. They were only Jesus' apostles because of His grace, of course, and I'm sure Jesus needed to keep showing them a lot of grace when they were in His presence! It was a shame they didn't extend the same principle of grace to others!

"Then John answered and said, "Master, we saw someone casting out demons in Your name, and we forbade him because he does not follow with us"" (verse 49). John had the attitude, "Master, You'll be glad to hear this!" Someone, who was clearly a believer, had been successfully casting out demons in the name of the Lord Jesus. Needy people were being set free through this other man's ministry, but John, so filled with party spirit for his own group, proudly stated, "I stopped him, Lord, because he's not one of us! Isn't that marvellous?"

This is an example of one of the beginnings of *denominationalism* in the New Testament. John did not understand. God's grace was bigger than their band. It was *much* bigger than that! It could extend to any believer.

---

[1] *The word 'Boanerges' may come from the Hebrew for 'sons of tumult' or 'sons of rage/anger'. It clearly pointed to their fiery, zealous, volatile dispositions. The gospels reveal that, in their youth, James and John were ambitious, wanted preferential treatment and tended towards misguided 'righteous' indignation—motivated more by a sense of superiority or vindictiveness than true righteousness. They tended to see everything and everyone in 'black and white', either for or against the Lord, and then judged accordingly.*

Jesus had to teach John a lesson about grace. "**But Jesus said to him, "Do not forbid him, for he who is not against us is for us""** (verse 50).

The story does not end there. "**Now it came to pass, when the time had come for Him to be received up, that He steadfastly set His face to go to Jerusalem, and sent messengers before His face. And as they went, they entered a village of the Samaritans, to prepare for Him**" (verses 51-52). The Samaritans despised anyone who worshipped in Jerusalem; they worshipped on their own mountain. Now Jesus had set His face as flint to go to Jerusalem. Therefore, He was not going to get a very good reception in Samaria. "**But they did not receive Him because His face was set for the journey to Jerusalem**" (verse 53).

"**And when His disciples James and John saw this, they said, "Lord, do You want us to command fire to come down from heaven and consume them, just as Elijah did?""** (verse 54). Was this a gracious attitude? No, it certainly was not! But it was characteristic of James and John: lots of noise; lots of thunder! They wanted to command fire to come down; and they spoke as if they were great men of God, able to do this! But *they* couldn't do it. They didn't have the authority to do it. They were not representing the Lord's attitude. Rather, it was just *them*—offering judgment before grace!

Jesus wasn't going to allow these young disciples to continue with such a misconception, of course: "**But He turned and rebuked them, and said, "You do not know what manner of spirit you are of. For the Son of Man did not come to destroy men's lives but to save them**" (verses 55-56a).

To be fair to James and John, they didn't always remain like this. They were among Jesus' closest disciples and friends, and they were gradually transformed. After Pentecost, when the Holy Spirit came upon them in power, and after further years of being disciples of the Lord, we find a new James and a new John.

James was actually the first of the twelve apostles to die as a martyr (Acts 12:2), and his brother John, as the Lord designed it, was the last to die. James was martyred for Jesus, killed by Herod Agrippa I. What a privilege! And John had the equal privilege of living for the Lord Jesus.

Before John died—that Son of Thunder—he wrote one of the most beautiful pieces of prose there has ever has been—John's Gospel. He also wrote three sublime letters. And what were they about? *Love!* There was no more commanding fire to come down, no more seeking to prove himself, no more looking for the judgment of others. Rather, there was love pouring out through him, and his message was about the need for love. John had changed. He was still a Son of Thunder, but now a very different one—because, at the end of the Bible, the thunderous voice of John booms out as the inspired author of the Book of Revelation.

I always try to remember John not as he was in the gospels. I remember him as he was on his death-bed: an old man, probably aged about 100, who had witnessed the Church already splitting apart—and this had crushed him so much. We learn from history that, in Ephesus, as he was dying—a frail man, with many brethren around him—his last act was to lift his hands to heaven to ask a blessing upon the Church. His last words were reported to be these: *"Little children, love one another, because such was the Lord's command; and if this only be done, it is enough."*[2] Here is our Son of Thunder at the end of his life, transformed by the love of His Lord.

There is no replacement in the Christian life for experience. I do not believe there ever can be; I really don't. I believe that the gifts of God can be given to anyone; but the fruit of the Spirit only come when our lives have been dealt-with by God.

Just consider these beautiful words: *"Little children, love one another, because such was the Lord's command; and if this only be done, it is enough."* It is so easy to say these words, isn't it? It is so easy to think that we've got the meaning of them. But I believe we need really to understand the meaning of them, all of us, throughout the whole Body of Christ.

We need to beware of the attitudes James and John had in their early days—their party spirit, their denominationalism, their excessive zeal, their failure to rejoice when others were blessed. Rather, we should rejoice when *Jesus* is blessed; that is real submission to the Spirit of God. When the local church down the road is growing, we should be saying, "Praise You, Lord, because Your name is being uplifted in this place! People are being saved and set free—Thank You, Lord!" That is loving one another. That is preferring one another (Romans 12:10). When we can say, "Thank you, Lord," even if we are being trodden into the ground, and can say, "For my brother I'd do anything, Lord, because I'm doing it for You"—*that* is love. There is such a contrast between thunderous judgmentalism and God's love.

---

[2] The source of this quotation is probably Irenaeus or Eusebius. Irenaeus was a 2nd Century disciple of Polycarp, bishop of Smyrna. Polycarp had learned the gospel directly from John and others who had seen the Lord personally. Irenaeus noted that John lived until the time of the Roman Emperor Trajan. John therefore lived to a great age, since Trajan was emperor from AD 98-117. Eusebius, who wrote in the 4th Century, also said (quoting Polycrates, an earlier bishop of Ephesus) that John returned from exile on Patmos to live in Ephesus until the time of Trajan.

These two brothers did not understand the grace of God at first, but they came to understand as they began listening to Jesus and to the Holy Spirit who taught them and changed them. Soon, their whole lives were dedicated to God's love and grace.

Now I want to concentrate on one man in the Old Testament who resisted learning the lessons God wanted to teach him about grace. He was a prophet; so first we need to know a little about the Old Testament prophets.

THE PROPHETS

There is a common misconception that all the prophets were only messengers of doom. However, that is a mistaken idea. If we believe this and then we try to read our way through the Books of Isaiah, Joel or Habakkuk, for example, we will not understand much of them; or the Book of Nahum will defeat us.

However, if we understand the prophets in the context of God's grace, then we will find that they were not so much prophets of doom; they were first and foremost prophets of *grace*—of grace before judgment!

If God had wanted to destroy Edom immediately He could have done so. He could have blotted the Edomites out without giving them any notice. But He *didn't* do that. Instead, He first raised up a wonderful believer, called Obadiah—one of my favourite believers, in fact. Obadiah declared the word of God concerning Edom to the people there who hated God and hated him. What was God doing? He was warning the Edomites of the judgment that was coming in view of their pride and their violence against Israel (see Obadiah 3, 10). He was telling them what they had done to deserve judgment, to give them an opportunity to repent.

God could have destroyed Babylon with no notice. But He *didn't* do so until He'd first revealed their impending destruction through prophets such as Jeremiah, Habakkuk and Daniel. God first told the Babylonians what they had done wrong and what was going to happen to them—unless they repented. That was grace.

If God warns us, "If you carry on the way you're going, the consequence will be... ," then that is grace, because God is giving us an opportunity to repent. He wants us to repent so that He can bless us and show us His goodness, rather than judge us.

The prophet Jeremiah, for example, was a wonderful believer. As well as prophesying to Judah (Jeremiah chapters 2-45), God gave him messages for a number of Gentile nations (chapters 46-51): Egypt, the Philistines,

Moab, Ammon, Edom, Damascus, Kedar and Hazor (Arabia), Elam and Babylon. What message did he preach? "God will have to judge you soon—unless you repent!" He even went to Egypt and prophesied there. Ezekiel prophesied to a similar list of nations that were neighbours of Judah, including Tyre and Sidon.

The prophets were truly wonderful servants of God. Every single prophet, to me, speaks primarily of grace, not of judgment and doom. God could simply have obliterated the nations to which they preached, but He did not; and He could simply have judged Israel and Judah without warning too.

Do you realize what the prophets had to suffer? They dedicated their whole lives to the LORD and, as a result, they suffered terrible persecution. They were reviled; they were imprisoned; they were maimed; they were tortured; and some were killed—because God loved Israel, Judah and all the nations so much. These wonderful believers didn't think of their own comfort. Instead, they obeyed God and took the message of His love to those who needed to hear it.

Have you read what Jeremiah, for example, endured? It is a fascinating Bible study, if you have not. He suffered terribly.[3] And it is said that Isaiah was sawn in two by King Manasseh (cf. Hebrews 11:37), a king to whom he had preached the word of God so faithfully. This is the type of suffering these men went through. It is no wonder the Book of Hebrews describes them as people "**of whom the world was not worthy**" (Hebrews 11:38a).

However, there is one prophet who sticks out like a sore thumb, and that's Jonah! We are going to concentrate now on the Book of Jonah, and we shall see how God showed Jonah nothing but grace, yet how Jonah showed the Ninevites, and the LORD, nothing but bitterness, all the way through.

JONAH: WONDERFUL LESSONS ABOUT GRACE

God could have destroyed the Ninevites very easily but, instead, He chose to preach a message to them first. And the man He chose to preach that message for Him was Jonah.

---

[3] See for example Jeremiah chapters 26-29, 37:11-16 and 38:1-13. Jeremiah faithfully proclaimed God's word to Judah for 40 years, but was rewarded with opposition, beatings, isolation, imprisonment and a charge of treason. His life was one of continual conflict, because he faithfully foretold God's coming judgment on Judah through the Babylonians. He was persecuted by his own family, threatened in his home town of Anathoth, put on trial for his life by the priests and prophets in Jerusalem, put in stocks, forced to hide from King Jehoiakim who burnt his prophecy, publicly confronted by the false prophet Hananiah, thrown into a cistern, and so on.

Jonah chapter 1

"**Now the word of the L**ORD **came to Jonah the son of Amittai, saying, "Arise, go to Nineveh, that great city, and cry out against it; for their wickedness has come up before Me**" (verses 1-2). Nineveh was a great city of Assyria. It was to become the vast capital of the Assyrian Empire—the mightiest city on earth.[4] However, the 'smell' of Nineveh—the stench of that city, because it was so full of idolatry and of people who hated God—had come up to heaven.

The Assyrians are reckoned to have been probably the most cruel people that the world has ever seen—they have not been surpassed. They excelled in violence and war. Even to read about some of the vile things that their armies did is enough to make one's hair stand on end. If I told you some of the things that the Ninevites boasted of doing, you'd probably say they deserved to be smashed: and they did—just as we also do. However, we are dealing with the wonderful principle of Grace before Judgment. Therefore God—instead of smashing them into the ground immediately (as I would have done and as Jonah certainly wanted to do)—said to Jonah, "Jonah, I want you to go and cry out against that city! I want you to go and tell the Ninevites what is going to happen to them!"

Notice how verse 3 begins with "**But Jonah...**", whereas verse 4 begins "**But the LORD...**". A struggle was now on. Jonah did not want to go and preach to the Ninevites. In fact, it is clear that he did not want Nineveh to be saved. He was bitter towards the Ninevites and he loathed them. The thought of them being saved and blessed was too much![5]

Jonah thought, "The LORD might have called me to this, but I'm going in the opposite direction!" "**But Jonah arose to flee to Tarshish from the presence of the L**ORD**. He went down to Joppa, and found a ship going**

---

[4] At its peak, Nineveh is described as having several walls, some 100 feet (30 m) tall (or 100 bricks tall), with 1500 huge watchtowers reaching a further 100 feet up and 15 magnificent gates. The inner wall was so wide that three or four chariots could travel abreast along the top. The walls were surrounded by a moat 150 feet wide and 60 feet deep. The wealth in the city was fantastic. It had magnificent palaces, gardens, canals and more than thirty gold- and silver-covered temples. Nineveh became probably the richest city there has ever been.

[5] The Assyrian Empire lasted from about 960 BC to 612 BC, with its peak from about 750 to 650 BC. During the mid-9th Century BC, particularly under Ashur-Nasir-Pal (c.883-859 BC), Assyria expanded greatly and its domination of other peoples by terror increased sharply—including of Israel. However, during the reign of King Jeroboam II (793-753 BC) in Israel—the probable time of Jonah's ministry—Israel expanded and prospered again, following a time of affliction (2 Kings 14:25-26). Assyria meanwhile was in period of mild decline, due to internal strife, but remained a threat. The Assyrian army (of perhaps 2 million soldiers) practised genocide and the deportation of whole populations. Its cruelty, already legendary, meant that the Jews would have longed for the destruction of Nineveh.

to Tarshish; so he paid the fare, and went down into it..." (verse 3a).[6] There are two things we need to know about Tarshish. First, it was in the opposite direction to Nineveh. Second, it was the furthest place Jonah could go to in his day—the edge of the world. It was probably a trading port in southern Spain, on the Mediterranean Sea coast. Beyond were the "Gates of Hercules", or what we call the Straits of Gibraltar. The Phoenician sailors of that time believed that, just beyond, the sea fell off the world.[7]

Therefore, Jonah was going to go as far as he possibly could in the opposite direction to Nineveh! He was determined to go directly against the will of God, away from the commission he had received. He went down into the ship, "**...to go with them to Tarshish from the presence of the LORD**" (verse 3b).

Now we begin to see God's grace. God wanted Jonah to preach in Nineveh; and He so loved the Ninevites that He was determined to have Jonah preach. A legalistic believer might conclude that God chose the wrong man, but that was not true! God had chosen exactly the *right* man for the job. A legalistic believer might also wonder why God did not smash Jonah, send fire down on him and destroy him. But no! There is *grace* before judgment—*always* grace before judgment. Instead, God sent a storm.

"**But the LORD sent out a great wind on the sea, and there was a mighty tempest on the sea, so that the ship was about to be broken up. Then the mariners were afraid; and every man cried out to his god, and threw the cargo that was in the ship into the sea, to lighten the load**" (verses 4-5a). Can you imagine this scene of panic in the middle of the Mediterranean? Ancient wooden ships were not always well built; and this one was about to fall apart. But it must have been an exceptionally violent storm if even these accomplished Phoenician sailors were afraid and wailing to their gods to intervene. They were doing anything they could think of to calm the storm.

---

[6] Joppa is present-day Jaffa (Yafo in Hebrew), the Mediterranean port just south of Tel Aviv.

[7] Between about 1000 and 500 BC the Phoenicians were responsible for most sea traffic in the Mediterranean. They were great sailors, and they pioneered exploration and trading by sea. It is therefore very likely that the vessel Jonah joined was a Phoenician merchant ship.

About 600 years after the time of Jonah, the Phoenicians probably discovered America, landing near present-day Baltimore. However, it was at the time when the Romans were fighting the Carthaginians (who were Phoenicians) and the Romans killed them, preventing them from escaping to the new land they had discovered. At the time of Jonah and the Assyrian empire, however, they had only reached Tarshish and no further.

What was Jonah doing? He should have been praying, "Oh Lord, deliver us! I've got to get the gospel out to these sailors before we all die. I've got to make sure that they know about You!" "**But Jonah had gone down into the lowest parts of the ship, had lain down, and was fast asleep**" (verse 5b).

Sadly, I think this is a picture of many Christians today. While the 'ship' of this world is breaking up all around them they are fast asleep. In some ways I admire Jonah's faith at this point; I don't think I would have slept much on that ship in such a storm! We can see how Jonah didn't really care about the sailors he was with, just as he didn't really care about the Ninevites.

In fact this summarizes the life of Jonah: *he cared more about himself than he did about anyone else*. "**So the captain came to him, and said to him, "What do you mean, sleeper? Arise, call on your God; perhaps your God will consider us, so that we may not perish." And they said to one another, "Come, let us cast lots, that we may know for whose cause this trouble has come upon us." So they cast lots, and the lot fell on Jonah**" (verses 6-7). Thus the LORD revealed to the unbelievers that Jonah held the key to what this trouble was all about.

"**Then they said to him, "Please tell us! For whose cause is this trouble upon us? What is your occupation? And where do you come from? What is your country? And of what people are you?" And he said to them, "I am a Hebrew; and I fear the LORD, the God of heaven, who made the sea and the dry land." Then the men were exceedingly afraid, and said to him, "Why have you done this?" For the men knew that he fled from the presence of the LORD, because he had told them**" (verses 8-10).

These men were so gracious to Jonah. He effectively admitted to being the cause of the crisis and they listened patiently while he explained it all. "I've disobeyed my God, who made the sea and the dry land, and this is His way of showing His displeasure and getting my attention!" The sailors understood; and they were very afraid. "**Then they said to him, "What shall we do to you that the sea may be calm for us?"—for the sea was growing more tempestuous. And he said to them, "Pick me up and throw me into the sea; then the sea will become calm for you. For I know that this great tempest is because of me"**" (verses 11-12).

Did the sailors immediately throw Jonah overboard to save their own skins? They did not: "**Nevertheless the men rowed hard to bring the ship to land, but they could not, for the sea continued to grow more tempestuous against them**" (verse 13). What grace this was! Here were *un*believers, showing grace to Jonah—a miserable, self-centred, out-of-fellowship believer. It is indeed the case that unbelievers sometimes show believers up terribly and this is an example. Jonah could not have cared less about the Phoenician sailors; but they cared for him—much more than he did for them or for the Ninevites.

Can you see how God was trying to teach Jonah about grace through these unbelievers? He was saying, "Look, Jonah! Even these Phoenicians care about you. How much more do I care for the Ninevites? Yet you stubbornly refuse to go to them!"

"**Therefore they cried out to the LORD, and said, "We pray, O LORD, please do not let us perish for this man's life, and do not charge us with innocent blood; for You, O LORD, have done as it pleased You." So they picked up Jonah and threw him into the sea, and the sea ceased from its raging**" (verses 14-15). Here is an example of God's overriding grace—of the Romans 8:28 principle. The sailors cried out to the LORD and prayed to Him! "**Then the men feared the LORD exceedingly, and offered a sacrifice to the LORD and made vows**" (verse 16). Already Jonah had won 'converts'! The sailors began worshipping the LORD. Jonah was soon going to have many more converts, but he had started reaching others already. Praise God! This shows us that even if our attitude is totally wrong, like Jonah's, God can still use our life. It was His grace every step of the way. It demonstrates the greatness of our God and reflects nothing at all on Jonah's life or ability. God had used the calming of the storm to demonstrate His might.

Now we come to a beautiful thing. Jonah deserved to drown. He hadn't obeyed his calling. In my natural reasoning I would say, "Let him sink to the bottom!" But no! God knew what was going to happen with Jonah and He'd already prepared for it. "**Now the LORD had prepared a great fish to swallow Jonah**" (verse 17a). God sent a huge fish[8]—a 'living submarine'—and it was God's ordained vessel for that precise moment. When Jonah was thrown overboard, the fish just came along and snapped him up.

---

[8] The Hebrew word speaks of a great fish. It was not a whale. A whale is a mammal and not a fish. The AV uses the word 'whale' in Matthew's Gospel, but the Greek word used (ketos) in Matthew 12:40, as well as in the Septuagint's Book of Jonah, means 'sea monster' or 'huge fish'. Our present knowledge of whales confirms that it could not have been a whale. In the 17th Century, however, 'whale' would have seemed a sensible word to the Bible translators.

There is no need to give an apology for the great fish swallowing Jonah or to quote articles about other men who have been swallowed by great fish in an effort to prove it can happen. Our God is God of the 'impossible'! It was a miracle. It really happened. It is in the Word of God; and that is all that needs to be said on the matter.

Why didn't God let Jonah just die? After all, he'd been disobedient—so why not let him drown and be finished with him? First, God rescued Jonah because He happened to love Jonah. And He didn't just love him—He loved him a great deal! This fish represented God's love and grace to Jonah. Second, God loved the Ninevites and He still wanted to use Jonah to preach to them. Jonah was still God's man for the job!

In fact, the great fish represented more, because one of the things we know about the Ninevites is that they worshipped a fish-god.[9] The counsels of God are so miraculous and so wonderful. What an example this is of the Romans 8:28 principle! As Jonah walked through Nineveh later, every time he saw a temple dedicated to their fish-god, he could say, "You worship a little fish, but my God prepared a huge fish that obeyed Him. My God is much greater than your little gods. He is God of all gods! Therefore, you'd better turn to Him!"

This was grace upon grace! God was not just saving Jonah's life so that he could at last go and bring God's word to Nineveh; He was giving him an even more wonderful message to proclaim as well. God could have rescued Jonah in many different ways, but He happened to know that the Ninevites needed Jonah to be rescued by a big fish!

"And Jonah was in the belly of the fish three days and three nights" (verse 17b). There are wonderful ways, of course, in which this was a type of the Lord Jesus (see Matthew 12:40), but we don't have time to go into that here. The important thing to note is that God was prepared in advance for Jonah's disobedience. God knew that Jonah was going to need some coercion to fulfil his commission!

Jonah chapter 2

In chapter 2 we find Jonah 'back in fellowship', praying to the LORD and praising Him for His mercy. He'd come back to his right mind now. Remember that this probably took place 40 fathoms down and travelling at

---

[9] The Assyrians had many gods, whom they tried to appease and gain the favour of. There was probably a whole hierarchy of these capricious gods, ranging from individual and family gods right up to national deities. The chief gods were Ashur and Ishtar (who was sometimes represented with the sign of a fish or riding on the back of a lion). The symbol of Nineveh itself was a pregnant woman or a house containing a fish. Nineveh might have been named after the goddess of fish, Nina or Nanshe. The Ninevites also worshipped Ea, god of the waters and wisdom, whose priests were represented as half man and half fish. The Ninevites may also have adopted the god Dagon (or Dagan), who was worshipped in the Near East for some 1500 years. He was thought to be a fish-god, but is now understood to have been a god of grain, storms and weather. Dagon was the chief god of the Philistines (Judges 16:23; 1 Samuel 5:2ff).

several knots back towards Nineveh! Jonah was deep down under the sea and it was completely dark.

"**Then Jonah prayed to the LORD his God from the fish's belly. And he said, "I cried out to the LORD because of my affliction, and He answered me. Out of the belly of Sheol I cried, and You heard my voice"**" (Jonah 2:1-2). Jonah knew a bit about the LORD—that He hears the cries of His people. He recognized how God had saved him from the brink of death by sending the fish, immediately after he'd cried out for help. Jonah was still in a major dilemma, inside the fish, but he was now praising and thanking God for his miraculous deliverance. There was now praise issuing up from the depths of the sea, and God heard it.

Isn't God amazing! No *man* can hear what is spoken inside a submarine that is 40 fathoms down; but *God* can hear and, what is more, He hears every word that is being said inside someone's *heart* down there—or anywhere else. He happens to be God down there as well!

"**For You cast me into the deep, into the heart of the seas, and the floods surrounded me; all Your billows and Your waves passed over me. Then I said, 'I have been cast out of Your sight'; yet I will look again towards Your holy temple**" (verses 3-4). Notice how Jonah did not say, "The Phoenicians cast me into the deep," but rather, "*You* did it, Lord." He recognized God's hand in his life, just as we should. "**The waters encompassed me, even to my soul; the deep closed around me; weeds were wrapped around my head. I went down to the moorings of the mountains; the earth with its bars closed behind me for ever; yet You have brought up my life from the pit, O LORD, my God**" (verses 5-6).

Sometimes God has to bring us to the end of ourselves to show us His tremendous provision. Jonah continued, "**When my soul fainted within me, I remembered the LORD; and my prayer went up to You, into Your holy temple. Those who regard worthless idols forsake their own Mercy**" (verses 7-8). The last sentence contains a Hebrew idiom and means "Those who *kid themselves* forsake their own Mercy." There should be no place in our lives for kidding ourselves, because it is deception and idolatry. Jonah had thought that he could escape God's presence and assignment; but it was not true. We cannot do it either!

We are here to serve the Lord. Are you deceiving yourself, perhaps, that you could be happy doing something else? Are you saying to yourself, "If only I had this...," or, "If only I had that..., *then* I'd be happy." You would *not* be happy for long! As a Christian you are designed to serve God, and the *only* way you are ever going to be fulfilled is by serving the Lord with all your heart. If you kid yourself about this, then you are forsaking God's mercy. I feel sorry for Christians who are trying to gain satisfaction from the world—because they don't enjoy the world, and they don't fully enjoy the Lord either. The most miserable Christians are certainly those who are trying to live in two camps. Rather, we should say, "**But as for me and my house, we will serve the LORD**" (Joshua 24:15b). There is "**joy unspeakable and full of glory**" in serving the Lord (1 Peter 1:8b, AV). Don't fool yourself.

Jonah had come to his right mind again. He was effectively saying, "Lord, I've stopped kidding myself now, and am glad to be experiencing Your mercy once again." In verse 9 we find his sacrifice of praise: "**But I will sacrifice to You with the voice of thanksgiving; I will pay what I have vowed. Salvation is of the LORD.**"

"**So the LORD spoke to the fish, and it vomited Jonah on to dry land**" (verse 10). The fish obeyed the LORD. Jonah needed to be back in fellowship with God before he could preach; and now he was. You cannot truly serve the Lord if you are out of fellowship.

Jonah chapter 3

"**Now the word of the LORD came to Jonah the second time, saying, "Arise, go to Nineveh, that great city, and preach to it the message that I tell you." So Jonah arose and went to Nineveh, according to the word of the LORD. Now Nineveh was an exceedingly great city, a three-day journey in extent**" (Jonah 3:1-3). Now that Jonah was back in fellowship, God, in His grace, called him again. This time, Jonah started going, although he still didn't really want to go, as becomes clear later on—he still resented having to preach to Nineveh. He'd experienced God's mercy and grace dramatically, yet he still knew very little about being gracious himself! However, he'd learnt an important lesson—that it was fruitless to try to escape from God.[10]

Verse 3 could mean that it was a three-day journey around the outside of Nineveh, or that it would take Jonah three days to visit all parts of the city. It was a major city: "**...Nineveh, that great city, in which are more than one hundred and twenty thousand persons who cannot discern between their right hand and their left...**" (Jonah 4:11b). This idiom

---

[10] It seems likely that the fish deposited Jonah back at Joppa, from where it was an approximately 500 mile (800 km) journey to Nineveh. This would take almost a month by camel or donkey caravan, or perhaps five or six weeks on foot.

probably means there were 120,000 children in Nineveh, indicating that the total population might have been one million. Therefore, Jonah was going to preach to a million people. What a privilege! Only Billy Graham and a few other evangelists have sometimes been able to preach to that many people at once in recent times. Jonah was going to do it by walking through the city, in just three days.[11]

"And Jonah began to enter the city on the first day's walk. Then he cried out and said, "Yet forty days, and Nineveh shall be overthrown!"" (Jonah 3:4). I imagine Jonah really concentrated on his message: "You're all going to be smashed to pieces in 40 days!" We can't be sure if this was the whole message God gave him to preach, but I bet he preached nothing but judgment—and I expect he enjoyed himself as well. We are not told that he mentioned repentance or the mercy of God. He didn't tell the Ninevites that he was going to sit up on a hillside, so that he wouldn't miss seeing the destruction of their city!

Look at verse 5. **"So the people of Nineveh believed God..."**. Oh, hallelujah! The word translated **"believed"** here (*aman*)[12] is the same word used of Abraham in Genesis, where it says, **"And he believed in the LORD, and He accounted it to him for righteousness"** (Genesis 15:6). The whole city of Nineveh believed the message. Imagine that: one million 'converts' in just one day!

We considered Noah in the previous chapter. He preached faithfully for 120 years and didn't win a single convert, except within his own family. Yet here was Jonah, who did not want to preach; yet he won a million converts in one day! Was it any reflection on Noah? Absolutely none. Was it any reflection on Jonah? Absolutely none. Only God gets all the glory. Praise His name!

We need to understand that gifts are *given*—they tell us something about the giver, and nothing at all about the receiver. The fruit of the Spirit are

---

[11] It is possible that the phrase "a three-day journey in extent"—implying about 60 miles (100 km)—referred to the distance around the whole area of 'Greater Nineveh', which included several cities. Later, it was some 80 miles (130 km) around Greater Nineveh, while it was more than 6 miles (10 km) around Nineveh itself and about 11 miles (18 km) including the surrounding settlements, allotments and gardens. Archaeology has revealed three main cities in close proximity, which were probably all royal capital cities of Assyria at various times: Kouyunjik (Nineveh), Khorsabad and Nimrod, with Ashur also nearby to the south. It is an interesting thought that the text could refer to Jonah needing three days to visit these three main population centres. However, it could simply mean that Jonah would require three days to fulfil his mission.

[12] Aman means 'to believe', 'to have faith in' or 'trust'. It is the root word from which the Hebrew word Amen is derived. Amen means '(this is) true', 'fixed', 'certain', 'faithful'.

altogether different. A gift can be given to me in a moment of time, but the fruit of the Spirit take years to develop. I am convinced of this.

The Ninevites turned to the LORD and sought to get right with Him: "**So the people of Nineveh believed God, proclaimed a fast, and put on sackcloth, from the greatest to the least of them. Then word came to the king of Nineveh; and he arose from his throne and laid aside his robe, covered himself with sackcloth and sat in ashes. And he caused it to be proclaimed and published throughout Nineveh by the decree of the king and his nobles, saying, "Let neither man nor beast, herd nor flock, taste anything; do not let them eat, or drink water"**" (verses 5-7). The king of Nineveh[13] did not only want the people to stop eating and drinking, but the cattle and sheep as well. This Assyrian king, who had been vile, was cut to the quick when he heard God's message through Jonah, and he was determined to get right with God. He repented; and the whole city repented with him. **"But let man and beast be covered with sackcloth, and cry mightily to God; yes, let every one turn from his evil way and from the violence that is in his hands. Who can tell if God will turn and relent, and turn from His fierce anger, so that we may not perish?"** (verses 8-9). Sackcloth was a sign of repentance.

Note that the word "**relent**" ("repent" in the AV) does not mean to 'feel sorry'. It means 'to change one's mind or attitude'. The king was saying, "If we get right with God, who can tell if He will change His attitude toward us? At the moment He is intent on destroying us; but who can tell if He won't change His mind and save us from the wrath that's coming, if we turn from our wicked ways and cry out to Him?"

It is interesting that the king said, "**Who can tell...?**" *Jonah* should have told them that God is merciful and that He might relent from sending judgment! There *was* opportunity to repent! But Jonah clearly never did tell the Ninevites this. Instead, he had concentrated on announcing, "Yet forty days, and Nineveh shall be overthrown!" because that was what *he* wanted to happen. He had not told them that God is a gracious God, who offers grace before judgment. Nor, it seems, had he told them how God had given him such grace—even during the past few weeks! He had ignored his

---

[13] The King of Nineveh probably means the King of Assyria who, at the time, was probably Ashur-Dan III (c.772-754 BC). The Book of Jonah is traditionally placed during the first half of the 8th Century BC, during the reign of Israel's King Jeroboam II (782-753 BC)—since 2 Kings 14:25 tells us that Jeroboam II expanded Israel's territory in accordance with God's word through Jonah. The Book is sometimes placed earlier in view of reforms that took place under earlier Assyrian kings, such as Adad-Nirari III (810-783), that could be associated with the repentance under Jonah's preaching. Succeeding kings nevertheless resorted to further reigns of terror and systematic cruelty.

own rebellion. He had ignored the fact that he had been plucked from the Mediterranean Sea and been saved from death. God had forgiven Jonah so much, then empowered him by the Holy Spirit to preach. Jonah should have told the Ninevites, "The LORD is a wonderful, gracious God! If you get right with Him, He may show you the same mercy and grace that He has shown me!" Yet it seems Jonah didn't mention this.

Jonah had deserved to be destroyed, but he had been delivered. Now here he was preaching destruction, not grace, to Nineveh. Yet the people repented at his preaching (Matthew 12:40)—every one of them! "**Then God saw their works, that they turned from their evil way; and God relented from the disaster that He had said He would bring upon them, and He did not do it**" (Jonah 3:10).

What a shame it is for Jonah that the Book of Jonah does not end here! If it had, then we would simply have a wonderful account about a missionary who did not want to go to Nineveh, but finally came to his right mind, went, and then led a million people to repentance. We would not know too much about the real attitude of Jonah's heart. However, unfortunately for Jonah, but very fortunately for us, God had more to say about grace. Now we come to the object lesson.

Jonah chapter 4

"**But it displeased Jonah exceedingly, and he became angry...**" (Jonah 4:1). Jonah was furious. A million Ninevites had turned to the LORD and God did not destroy the city. Now he was absolutely fuming at God.

I just do not understand this man. I think I'd have been angry if no one had turned to the LORD; but Jonah was angry because God had chosen *not* to destroy the city. Jonah had wanted the Ninevites to be obliterated; but God happens to be a gracious God. We should be so glad that God is not like Jonah! We would not last five minutes under Jonah's regime; and neither would Jonah himself, of course!

"**So he prayed to the LORD, and said, "Ah, LORD, was not this what I said when I was still in my country? Therefore I fled previously to Tarshish"**" (verse 2a). What an admission this was! Jonah had realized that, if he started preaching, the Ninevites might turn to the LORD. That's why he'd fled to Tarshish! Jonah had foreseen this sequence of events, but had not wanted Nineveh to be saved. Now he was angry because God had used him, of all people, to save them.

What a terrible attitude! Jonah was now out of fellowship again. "**...For I know that You are a gracious and merciful God, slow to anger and** abundant in loving-kindness, One who relents from doing harm" (verse 2b). Jonah had been dreading the fact that God might be gracious to Nineveh and spare the city!

"Therefore now, O Lord, please take my life from me, for it is better for me to die than to live!" (verse 3). "I'm so angry about this that I want to die, Lord. Please kill me!" This is Jonah, the prophet. The Book of Jonah is so misrepresented, I think. The story is often told to Sunday School classes, for example, but the main point is missed. The Book contains a great message; and it's a wonderful message about God's grace—not only to the Ninevites but to Jonah himself. Jonah demonstrates the graciousness of God more than anyone else I can think of. God showed Jonah grace upon grace, even though Jonah did not want God to show any grace to the Ninevites.

There are Christians who suddenly react to circumstances and say, "I just want to die, Lord!", and it is self-pity from beginning to end! Jonah was so full of himself that all he could say was, "Lord, kill me off now!" He did not mean it for one second, of course; but he was so angry at that moment that he felt he wanted to die. The Lord then asked him a question.

"Then the Lord said, "Is it right for you to be angry?"" (verse 4). God was asking him, "Is it right that you're angry, Jonah, when I've given grace upon grace to you? I've forgiven all your transgressions, I showed you grace through the Phoenicians, I prepared a fish big enough to swallow you and then I arranged for you to be vomited out on to dry land. Yet now you're furious because I've forgiven other people for their sins, too! Is this right, Jonah?" The answer was of course "No!"

Jonah now showed his inconsistency. When the Lord asked him, "Are you right to be angry?", Jonah jumped to the wrong conclusion. He thought, "Oh good, You really *are* going to destroy Nineveh after all, Lord. My anger is premature." But that was not what God meant.

"So Jonah went out of the city and sat on the east side of the city. There he made himself a shelter and sat under it in the shade, till he might see what would become of the city" (verse 5). Jonah wanted to sit in comfort. However, he wanted to sit in *that* particular place so that he could see fire fall from heaven and destroy the city—so that he could rejoice. He therefore picked the best possible spot to ensure that he would have a grandstand view! This is not twisting the story at all; it is all there in the Book, or at least very strongly implied!

Unfortunately for Jonah, in a desert climate, if you build a shelter for yourself it usually becomes hotter inside the shack than outside, because the shack traps the heat. It is like being inside your shed in summer; it gets hotter and hotter. Here then was Jonah—he was not going to suffer from sunstroke because he was in the shade, but he was going to get very hot indeed. If I were God, I would have said, "Good. Let him steam up a bit!"

The Object Lesson

However, God had another lesson about grace to teach Jonah now, designed to help him discover God's perspective on Nineveh's repentance. **"And the LORD God prepared a plant and made it come up over Jonah, that it might be shade for his head to deliver him from his misery. So Jonah was very grateful for the plant"** (verse 6). God prepared a plant to give Jonah relief from his misery. This plant (a '*qiqayon*' in Hebrew, translated "gourd" in the AV) was probably a Palma-christi tree—a castor-bean plant. These still grow in the Middle East; and they stand about 10 feet (3 m) tall and have huge leaves that provide excellent shade. If you sit under the shadow of any tree it is significantly cooler than if you are inside a shelter. God in His grace was saying, "Jonah, I don't want you to be uncomfortable while you sit there watching what's going to happen to Nineveh!"

Now, for the first time in the whole book, Jonah was happy about something! He was happy because *he* was comfortable. He hadn't been happy at all when a million people had been delivered from destruction, but he was exceedingly happy now. One plant had made him happy!

Perhaps I am painting a picture of you, am I? You will know whether I am. Are you more concerned with the comforts that give you a little bit of pleasure now than you are about the destiny of millions of people in this country, or in other places, who are going to a lost eternity without Christ, cut off from the love of God? We need to consider seriously whether we are more preoccupied with the blessings God gives us than we are with the tasks God has called us to, which include preaching the gospel. Or are you happier when you're preaching the gospel at your own discomfort than when God supplies you with blessings galore for yourself? Of course God desires to bless us, but the point is our motivation. Are we more concerned with our own comfort or with spreading the gospel?

"But as morning dawned the next day God prepared a worm, and it so damaged the plant that it withered" (verse 7). There is no pesticide that could have killed *that* worm. There wasn't a boot that could have stamped it into the ground—not one. Do you know why? Because *God had prepared it*, and He had a task for that worm to do. That little worm killed the small 'tree' in a few hours. It was miraculous. Now Jonah's beloved plant was gone.

"And it happened, when the sun arose, that God prepared a vehement east wind; and the sun beat on Jonah's head, so that he grew faint. Then he wished death for himself, and said, "It is better for me to die than to live"" (verse 8). As the sun arose and a scorching east wind came, Jonah was wallowing in self-pity again. "Lord, kill me off," he repeated.

"Then God said to Jonah, "Is it right for you to be angry about the plant?" And he said, "It is right for me to be angry, even to death!"" (verse 9). God repeated His question, in reference to the plant this time; and this time Jonah answered quickly. He was furious again.

We need to see the irony here. Jonah was upset now because God had destroyed one plant. But he had been upset earlier when God had *not* destroyed one million people. The terrible fact is clear: *Jonah loved a plant more than he loved a million souls*. He would have been quite happy to see Nineveh destroyed—to see fire come down and burn up the people in Nineveh. But he was not at all happy that God had destroyed the one plant that had relieved him of his discomfort!

God was trying to say something to Jonah: "Your heart is not filled with love, Jonah! You've got your priorities wrong. You prefer one tree, that brings you a day's relief, to a million people who can bring Me joy for all eternity. I gave the plant to you when you didn't deserve it, Jonah, so why are you angry after I gave a million people in Nineveh some grace too? Why is there this inconsistency in your life?"

Grace always flows from love. Jonah did not love the people of Nineveh, so he did not want God to give them grace. Beloved, we have got to love one another. We are all too quick to judge one another instead of showing grace before judgment. It is love that is needed—much more love.

Let's read on to the end of the Book: **"But the LORD said, "You have had pity on the plant for which you have not laboured, nor made it grow, which came up in a night and perished in a night. And should I not pity Nineveh, that great city, in which are more than one hundred and twenty thousand persons who cannot discern between their right hand and their left, and also much livestock?""** (verses 10-11). God reminded Jonah that there were also many innocent people and animals in the city. Jonah felt he had the right to be concerned for one temporary plant. "*You* didn't even plant that tree, Jonah! *You* didn't water it; *you* didn't tend it; but *I* did," God said, "Therefore, do you not think that I have the right to be concerned for Nineveh?" Jonah had no basis for resenting the graciousness of God. The Book of Jonah ends abruptly at this point. God had got His message across. He had provided grace all the way along for Jonah and now He'd given grace to the Ninevites. The events were a stark lesson in grace for Jonah—and now they are a lesson in grace for us as well.

Lessons for Us

What God was teaching Jonah also applies to us. We have already noted a number of lessons; but I want to highlight two things we should learn.

The first I've just mentioned—that *grace and love go hand in hand*. To be gracious, we first need to have love. We need to ask God to enlarge our hearts, with His love, so that the people around us who are going to a lost eternity will be encompassed by the love that we have for them. Then we will be determined to preach the gospel to them and will not be complacent when God starts revealing His judgment in our nation. Rather, we will be earnestly concerned.

The other lesson that I want to emphasize is this: God prepared a fish; He prepared a plant; He prepared a worm; and He prepared an east wind. These each fulfilled the tasks that God intended them to do. God has prepared us to be ambassadors of Christ. My question is: "Are you fulfilling your ministry?" Is the Lord Jesus being revealed in you—through what you say and do, and through who you are? If He's not, then is it perhaps because your heart is not big enough towards God and has not embraced His love?

---

[14] There are a number of other lessons we can learn from the Book of Jonah. Jonah learned the hard way that God not only wanted him to obey His commission, but to yield to His purpose. Jonah knew that God is gracious, but felt he knew best how God should work.

The example of Nineveh repenting would serve as a reminder to Israel and Judah in future years that God responds to true repentance. Jonah was one of the earliest prophets and, when other prophets arose announcing God's judgment on His own people, Nineveh—then a much greater city—would stand as a vivid reminder of God's mercy. The fact that Nineveh had been delivered would also remind God's people of His love and mercy towards all mankind, warning them not to be blinded to His purpose of worldwide salvation.

Under Jonah's preaching Nineveh experienced the mercy of God. Nevertheless, Assyria quickly returned to violence, pride and idolatry and, only 100 years later, Nahum proclaimed Nineveh's downfall once again. Babylon so destroyed the city in 612 BC that it remained undiscovered until AD 1842 (see Chapter 12)! God indeed had shown grace before judgment, but His judgment eventually came, since the Ninevites—despite coming to know the one true God—turned back to their wickedness.

5. THE THREE FALLS OF SATAN

UNDERSTANDING OUR ENEMY

In this chapter we consider the subject of Satan and, specifically, the judgment of Satan. But the real subject—as in any Bible study—is the glory of the Lord Jesus![1] It is God's victory over His enemy that we are really dealing with. It is important to understand Satan, our enemy, and know what he's up to—especially in these days when he is so active. However, we first of all need to get to know God in a personal and practical way, to enable us to stand in His victory in these days.

The subject of Satan could be covered from many different angles. For example, we could take the character of Satan, the history of Satan or the attack of Satan on the blood-line of Jesus. We could consider Satan's attacks on believers. We could follow the whole course of Satan through the Tribulation. We could find out what he's going to be doing (or rather, *not* doing!) during the Millennium. Or we could examine how he operates, with the evil demonic army that he controls. However, I have called this study "The Three Falls of Satan", because our theme is judgment; and the three 'falls' of Satan cover the sin of Satan and his judgment by God.

This is a very important topic. It concerns God's dealings with the most wonderful and the most beautiful creature that He has ever made. This is an essential point to grasp, because Satan has, according to the Bible, a position of prominence and power second only to that of God Himself. That is the significance of the enemy—*our* enemy. There is no other man or angel in the whole Word of God who has his history traced right through from the very beginning of creation to the end.

---

[1] All the Scriptures testify of Christ (John 5:39). Therefore, the subject of every Bible study is really the Lord Jesus, and it is with Him that our souls have to do. Therefore, no matter what we are studying in the Bible or what we are doing or going through in our lives, it should be the Lord who is central. Our goal should be to know Him more.

Yet it is a most surprising thing that Satan's biggest trick today is to try to convince everyone that he doesn't really exist. If you as a believer are not quite sure of the existence of the enemy, then I am sorry for you, really; the Bible is so abundantly clear. If you do not believe that you've got an enemy, then he can get away with almost anything in your life and in the lives of those around you.

A tactic Satan is busy using, of course, is to design false images of himself. I believe that it is Satan who stands behind every cartoonist who draws a picture of him. He is deliberately trying to make himself a character of such fun that not even young children will believe he is real. When children open their magazines or comics and see an odd looking creature staring out with the title "The Devil" written underneath, he *wants* them to laugh at him. But behind this there is a very serious-faced enemy, who knows what he is doing. I am not amused by the caricaturing of Satan that we see around us, because it's a dupe. He is trying desperately to convince everyone that he does not exist or that he has no real influence. It is terribly serious; and his plan is having an effect. The majority of people in the world today do not believe that Satan is a real personality—but he is. On this point the Bible is extremely clear.

THE NAMES OF SATAN

Satan's original name was *Lucifer*—a beautiful name, with a glorious meaning. It literally means 'light bearer', and is used in Isaiah 14:12 to translate a Hebrew word meaning 'brilliant one' or 'shining one'. He was a mighty celestial being, the brightest of all the 'stars' (the angels)—the morning star.[2] Yet this name is only mentioned once in the Bible, because the name Lucifer describes Satan's *original* character.

Most of Satan's other names are the ones we are more familiar with, and they describe his *present* character:

---

[2] The Hebrew word translated "Lucifer" is 'helel' which means 'brilliant one' or 'shining one': the root denoted the giving off of light by celestial bodies. The alternative translation "morning star" suits the context and parallelism where Satan is called "**Lucifer, son of the morning**" (literally "Shining-one, son of the dawn"), which alludes to the planet Venus, known as 'the morning star' or 'day star' because of its brightness at dawn. The verse implies that Satan was the brightest, shining star among all the other stars (angels)—the word 'star' is used to refer to angelic beings (see Job 38:7; Revelation 12:3-4). Lucifer, Latin for 'light bearer', was the Latin name for the planet Venus, hence why translators traditionally have used it in English Bible translations. The Greek translation used in the Septuagint meant 'morning star'.

1. *Satan*. The Hebrew word *satan* means an 'adversary', 'resister', 'opponent' or 'enemy'—in other words, 'one who comes against (you)'. With the article 'the' it becomes the proper name of Satan himself (Job 1:6ff; Zechariah 3:1-2). He is called *Satanas* in Greek, which also means 'adversary'.

2. *The devil*. The word translated "devil" in the New Testament (Greek *diabolos*) means 'false accuser' or 'slanderer'. Satan is very good at accusing us and slandering us. He is called "**the accuser of our brethren**" in Revelation 12:10.

3. *Apollyon*, meaning 'destroyer', is another name in Greek used to describe Satan in Revelation 9:11. It is equivalent to the Hebrew name *Abaddon*, from a root meaning 'destroy' or 'destruction'. This verse reveals that he is the angel of the bottomless pit (Abyss) and king over a demonic army.

4. Another name used in reference to Satan himself is *Beelzebub*, the prince or ruler of the demons (Matthew 12:24).[3]

5. Another descriptive title is *the evil one* or *the wicked one* (Matthew 13:19, 38). Jesus taught His disciples to pray that God might keep them from the evil one (Matthew 6:13b; see also John 17:15).

6. *The great dragon*. This title portrays Satan's great power (Revelation 12:9).[4]

THE CHARACTER OF SATAN

Now let us consider quickly what the Bible says about the *character* of Satan. We will look at just four aspects.

1. In 1 John 3:8a, John tells us, "**He who sins is of the devil, for the devil has sinned from the beginning.**" Here then is one thing we know about Satan: he has been sinning right from the beginning.

---

[3] It derives from the Hebrew names Baal-Zebub and Baal-Zevul. The god Baal was the chief male god of the Phoenicians and Canaanites, whose name meant 'lord' or 'master'. Baal-Zebub was a Philistine god, the god of Ekron (see 2 Kings 1:2-6), meaning 'lord of flies'. Baal-Zevul means 'lord of heaven' or 'lord of a high abode', but is a word play on zevul meaning 'dung', 'rubbish' or 'excrement'.

[4] The reference to Satan being a great dragon is linked to his appearing as a serpent in the Garden of Eden in Revelation 12:9. He is a powerful dragon, but he deceptively appeared as a tiny dragon—a serpent.

2. In John 8:44, Jesus said to some religious Jews, **"You are of your father the devil, and the desires of your father you want to do. He was a murderer from the beginning..."**. Satan has also been a *murderer* from the beginning—he brought death to the whole human race and continues to seek our destruction; **"...and does not stand in the truth, because there is no truth in him. When he speaks a lie, he speaks from his own resources, for he is a liar and the father of it."** Satan is also a *liar* and he continues to be a liar to this day. He is the enemy of God and all truth.

3. In Revelation 12:9 Satan is described as one who **"deceives the whole world"**. He is a *deceiver*.

4. In 1 Peter 5:6-7, Peter told us to humble ourselves, casting all our care upon God, who cares for us. Then he said, **"Be sober** [right-minded]**, be vigilant; because your adversary the devil walks about like a roaring lion, seeking whom he may devour"** (verse 8). Satan is our adversary. He seeks to be a *devourer* whenever he can.

That is Satan's character.[5] Satan's original name was 'shining one'—the morning star, son of the dawn—but he became the sinner, the murderer, the liar, the deceiver, the devourer, the adversary, the accuser, the destroyer, and so on. What happened to Satan between the time he was called *Lucifer* and the time he became known by his present names *devil, Satan, the evil one,* and all the others? What was it that changed the course of Lucifer's life? It is that which constitutes the first fall of Satan.

The First Fall of Satan: the Sin of Lucifer

When Satan (then called Lucifer) was created, he was absolutely perfect in all of his ways. Like all higher creatures, he had complete free will; and he also had certain advantages that we do not have. Lucifer beheld the glory of the Lord in the heavenly realm. He beheld the whole glory of God's throne room in heaven, where God was enthroned above all the angelic beings.

There is some scriptural evidence (we'll deal with some of it later on) which indicates that Lucifer was the closest servant of the Lord Jesus Himself. There is some suggestion that it was he who personally waited on

---

[5] Other descriptions of Satan include: "**the god of this age**" (2 Corinthians 4:4); "**the prince of the power of the air**" (Ephesians 2:2); "**the ruler of this world**" (John 12:31; 14:30; 16:11); and "**the tempter**" (Matthew 4:3; 1 Thessalonians 3:5), who wants to entice men to sin through deception. Paul was also probably referring to Satan when he used the name "**Belial**" in 2 Corinthians 6:15, which means 'worthlessness' or 'without profit'.

the Lord. That was Lucifer. And while he loved God, he was a faithful servant of the Lord.

However, Lucifer's love for the Lord started dimming and he turned against God. One day, his positive volition—his free will that had been positive towards God—suddenly became negative.

There is a lesson for us in this—the same lesson we saw in Chapter 2. We have got to keep the Lord as our first love. The apostle John recorded Jesus' warning to a church, **"You have left your first love....Repent!"** (see Revelation 2:4-5). If you have left your first love, you need to repent; that is the only way through. While your first love for the Lord remains intact, you dwell in the secret place of God, under the shadow of the Almighty (Psalm 91:1)—and it is wonderful!

All of us who have the Lord as our first love show forth His life and glory. But if we allow our love for Him to grow cold in any way, the result will be negativity towards God. Soon, we will find that we don't love Him as much as we ought to—not as much as we love other things. We will find self rearing its ugly head and the cares of this world taking over and getting out of proportion in our lives.[6] We will begin to turn against God.

This is what happened to our enemy, Satan. When Lucifer, the shining one, found that other things were occupying his heart, he became negative towards God, and pride started rising in his heart with disastrous consequences. It was then that he began a revolt.

Satan's revolt probably was not a sudden attack on the throne room of God. He probably did not storm the gates of heaven or anything like that. I imagine that it was like the attack which Absalom led against King David. Absalom went around gathering those who were discontent. He collected one person and then another, until soon he had a significant army that could try to unseat David.

I imagine that Lucifer went around from one angel to the next, saying, "I'm going to establish myself. Are you going to follow me? Lots of other angels are going to join me!" And Revelation 12:4 indicates that one third of all the angelic hosts started following Lucifer; a major revolt was in progress. "I'm going to take over," he was saying, "it's either got to be God in charge, or me; and *I* want to be in charge!" A wave of horror must have

---

[6]Many scriptures exhort us to love God above everyone and everything else. This is in fact the first great commandment (see for example: Deuteronomy 6:4-5; Deuteronomy 10:12; Matthew 22:37-40; Mark 12:28-31; Jude 21).

swept through the universe when Lucifer first set himself against the authority of God. God knew what was happening of course, and, at that point, Lucifer fell out of God's favour.[7]

It is important to remember that Satan is the 'antithesis' of the Lord Jesus. Whatever we see in Satan, the opposite is true of the Lord. Therefore, as we consider the fall of Lucifer in more detail, I'm going to contrast what Satan wanted to do—his rebellious self-exaltation—with what the Lord Jesus has actually done. There is a world of difference between the two.

Isaiah chapter 14: The five "I wills" of Satan

The details of how Satan fell are given in a marvellous passage in Isaiah chapter 14, the first verse of which we've already referred to. **"How you are fallen from heaven, O Lucifer, son of the morning! How you are cut down to the ground, you who weakened** [overwhelmed] **the nations!"** (verse 12). At first, Satan was called Lucifer (shining one), son of the dawn.[8]

Satan's first fall—his fall from God's favour, when pride rose in his heart and turned him against God—is described in verses 13 and 14. This passage is sometimes called "The five wills" or "The five I wills" of Satan. It records Lucifer saying "I will" five times.

"For you have said in your heart..." (verse 13a). Isn't the Bible a marvellous book! It is the only historical book that tells us what a person was actually thinking—because God is the only One who can give a true commentary on what was going on inside someone's heart. Lucifer appeared beautiful on the outside, but the Bible cuts right through the outward appearance to describe the rebellion that was going on inside his heart.

1. "I will ascend into heaven"

First of all, Lucifer said in his heart, **"I will ascend into heaven"** (Isaiah 14:13b). He wanted to go up, or scale, the heavens. Lucifer had always

---

[7] When Lucifer decided to establish his own claim, he substituted his own will for God's, resulting in a conflict between God's will and that of a created being for the first time.

[8] The Hebrew word for the "serpent" in the Garden of Eden was nachash. In the first series of Basic Bible Studies it was mentioned that a related word means 'shining' or 'sparkling'. There was thus a similarity in meaning with Lucifer here. These associated words could imply that the serpent—indwelt by the fallen Lucifer (Satan)—was shining in some way. Undoubtedly, the serpent was very beautiful in appearance.

been allowed into very the presence of the Lord. It is important to be clear on that.[9] So what did he mean by, "I will ascend into heaven"?

What Satan wanted was for the very throne room of God in heaven to become *his own*. He was no longer content to be the highest angel; he wanted to be *far above* all other principalities and powers, just as God was. He wanted to be the king, like God—or even to remove God as the sole king. It was pride that drove him on.

Pride could never achieve this, however; but *humility* could! Do you know where the Lord Jesus Christ is today? He is ascended, and He is seated at the right hand of God the Father in the throne room of God, far above every principality and power (Ephesians 1:20-21). He has ascended into the third heaven, right into that glorious, magnificent throne room. The Lord Jesus did not get there through pride. He entered through humble obedience.[10] And we should be humble, just as He was humble—so that "**as He is, so are we in this world**" (1 John 4:17b).

What Satan tried to gain through pride he didn't succeed in obtaining. What the Lord came to do He succeeded in, because of His humility. And we, brothers and sisters in Christ, must learn the lesson. If you are in any way motivated by pride in your spiritual life, or in any other aspect of your life, then you are in Satan's territory. There are Christians who are seeking to 'get somewhere' with God, who are trying to get a great ministry for themselves; but there's only way, and that's down. As you humble yourself, God can exalt you. As you are prepared to let all of your service

---

[9] Even after his first fall, Satan was still permitted into heaven. For example, a wonderful passage in Job chapter 1 tells us, "**Now there was a day when the sons of God came to present themselves before the LORD, and Satan also came among them**" (verse 6). In this context the phrase "sons of God" refers to angels. "**And the LORD said to Satan, "From where do you come?" So Satan answered the LORD and said, "From going to and fro on the earth, and from walking back and forth on it"**" (verse 7). Satan's answer involved an idiom meaning ownership. He was saying, "I've been walking throughout my estates. I've just been having a look at everything I own." However, God immediately said something marvellous as a rebuff: "**Then the LORD said to Satan, "Have you considered My servant Job?"**" (verse 8a). Satan had come into God's presence boasting, "I own everything," but God replied, "What about Job?" Hallelujah! Job happened to be a believer, so he did not belong to the devil; rather, he belonged to God, his Father. Suddenly Satan was thrown off balance. "Well, there are reasons," he replied. The whole Book of Job then goes on to describe the remarkable conflict that ensued. Isn't it interesting that the Book of Job—probably the earliest book of the Bible—deals with angelic conflict? How important that is.

[10] Several passages tell us about the ascension of Jesus. Ephesians 1:19-22, for example, concludes that all things (including Satan!) have now been put under Jesus' feet. Praise God! Philippians 2:5-11 tells us that, because of Jesus' humble attitude and obedience to His Father, "**God also has highly exalted Him and given Him the name which is above every name, that at the name of Jesus every knee should bow**" (verses 9-10a). Even Satan will have to bow before Jesus!

and ministry be sown to God and for others, so *God* will exalt you in His time. Humility is *always* the way for us. We have got to learn this lesson. To count others better than ourselves, to serve one another, is the best and only true way of exaltation (Mark 9:35b).[11]

Satan thus began by thinking, "I am going to ascend to take over the throne room of God." That was his plan. However, God knew what was in his heart even before he put his plan into operation!

2. "I will exalt my throne above the stars of God"

The second "I will" that Lucifer said in his heart was, "**I will exalt my throne above the stars of God**" (verse 13c). A throne, as we have seen before, represents authority. Thus, Satan intended to raise, or increase greatly, his authority over all the other "**stars of God**"—which refers to the other angelic beings (see Job 38:7; Revelation 12:3-4). He wanted his authority to be lifted on to a different sphere. Satan did not simply want to be head among all of the angels. His idea was to be *much* higher than them all. In other words, he did not want to be one of them any more! It was false, unrealistic ambition. The thing that follows from pride is this type of ambition.

When the Lord Jesus came to the earth He did not have any ambition except to do the will of His Father. Our ambition as Christians must be the same. Every Christian is truly a full-time servant of the Lord and a full-time priest. You might be a car mechanic, a nurse, a teacher, or whatever else; but you are full-time for God! If God has some other specific ministry for your life, you won't move into it by being ambitious for yourself. What you have to do is rest in the Lord and be faithful to Him. Let Him do the pushing! Sometimes I see Christians who realize that God wants to use their lives—and they're right—but *they* have decided how God should use their lives, and off they go! They are determined to have a particular ministry, whether God wants them to or not; and it is often sheer ambition on their part—exactly what Satan had. "I don't want to be just an ordinary Christian, one of the riff-raff," they think, "I'm going places with God!" However, it is important to realize that we are *all* going places with God! God may simply want you to pray faithfully for the rest of your life, or do some other essential ministry that goes largely unrecognized. If that is what *He* wants you to do, then truly you will be going places with God.

---

[11] It may be only in the next age that we will be exalted, the results of our labours recognized and any reward received.

I am convinced that it is not the famous names who will get the biggest prizes in heaven. It's going to be the people who have faithfully served the Lord, despite everything being against them. The desire for popularity, for a 'great' ministry and for recognition, that is so prevalent today, is a snare for Christians. If *you* get the glory now, then *He* isn't getting the glory. We have got to learn this lesson. *Satan* was ambitious, so if there is any such ambition in us, may God deal with it.

It is vital to understand this: *if we cannot be content where we are, then we will not be content anywhere else*. We need to learn to live in victory in our current job or situation; then we will also have victory if the Lord happens to call us to some other ministry. If we are not living in victory in our home today, then certainly we wouldn't have victory out on the mission field. If we cannot lead people to the Lord now in our own language and culture, then we certainly wouldn't be able to lead people to the Lord in another place. Let us not deceive ourselves and be blinded by our ambition.

One more thing needs to be said, however. It *is* a good thing to *desire* a position of responsibility. 1 Timothy 3:1 says, "**This is a faithful saying: If a man desires the position of a bishop, he desires a good work.**" The type of ambition that is wrong is that which drives us to push ourselves in front of others. But if we pray and ask God to bring out the ministry *He* wants us to have, that is something quite different. If we are seeking to obey the Lord and glorify Him, that is entirely different. However, take heed, because the same passage also warns that an overseer must be "**not a novice, lest being puffed up with pride he fall into the same condemnation as the devil**" (1 Timothy 3:6). Pride is a major obstacle to Christian service.

3. "I will also sit on the mount of the congregation, on the farthest sides of the north"

A well known chorus includes the words, "Beautiful for situation, the joy of the whole earth, is Mount Zion in the sides of the north...". This song is based on Psalm 48:1-2, "**Great is the LORD, and greatly to be praised in the city of our God, in His holy mountain. Beautiful in elevation, the joy of the whole earth, is Mount Zion on the sides of the north, the city of the great King.**" I wonder how many people who sing these words actually know what they mean?

Mount Moriah, where the Temple was built in Jerusalem, was on the north side of Mount Zion. And it was from the Temple that God's rulership went forth (and is going to go forth again in the future). Therefore, the psalmists were saying, "How wonderful are the sides of the north—the place God has chosen to have His throne of rulership!"

In the future, the Temple is going to be established again on the sides of the north—on the northern side of Mount Zion—and from that Millennial Temple the Lord Jesus Christ shall rule the nations with a rod of iron (see Revelation 2:27). You've probably read the prophecies, just as I have. Jesus will rule from there, in Jerusalem.

Satan of course wants to rule. He wants nothing less than what Jesus has and what Jesus will inherit. Therefore, he wants to own the sides of the north now. When Satan said in his heart, **"I will also sit on the mount of the congregation, on the farthest sides of the north"** (verse 13d), he was effectively saying, "I want rulership over Israel; and I want rulership over the whole earth as well." He wanted God's palace (the first "I will"); he wanted God's authority (the second "I will"); and third, he wanted God's rulership, extending over Israel and the whole earth. He wanted everything for himself!

What did the Lord Jesus do? He laid down His life at Golgotha. Golgotha is therefore a beautiful place too, because the very life-blood of the Lord Jesus was shed there for each one of us. Jesus did not come to usurp authority and rulership. Rather, He came to give Himself. And now He has *received* authority and rulership from His Father. Glory to Jesus! Satan wanted to take over the whole world. But the Lord Jesus died for it—and all authority has now been given to Him (Matthew 28:18).

4. "I will ascend above the heights of the clouds"

Satan's fourth "I will" was this: **"I will ascend above the heights of the clouds"** (Isaiah 14:14a).

There are approximately 150 references to clouds in the Bible, many of which deal with clouds as a picture of the glory, power and majesty of God.[12] When the Lord Jesus Christ returns, He will come **"on the clouds of heaven, with power and great glory"** (Matthew 24:30b). Therefore, when Satan said, **"I will ascend above the heights of the clouds"**, he was effectively saying, "I want as much glory and majesty and power as God."

Jesus Christ humbled Himself and went to the Cross. There He won the most tremendous and glorious victory over Satan and all his forces (Colossians 2:14-15). Now Jesus has been glorified and He shares the same glory as His Father (John 17:5).

---

[12]One example is Exodus 16:10. "Now it came to pass, as Aaron spoke to the whole congregation of the children of Israel, that they looked toward the wilderness, and behold, the glory of the LORD appeared in the cloud." Other examples are Exodus 40:38, Isaiah 19:1 and Revelation 1:7.

There is an important principle for us to learn here—*the cross comes before glory*. Satan wanted the glory, but he didn't want a cross—not at all. Yet, through the Cross and all His suffering, the Lord Jesus has received the glory. Hallelujah!

It is staggering, isn't it, that Satan should have seen the Lord Himself so clearly—the whole glory of God—and then these thoughts entered into his heart? However, the four "I wills" we have seen so far were minor compared with the final one.

5. "I will be like the Most High"

Satan thought to himself, **"I will be like the Most High"** (verse 14b). What a stupendous project this was in the heart of the devil! Pride had now produced madness in his mind. He wanted not only as much as God had, but also to make himself like God. He probably intended that God should eventually serve him! This was utterly impossible. Satan was created; he could never become like God, the Creator. A created being can never become like God Himself. No angel or human can ever have the very nature of God.[13]

- God is *eternal*, with no beginning and no end. Satan was created by God and, therefore, there was a time when he did not exist.

- God is *immutable*: He never changes. However, Satan had changed. He had changed from being a servant of God to a rebel against God.

- God is *omnipotent*. Many Christians act as if Satan is omnipotent; but he is not.

- God is *omniscient*. Satan is not omniscient. There are many things that he does not know.

- God is *omnipresent*. This is the difference that I love above all the others. Satan is *not* omnipresent. Think about what it means! For example, if I receive four telephone calls within a few minutes from four different places, and each person says to me, "The devil's after me," then three of them, at least, must be mistaken!

Pride was thus the great sin of the devil; and it led to this incredible ambition in him. I believe that pride is the greatest sin in the life of any

---

[13] No created being can ever have the infinite, natural attributes of God (omniscience, omnipotence, omnipresence, sovereignty, everlasting existence, etc.), although we can and should develop the character attributes of God, through the work of the Holy Spirit in us. This is God's intention for us. All believers are predestined to be conformed to the image of Christ (Romans 8:29).

believer. It must be so, because pride was the very sin of Satan himself—the sin that led to his downfall and judgment.[14]

God's Judgment on Lucifer

We thus know what went on in Lucifer's heart, because God recorded it for us in Isaiah 14:13-14. Now let us read on to verse 15: **"Yet you shall be brought down to Sheol, to the lowest depths of the Pit."** God did not say, "to the sides of the north," but, "to the lowest depths of the Pit"! This was God's *judgment* upon Lucifer. This was the sentence God passed on him. Satan wanted to exalt himself—to usurp a position, authority and glory that can belong only to God Himself. However God declared that, instead, He would bring Satan right down.

The status of Satan is therefore this: *he has been judged and sentenced, but his sentence has not yet been fully carried out* (cf. John 16:11). We are thus living during the time when Satan knows what is going to come upon him, but God's word—His judgment on him—has not yet been fully carried out.

God has frequently pronounced judgment in this way. If we consider the life of King Saul, for example: after he had reigned for just a short time as king of Israel, God rejected him as king (see 1 Samuel 15:26). Nevertheless, he continued to be king for many more years before he actually lost the throne to David. As far as God was concerned, Saul was not the true and rightful king. His chosen king was David, although David was not yet recognized as king.

In the same way, Satan has been sentenced at this present time, but God's judgment is yet to come upon him in full. Jesus Christ is God's true and rightful King; and one day every knee will bow before Him (Romans 14:11; Philippians 2:10-11).[15]

This brings us on to consider the second and third falls of Satan. These are, of course, the remaining stages of God's judgment upon him—when God will carry out the sentence already pronounced upon him.

---

[14] I believe the enemy is far more interested in what's going on in heaven, and in any damage he can do to us there through accusation, than he is in what he personally can do to us on earth. Satan directs an organized host of wicked spirits in the heavenlies—demonic forces, who do his bidding. It is they who also operate on the earth; Satan doesn't have to come himself. He hands out most of his trouble-making to them.

[15] God thus still allows Satan to operate as a 'dethroned ruler' over those who choose, either willingly or ignorantly, to accept his authority.

Satan's Second Fall: his fall from heaven

The second fall of Satan is his permanent fall from heaven. This will take place in the future. Today, Satan dwells in the heavenly realm, and he still has some access to God's throne room in heaven itself. In fact, he commutes! He can come to the earth if he wants to, but he spends most of his time in the heavenlies as **"prince of the power of the air"** (see Ephesians 2:2).

Satan's main activity today, I believe, is slandering believers. He accuses us before God. At this very moment, Satan is accusing the brethren. He might be mentioning your name right now. He might be saying, "Look at her. Call herself a Christian? Look what she's just done!" or, "How can he say he loves everyone when he's talking like that?"[16]

The good news is that soon Satan is going to fall from heaven permanently. He is going to be thrown out of heaven forever. This second fall of Satan will happen three and a half years after the start of the Tribulation. One day soon, the Church is going to be taken up from the earth, or "raptured". Then, for three and a half years the earth will continue much as it is today. Conditions will probably be slightly worse than now, deteriorating as time goes on. However, after three and a half years there is going to be a war in heaven—which Satan will lose. And at that point, he is going to be thrown down to the earth. This will be the second major stage of his judgment by God.[17]

Revelation chapter 12 describes this. **"And war broke out in heaven: Michael and his angels fought against the dragon; and the dragon and his angels fought, but they did not prevail, nor was a place found for them in heaven any longer. So the great dragon was cast out, that serpent of old, called the Devil and Satan, who deceives the whole world; he was cast to the earth, and his angels were cast out with him"** (verses 7-9).

This will take place three and a half years after you and I, who are members of the Body of Christ, have been snatched away from the earth

---

[16]We will see how God deals with Satan's accusations in Chapter 8, which introduces the judgment of believers. God does something wonderful, the principle of which is liberating for every Christian.

[17]For three and a half years, the Church will have been occupying heaven with the Lord, and He will have been dealing with us up there. There will be no room for Satan anymore! Therefore, Satan will be cast out of heaven. (The timetable of future events is explained more fully later in this chapter.)

and caught up to heaven.[18] We are not going to fight in this battle. Michael is the great warring archangel, who watches over Israel (Daniel 12:1) and who regularly contends with the devil (Jude 9, for example). Michael's angels are from among the two-thirds of all angels who did not rebel with Lucifer in the beginning.

After Satan is thrown out of heaven to the earth, the second half of the Tribulation will be the most terrible period that the world shall ever experience. Satan himself, and every demonic force, will be living on the earth. The Lord Jesus prophesied much about this time, describing the dreadful things that will take place.

Jesus referred to this second fall of Satan in Luke chapter 10. He had given 70 of His disciples power and authority to go forth and preach that the kingdom of God had come near. They went out from Him and then they came back. **"Then the seventy returned with joy, saying, "Lord, even the demons are subject to us in Your name." And He said to them, "I saw Satan fall like lightning from heaven""** (Luke 10:17-18). When He heard their report, Jesus, whose whole thinking was shaped by the Word of God, knew that this was a sign of Satan's certain defeat. Immediately, the thought came to Him, "Satan is soon going to be thrown down from heaven"—in fulfilment of Isaiah 14:15. The second fall of Satan came to His mind, so He said, "I saw Satan fall from heaven—just like a lightning streak, I saw him come down." (Similarly, when we see demonic forces being defeated and crushed, we should be reminded that Satan's time in heaven is now very limited indeed.)

Jesus didn't stop there, however. Look at what He said next: **"Behold, I give you the authority to trample on serpents and scorpions, and over all the power of the enemy, and nothing shall by any means hurt you"** (Luke 10:19). It is time, my beloved brothers and sisters, for us to apply this passage in the Church today. It is time for us to be alert to the devil's schemes and to stop being pushed around by him. The Lord has given us authority over all the power of the enemy, so we should give him no foothold in our lives (Ephesians 4:25-27).[19]

---

[18] That is, halfway through the seven-year Tribulation period—three and a half years (1260 days) before it ends (cf. Revelation 12:6, 14).

[19] We need to recognize that, on the basis of Christ's victory, Satan is a defeated foe. If we resist him, he will flee from us (James 4:7; 1 Peter 5:8-9). If we give him no foothold in our lives through sin and we continuously resist him, Satan will have no power over us. God will also be able to use us to bring freedom and victory to others.

However, Jesus gave a warning in verse 20: **"Nevertheless do not rejoice in this, that the spirits are subject to you, but rejoice rather because your names are written in heaven."** It is the God of our salvation whom we should rejoice in, not the power and authority that He gives us. That is why I never laugh at the enemy—never! He is far greater than I am in terms of the natural power and abilities with which he was created. However, I am in Christ, whom God raised from the dead and made to sit at His right hand, far above Satan and all his evil forces (Ephesians 1:19-23). We are going to be the ones to judge the angels; but that day is in the future. For now we should be rejoicing that our names are written in the Lamb's Book of Life, and exercising our authority, in Christ, over the enemy—as God leads us.

SATAN'S THIRD FALL: INTO THE LAKE OF FIRE FOREVER

The third fall of Satan will occur right at the end of the Millennial Kingdom. For 1000 years, Satan will be bound up; and he will not be able to do any evil deeds at all on the earth. However, the Book of Revelation tells us that he will then be let out again for a short season (Revelation 20:3, 7).

What will he do? He will go out to deceive the nations (Revelation 20:8) and he will do exactly the same as he did at the beginning—lead a revolt against God. He will again start gathering 'converts'; and this time there will be a major rebellion *on the earth.*[20]

This time God will not merely pass sentence on Satan, but will finally say, "Enough is enough!" He will cast Satan away into the lake of fire forever—the everlasting fire **"prepared for the devil and his angels"** (Matthew 25:41). This third fall of Satan will be the time when the judgment of God upon His enemy will be complete.

TIMETABLE OF FUTURE EVENTS

The timetable of coming events can be summarized in seven points:[21]

1. Soon we will come to event number one: the *Rapture of the Church*. Satan is not going to like it, but the Church is going to be caught up into

---

[20] This is explained in greater detail in Basic Bible Study 61, entitled "The Millennium (Part 2)".

[21] The background, evidence for and details of this sequence of events are dealt with in the fourth series of Basic Bible Studies (BBS 43 to 63).

heaven! It will be a major testimony to Satan. The moment we go, he will know, "I've got just seven years before I'll be bound up," and he will be desperate. I pity the Jews particularly at that time. That's why we must pray urgently for them now, that many of them might be saved.

2. After the Church has gone, the *Tribulation* will begin. This will be a time of severe judgment on the earth. There is no judgment for those in Christ Jesus, so that is why all believers must be removed first.

3. Halfway through the Tribulation, *Satan will be thrown out of heaven.* As we have seen, this will be his second fall (Revelation 12:9). A terrible time will ensue.

4. Three and a half years later will be the *Second Coming of Jesus Christ*. He will come again in power and great glory, not as a humble Lamb this time, but as the victorious One, the King of kings and Lord of lords (Revelation 19:11-16). Our Lord will appear; and we are going to appear with Him! Enoch said, "**Behold, the Lord comes with ten thousands of His saints**" (Jude 14b). He knew all about this.

5. At this point Satan will be locked up and kept bound for 1000 years. This is the *Millennium*—which means 'one thousand years' (Revelation 20:1-6).

6. At the very end of the Millennium, *Satan will be released* for a short season, and he will lead his final revolt (Revelation 20:7-9).

7. Finally, the third fall of Satan will take place. *Satan will be cast into the lake of fire forever* (Revelation 20:10).

Ezekiel chapter 28

One major passage deals with all three falls of Satan: Ezekiel chapter 28. Try to identify his first, second and third falls as we read it through.

Up to verse 11, Ezekiel describes how God told him to address a man called the "prince of Tyre" (verse 1). This man was the king, but he claimed to be a god and not just a man (verse 2). The Tyreans were famous for having a man as their god. However, who was the real power behind the throne? *Satan* was. God then told Ezekiel to prophesy against the real 'king' behind the throne.

"**Moreover the word of the L**ORD **came to me, saying, "Son of man, take up a lamentation for the king of Tyre, and say to him, 'Thus says the Lord G**OD**: "You were the seal of perfection, full of wisdom and perfect in beauty"'"** (Ezekiel 28:11-12). This is the start of the 'funeral dirge' of Satan. Imagine someone altogether beautiful, with every beautiful facet. Lucifer was like that. He was the most magnificent and the most beautiful creature that God ever created.[22]

"You were in Eden, the garden of God..." (verse 13a). This probably does not refer to the historical Garden of Eden, but to a heavenly place. The Garden of Eden on earth was probably just a physical representation of this beautiful, spiritual garden of God in heaven. God was saying, "Satan, you used to be in the perfect heavenly environment—in the third heaven. You actually walked in Eden, the garden of God."

"Every precious stone was your covering: the sardius, topaz, and diamond, beryl, onyx, and jasper, sapphire, turquoise, and emerald with gold..." (verse 13b). It is interesting that all of these precious stones are also mentioned in relation to the breastplate of the High Priest of Israel (Exodus 28:17-20; 39:10-13).[23] God was saying to Satan, "You had precious stones like the High Priest. You too were a high priest who once ministered to Me." God was reminding Satan of the glorious position he once had in heaven.

"The workmanship of your timbrels and pipes was prepared for you on the day you were created" (verse 13c). This probably refers to Satan's beautiful voice. God was reminding him that he was a *created* being. "Satan, you were *created*. You are My workmanship. You are not ever-living. You are *not* like the Most High God."

"You were the anointed cherub who covers [protects]; **I established you"** (verse 14a). This suggests that it had been Satan's task to watch over or 'guard' the glory and holiness of God.[24] That was the privileged position Satan once held. What an astounding verse this is! God was reminding Satan that He had once *given* him such a mandate—by grace.

"You were on the holy mountain of God; you walked back and forth in the midst of fiery stones" (verse 14b). To walk back and forth is an idiom

---

[22] It is important to realize that, in general, Satan still does appear beautiful. That is another ruse of his deception. He transforms himself into **"an angel of light"** (2 Corinthians 11:14). His messengers likewise appear as **"ministers of righteousness"**, when really they are false apostles and deceitful workers (2 Corinthians 11:13,15).

[23] A list of such precious stones is only mentioned in the Bible in relation to three things: (1) Israel's High Priest; (2) the foundations of the wall of the heavenly New Jerusalem, the holy city (Revelation 21:2, 19-20); and (3) here, in relation to Satan before he fell.

[24] It was the task of cherubim to protect. For example, they guarded the way to the tree of life in the Garden of Eden (Genesis 3:24) and they 'guarded' the glory, righteousness and holiness of God as they overshadowed the mercy seat on top of the Ark of the Covenant (Exodus 25:20; 37:9).

for rulership or ownership; and the phrase **"fiery stones"** probably refers to the other angels. "You saw Me ruling everything in holiness, Satan, while you yourself ruled among the angels!"

"You were perfect in your ways from the day you were created, till iniquity was found in you" (verse 15). Satan had at first been sinless; but then iniquity was found in him. This refers to Satan's first fall. **"By the abundance of your trading you became filled with violence within, and you sinned"** (verse 16a). This means, "Because of your prosperity—your riches, your beauty, your wisdom, and so on—you became filled with anger, rage, bitterness and jealousy within, and you sinned."

"Therefore I will cast thee as profane out of the mountain of God" (verse 16b, AV).[25] This probably refers to Satan's second fall: "Satan, you're going to be thrown out of heaven!" **"And I will destroy thee, O covering cherub, from the midst of the stones of fire"** (verse 16c, AV).

"Thine heart was lifted up because of thy beauty [first fall again]**, thou hast corrupted thy wisdom by reason of thy brightness: I will cast thee to the ground** [second fall]**, I will lay thee before kings, that they may behold thee"** (verse 17, AV). Satan became proud because of his beauty and splendour. He became unwise. The last phrase means literally, "that they might squint at you". Kings will be appalled when they see Satan, and they will screw up their faces as they peer at him.

"Thou hast defiled thy sanctuaries by the multitude of thine iniquities, by the iniquity of thy traffic" (verse 18a, AV). The last phrase here ("iniquity of your trading" in the NKJV) probably refers to the time when Satan went around from angel to angel trying to gather converts. "You went here, there and everywhere trying to collect a group of rebels, Satan. It was sin; and it defiled you!"

"Therefore will I bring forth a fire from the midst of thee" (verse 18b, AV). This probably refers to the lake of fire. Satan's third fall is now in view: **"It shall devour thee, and I will bring thee to ashes upon the earth in the sight of all them that behold thee"** (verse 18c, AV). Every evil imagination of Satan shall utterly fail. Satan will collapse in ashes upon the earth and everyone will see his humiliation.

"All they that know thee among the people shall be astonished at thee: thou shalt be a terror, and never shalt thou be any more" (verse 19,

---

[25] The AV is used for the rest of the quotations from Ezekiel chapter 28, because the tenses used seem to represent more accurately the three falls of Satan.

AV). People will be aghast at Satan's downfall. The phrase "thou shalt be a terror" is literally "you shall be [in] terrors". Satan will be terrified. He will quickly meet his end.

Conclusion

Satan had no excuse—none whatsoever. He was indeed the most beautiful and magnificent creature of God but, because of pride, he rebelled. He is now under the judgment of God, awaiting the final stages of his punishment. Soon, his sentence will be carried out in full.

I want to end with two thoughts. First, may God reveal to us the fact that He is righteous and just in every way. May He also reveal, as part of this, how horrific the uprising of Satan was—when Lucifer, in pride, started leading a revolt against God. May God reveal this to us in all its wonder.

Finally, I want to turn back to Luke 10 because we, as believers, must never be preoccupied with the enemy. We should be occupied with the Lord. I can think of no more fitting verse on which to end than this: **"Nevertheless do not rejoice in this, that the spirits are subject to you, but rejoice rather because your names are written in heaven"** (Luke 10:20). We are never going to be cast out of the Lord's presence, my beloved. God has a mansion prepared for us up in heaven (John 14:2-3); and the enemy is not going to be there. Hallelujah!

6. CROOKED COUNSEL
The Unjust, irregular and illegal Judgment of Jesus by Men and Satan

The Cross stands as the hub of everything we believe. On the horizon of world history, it stands clear for all to see. It is also the unmistakable truth that the Holy Spirit is seeking to reveal to every single person on this earth. In this chapter and the next we have the wonderful privilege of being able to talk directly about the Lord Jesus Christ, to see Him as He was on this earth and to consider Him as He was judged.

The Bible reveals much about the judgment of Jesus. His specific judgment began at the time He was arrested by the soldiers in the Garden of Gethsemane, and continued until that glorious declaration on the Cross, "It is finished!" Jesus was proclaiming that He had borne our sins. He had taken the sins of the whole world and, from that time forth, no other sacrifice was necessary for our sins. His work was fully and perfectly completed forever.

THOSE RESPONSIBLE FOR THE JUDGMENT OF JESUS

The Bible assigns the judgment of Jesus and His death on the Cross to the account of eight personalities or groups of people, whom I view as being in two distinct sets.

Acts chapter 4 identifies four of those responsible. We will begin at verse 23 to see the context: "**And being let go, they** [Peter and John] **went to their own companions and reported all that the chief priests and elders had said to them. So when they heard that, they raised their voice to God with one accord and said: "Lord, you are God, who made heaven and earth and the sea, and all that is in them, who by the mouth of your servant David have said: 'Why did the nations rage, and the people plot vain things? The kings of the earth took their stand, and the rulers were gathered together against the L**ORD** and against His Christ.' For truly against Your holy servant Jesus, whom You anointed, both Herod and Pontius Pilate, with the Gentiles and the**

people of Israel, were gathered together…'" (verses 23 to 27). This passage ends with a list of two individuals and two groups of people who were responsible for the crucifixion of the Lord Jesus:

- Herod (Antipas), the supposed 'king' of Galilee at the time;
- Pontius Pilate, the Roman governor of Judea;
- the Gentiles;
- the people of Israel.

Herod Antipas and Pontius Pilate were, between them, responsible for governing most of the land of Israel at that time. The land had been taken over by the Romans; and the emperor had appointed a governor (a 'procurator' or 'proconsul') over the people in Judea, with military and administrative responsibilities. At the time of Christ's crucifixion, the governor was Pontius Pilate. Herod was the 'king' (or 'tetrarch') of Galilee, appointed by the Romans to help keep order.[1] All of the Gentiles were also responsible for the judgment of Jesus, as were all of the people of Israel. They were *all* gathered together against the Lord Jesus Christ.

This list thus includes every one of us—because, whether a Jew or a Gentile, this verse covers us all. Some people mistakenly think that only the Jews were responsible for the death of Jesus. That is not true. All the Gentiles were responsible too. Therefore, no matter whom you might blame for the judgment of Jesus, it was actually *you* who were responsible for the crucifixion of Jesus. It was *your* sins that caused Him to be put on the Cross.

However, I said there were *eight* parties named in the Bible as being responsible for the judgment and death of Jesus. Who were the other four? The fifth is not a surprise:

---

[1] Herod the Great was permitted by the Romans to rule in the land of Israel as king from about 40 BC (being officially instigated probably in 35 BC). He then ruled until the time of Christ's birth. His appointment by Mark Anthony was a political move to help settle unrest among the people, since Herod was an Idumean (a half-Jew) and not a Roman. It was in part a reward for Herod's past endeavours and for the help his father Antipater had given the Romans. Herod the Great was a great builder and was fervently Hellenistic.

Following Herod the Great's death, the land was divided between three of his sons: Herod Antipas ruled Galilee and Perea; Herod Philip ruled land in the north, east of the Jordan; and Herod Archelaus ruled Judea, Idumea and Samaria. However, the Romans quickly deposed the unpopular Herod Archelaus and took direct control of Judea, Idumea and Samaria. "Judea" became a province under a Roman governor, with the effective capital at Caesarea. Thus, at the time of Christ's crucifixion, the whole land was under the control of Pontius Pilate, Herod Antipas and Herod Philip, although the Romans had ultimate political and military control.

- It was Satan.

As the LORD God said to the serpent in Genesis 3:15, in that glorious first statement of the gospel in the Bible, **"He** [the woman's Seed, that is, Christ] **shall bruise your head, and you shall bruise His heel"**. The word translated "bruise" means 'to crush' or 'to break'. There is no question about it: Satan was instrumental in the betrayal and suffering of Jesus (Luke 22:3; John 13:2, 27)—although the precise extent to which he was involved in all the events is difficult to establish. Undoubtedly he was there, behind the scenes, inciting the chief priests and elders, stirring up the crowds against Jesus and provoking them to shout, "Crucify Him!" (Matthew 27:20-22; Mark 15:11-13). Undoubtedly Satan was also behind much of the terrible torture and cruelty that was inflicted on Jesus. I think it will break our hearts as we see it.

That covers five of the eight. But who were the other three? This is the glory of what we are in—of the remarkable plan of God—because the other three are these:

- God the Father;
- the Holy Spirit; and—you may find this surprising at first—
- Jesus Christ the Son of God as well.

The end of the passage in Acts confirms this. It tells us that the first four we have mentioned **"were gathered together to do whatever Your hand and Your purpose determined before to be done"** (Acts 4:27b-28). God the Father—and with Him the Holy Spirit and, amazingly, Jesus Christ Himself—were all involved in the judgment of Jesus on the Cross.

In this chapter we are going to deal with the first five who were responsible for Jesus going to the Cross. Then, in the next, we will see how God the Father, the Son and the Holy Spirit were involved. The difference between this and the next chapter is that, in the next chapter we will see *righteous* judgment, whereas in this chapter all the judgment we will examine was *illegal and false* and was a complete travesty of justice. Yet the Lord took it all without opening His mouth.[2]

---

[2] The judgment of Christ is in one sense still going on. There are many people today who are still judging the Lord and judging Him very falsely; and He is still taking it all, every single bit. Their judgment is entirely false because Jesus, no matter what they say about Him, was completely and utterly perfect in everything that He did.

Jesus was Sinless Throughout His Whole Life—including on the Cross

The Lord Jesus was *impeccable*. He was utterly perfect in every thought, word and deed. He did not sin. It is important to state this clearly before we begin. He was born without an old sin nature, and, although He was tempted and tested in every way, He never committed any personal sin whatsoever. When He hung upon the Cross, it was the fact that He was without blemish that meant He could take our sins upon Himself and be made the sin-offering for us. We need to look at a few scriptures on this.

"**For we do not have a High Priest who cannot sympathize with our weaknesses, but was in all points tempted as we are, yet without sin**" (Hebrews 4:15). What a wonderful verse this is! What a great comfort this is to me. Jesus was tempted in every way that I could be, as well as in ways that you or I could never be, yet He was without sin. And on the Cross He Himself was sinless. Praise His wonderful name!

The next scripture, in 1 Peter, was addressed to believers: "**Knowing that you were not redeemed with corruptible things, like silver or gold, from your aimless conduct received by tradition from your fathers**" (1 Peter 1:18). How I love that! Gold and silver are two of the things that are *least* corruptible in the world today. Yet Peter said, "You weren't redeemed with such *corruptible* things as silver and gold!", "**...but with the precious blood of Christ, as of a lamb without blemish and without spot**" (verse 19). Christ had no blemish or imperfection at all.

Another scripture is 1 John 3:5. "**And you know that He was manifested to take away our sins, and in Him there is no sin.**" This tells us that, still today, there is no sin in Christ. Hallelujah!

Jesus was crucified between two thieves. Luke records, "**Then one of the criminals who were hanged blasphemed Him, saying, "If You are the Christ, save Yourself and us." But the other, answering, rebuked him, saying, "Do you not even fear God, seeing you are under the same condemnation? And we indeed justly, for we receive the due reward of our deeds; but this man has done nothing wrong"**" (Luke 23:39-41). This passage is perhaps the most glorious of all concerning the sinlessness of Christ. One of the thieves crucified alongside Jesus recognized that He was righteous! Christ had done nothing to deserve being put on a cross, but He was there nonetheless. He was absolutely perfect; yet He was there suffering—for *our sins*.

With this in view, everything else we are going to see in this chapter was completely unjust and illegal. Because Christ was perfect, the very fact that any man or angelic being dared to stand against Him in judgment was a complete farce, and a hollow sham of anything that we call "justice". Yet, for almost a day, Christ was subjected to the most tragic travesty of justice that the world has ever seen.

The Irregular and Illegal Trials of Jesus

After Jesus was arrested, He was subjected to a series of trials. There was not just one trial. In fact, there were six trials. Jesus appeared before: (1) Annas; (2) Caiaphas; (3) the Sanhedrin; (4) Pontius Pilate; (5) Herod; and (6) Pontius Pilate again. To go through each of the six trials in detail would take a long time—although it's an excellent Bible study to do. Therefore, in this chapter we will consider just two of the trials, to see how unjust the judgment of Jesus really was.

The Jewish legal system was extremely fine and, usually, it was fair in every respect. However, the Jewish leaders conveniently ignored their own principles of justice when it came to Jesus. Therefore, first I am going to define six main ways in which the trials of Jesus were absolutely irregular or illegal as far as even the Jews themselves were concerned.[3]

1. The first two trials were held at night

A trial was not usually allowed at night, especially in a serious case. It had to take place during daylight hours. Also, a trial could not be held on a Sabbath or feast day, so a serious case would not usually be heard immediately prior to such a day either. Yet Jesus was tried at night before Annas and Caiaphas (Luke 22:66), because the religious leaders had to keep the Feast of Passover. They therefore wanted Jesus' case to be finished with quickly, so that they could take the feast with clean hands the following afternoon and evening! The tragic irony was that the Passover represented Christ dying for our sins. These religious leaders were now rushing the trials illegally that would result in the true Passover Lamb of God being sacrificed on the Cross!

---

[3] Even under the Romans, the Jews were allowed their own religious courts. Small, local courts are known to have had from 3 to 23 judges, but the highest religious court was the powerful Sanhedrin (or "the Council") in Jerusalem, which had 70 members who were effectively judges. This was the highest Jewish authority. In New Testament times it comprised mostly members of the aristocracy (chief priests, elders, Sadducees) under the leadership of the High Priest. It also included other nobles and scribes (who were Pharisees). It had great power and jurisdiction, although it was ultimately answerable to the Roman governor. It was allowed almost complete control over the internal affairs of the nation, so long as public order and tax revenues were maintained. It had complete control of Jewish religious affairs, and was allowed to try certain criminal cases too. The Sanhedrin was dissolved in AD 70.

2. The sentence should not have been passed on the same day that evidence was given in the trial

In normal practice, final evidence had to be given on one particular day and, only on the next day, could the verdict be given and a sentence passed. That was the rule as far as the Jewish legal system was concerned, just as it is the case in British courts and most others even to this day—especially for serious cases involving capital punishment. However, when we come to the trials of Jesus, it wasn't even the case that they were going to present the evidence and then pass judgment on the same day. It was much worse than that! The accusers of Jesus had already decided what the verdict was going to be *and* they had already decided on His sentence! Their problem was to find a crime! It was not a matter of making "the punishment fit the crime" (as in the Gilbert and Sullivan song); rather, it was a matter of making some crime fit the punishment they had already chosen. This demonstrates the wickedness of fallen man.[4] The religious leaders were determined to find some convenient excuse to pass a sentence of death. Jesus knew that this travesty of justice was going on, yet He didn't say a word.

3. The court was biased: the judges acted as the prosecution and extracted false testimony

In these 'courts', the 'judges', who should have been totally impartial, were generally the very ones who were firing the prosecution questions at Jesus. Pontius Pilate was an exception. In other words, those who were going to pass judgment were the very same people who were accusing Jesus. In Britain, as in any other country (apart from the most corrupt), that would not be tolerated even for a moment. Worse still, the judges actually went about seeking witnesses to give even false testimony—possibly by handing out bribes—in an effort to persuade anyone to come up with evidence to help their cause.

Mark chapter 14 describes this: "**And the chief priests and all the council sought testimony against Jesus to put Him to death, and found none. For many bore false witness against Him, but their testimonies did not agree**" (verses 55-56). The chief priests and others in the Council were

---

[4]The Bible defines every unbeliever as an enemy of God (see Romans 5:10; 8:7). Usually, however, the enmity is hidden and is latent within a person. Yet at the Cross and in the events leading up to the Cross—when the very heart of God was revealed, bursting with love for the world—that was also the time when the wicked heart of man was most clearly revealed, bursting with hatred towards the Son of God.

acting as judges *and* prosecutors, yet they could not find two witnesses to say anything substantial or consistent against Jesus.

I like to imagine that, as they went through the streets and asked people, "Would you be a witness in the case of the Council versus Jesus?" many people said, "Yes, I will…. I was lame, but now I can walk! I'll be a witness." Such a witness would have been told to go away. Others might have said: "Yes, I was blind, but now I can see! Jesus did that for me"; "I was deaf, but now I can hear everything you say to me! I'll stand up for Jesus any time"; "I was dead, yet now I live!" However, the chief priests would have said, "Go away, we don't want you!" Therefore they tried collecting false witnesses, but as soon as they brought in these witnesses and began to question them, the trials turned into a farce because their testimonies disagreed! They quickly had to dismiss them: "That's enough, thank you! Next witness, please!"

Jesus stood there, in His full regality, not taking part. He knew it was all a mockery of Himself and of justice, but He was loving those people as they did this to Him. Imagine it! He just stood there, with eyes full of love, gazing at the High Priest, gazing at all the men in the Sanhedrin, loving them and willing them to love Him. I think that the greatest heartache for Jesus was not what they were doing, but the fact that they rejected His love and would not love Him.

"And some rose up and bore false witness against Him, saying, "We heard him say, 'I will destroy this temple that is made with hands, and within three days I will build another made without hands.'" But not even then did their testimony agree" (verse 57-59). They finally found some 'witnesses' who said the same thing, so they thought, "Great. That's the charge!" However, as soon as they questioned them further, even the testimony of these witnesses was contradictory. In any normal, unbiased court of law, if the prosecution cannot find any reliable witnesses, the whole trial is immediately abandoned. However, this was not what happened.

4. No one argued on behalf of Jesus

No one at all supported Jesus. These were supposed to be trials, yet, in all six, Jesus was given no defence. Ironically, the closest Jesus ever came to having a defence spokesman was when Pontius Pilate, the Roman governor himself, appealed on His behalf. Pilate probably defended Jesus because he hated the Jews rather than because he liked Jesus. He was bemused by the Jews' unusual accusations concerning Jesus. The history of Pontius Pilate is marked with incidents when he deliberately riled the Jews. He never quite provoked them to riot, although he came close to it sometimes! He knew exactly how far to go. He simply wanted to put the Jews down.

5. All the witnesses were false

Deuteronomy chapter 19 gives important teaching concerning trials: "**One witness shall not rise against a man concerning any iniquity or any sin that he commits; by the mouth of two or three witnesses the matter shall be established**" (verse 15). The Jewish leaders acknowledged this law and therefore wanted to find two witnesses to prove that Jesus was worthy of death. If only they had chosen to ignore this particular scripture it would have been much easier for them; but they didn't!

However, notice what the passage goes on to say: "**If a false witness rises against any man to testify against him of wrongdoing, then both men in the controversy shall stand before the LORD, before the priests and the judges who serve in those days. And the judges shall make diligent inquiry, and indeed, if the witness is a false witness, who has testified falsely against his brother, then you shall do to him as he thought to have done to his brother; so you shall put away the evil person from among you**" (verses 16-19). Thus, if a man was found to have lied in order to bring the death penalty on another man, he had to be put to death himself. This was supposed to be a fearsome deterrent against giving false testimony—that is, perjury. The Jewish leaders at the trials of Jesus were thus seeking to observe the first part of these instructions, yet they were conveniently forgetting the next part. Their inconsistency did not seem to concern them.

6. There was violence in the courtroom

Violence simply is not permitted in our courtrooms, and it certainly was not permitted in theirs. Nevertheless, Jesus was subjected to terrible violence during His trials at the hands of His accusers and of the Roman soldiers.

All these trials were bogus. There was not a sound thing in any of them. Yet, on the basis of these trials, Jesus was sent to the Cross.

The Thirty Pieces of Silver

The chief priests had already shown exactly what they thought of Jesus. They had shown it very clearly when Judas Iscariot had gone to them, offering to hand Jesus over. "**Then one of the twelve, called Judas Iscariot, went to the chief priests and said, "What are you willing to give me if I deliver Him to you?" And they counted out to him thirty pieces of silver**" (Matthew 26:14-15).

The chief priests had done a clever and revealing thing. In Exodus 21:32, thirty pieces of silver was the amount that had to be paid to a master whose servant had been gored by an ox. They were therefore saying, "Jesus is worth as much as a maimed, useless servant to us. So, Judas, we'll give you 30 pieces of silver!" What *God* was saying behind this, however, was that Jesus was going to be *His* maimed servant—gored by our sins—so 30 pieces of silver *was* the appropriate price.

We shall now look at two of the trials of Jesus, or rather two parts of two of the trials, to see exactly how wicked they turned out to be.

THE TRIAL BEFORE CAIAPHAS

The trial before Caiaphas was the second trial that Jesus had to endure. It was probably one of the most prolonged. It is described in Matthew chapter 26 (as well as in the other three gospels).

"And those who had laid hold of Jesus led Him away to Caiaphas the high priest, where the scribes and the elders were assembled" (Matthew 26:57). This was a secret meeting held at night in the High Priest's house (Luke 22:54-55). It had been pre-arranged. It was clearly a meeting not to be missed by those who had gathered. It was a great event for them. Their adversary, the One whom they hated so much, because He had shown how false they were, was finally going to be put down.[5]

Verse 58 deals with the "carnal catastrophe" of Peter, but we won't deal with that here. The account continues: **"Now the chief priests, the elders, and all the council sought false testimony against Jesus to put Him to death, but found none"** (verse 59-60a). They had decided Jesus' sentence already, namely death. They therefore sought false witnesses against Jesus to justify putting Him to death.

The Greek text here suggests some shocking things. First, the aorist tense suggests not only that they wanted to put Jesus to death, but that they

---

[5] For all, that is, except two. There were two members of the Council (the Sanhedrin), at least, who were believers—Nicodemus and Joseph of Arimathea. I expect they were absent from the assembly. Perhaps they had not been told about the trial. However, at this stage we know that Joseph of Arimathea was a disciple of Jesus in secret, because he feared the Jews (John 19:38). He was a prominent Council member and was waiting for the kingdom of God to come (Mark 15:43). We are also told that he was a good and just man, and did not consent to the wicked counsel and deed of putting Jesus to death (Luke 23:51). We thus cannot be sure whether he was present at the trial, or whether he defended the Lord.

wanted to do so as quickly as possible, in a moment of time. Next, the active voice implies that they were determined to be involved themselves. The subjunctive mood, however, implies that they were not sure whether they could achieve their aim. The Lord Jesus of course knew exactly what their intentions were.

Notice how there was no bitterness in Jesus as He was hauled in front of them. What would you have done? You might say, "I'd have been like Jesus and not opened my mouth," but can you imagine the *thoughts* that would have been seething through your head? Jesus did not say a word; and *He did not sin in His thoughts*, either. Isaiah said of Him, "**He was led as a lamb to the slaughter, and as a sheep before its shearers is silent, so He opened not His mouth**" (Isaiah 53:7b). A slaughterer in Lincolnshire once told me how lambs are the most gentle creatures of all in dying. Pigs know they are going to die in the slaughterhouse, and they will rush to try and kill you if they are given the opportunity. Most other animals will put up a fight; but a lamb just lies down and submissively accepts death.

Jesus, knowing what was in the minds of his accusers, still went into their presence. There was not a wicked thought in His head; that would have been sin. Rather, there was love pouring out of Him for all the people. It would transcend anything that we have ever experienced, wouldn't it, to be in such an evil gathering with only love and no bitterness pouring out? Jesus was looking beyond His suffering and the injustice of it. He knew that unless He died sinless on that Cross, there would be no salvation for you and for me.

"**Even though many false witnesses came forward, they found none**" (Matthew 26:60b). We have already seen this. It would have been quite farcical, actually, to see the false witnesses being pushed forward and the religious leaders quite unable to extract two stories that agreed at any point!

"**But at last two false witnesses came forward and said, "This fellow said, 'I am able to destroy the temple of God and to build it in three days'"**" (verses 60c-61). As we have seen, two false witnesses did finally agree upon this one statement that Jesus was supposed to have made. But what was so bad about this statement anyway? The Jews were well known for boasting; and it could simply have been an idle boast.

In fact, when the Jews had asked Jesus (a few years earlier) to show them a sign, He had said, "**Destroy this temple, and in three days I will raise it up**" (John 2:19). "I will die, but I'm going to rise from the dead in three days," He was saying. Jesus wasn't talking about the Temple in Jerusalem. (If He'd been talking about the actual Temple, He probably would have said, "I will *instantly* raise it up again!" It would not take three days; it would take just a tiny movement of a little finger on one of His hands, and the whole Temple would reassemble immediately!) He was talking about His body: "**But He was speaking of the temple of His body**" (John 2:21).

Jesus had said nothing worthy of a death sentence, but now at last they had found one line on which two witnesses seemed to agree. There was absolutely no sin in it; but they were going to pounce on it. Incidentally, Mark's Gospel tells us that even the testimony of these two witnesses was soon found not to agree (Mark 14:59)!

Caiaphas decided to intervene. "**And the high priest arose and said to Him, "Do you answer nothing? What is it that these men testify against you?"**" (Matthew 26:62). Caiaphas stood in front of Jesus, saying, "There, that's Your crime! What have You got to say about it? This is what we are charging You with. How do You plead?" "**But Jesus kept silent**" (verse 63a). Jesus would not have anything to do with it. He remained completely silent in front of Caiaphas.

"**And the high priest answered and said to Him, "I adjure You by the living God that You tell us if You are the Christ, the Son of God"**" (verse 63b). The word "adjure" means 'to command'. Who is the living God? Jesus is! *There* was the living God standing right in front of him, and Caiaphas demanded of Him, "By the living God, You've got to tell us the truth!" How tragic! Caiaphas was completely blind to everything.

Jesus chose to answer at this point. "**Jesus said to him, "It is as you said. Nevertheless, I say to you, hereafter you will see the Son of Man sitting at the right hand of the Power, and coming on the clouds of heaven"**" (verse 64). How weak the English translation is here. The Greek is emphatic. Jesus was saying, "Yes! You've said it!" It was a definite "Yes". Mark's Gospel records Jesus' reply as, "**I am**" (see Mark 14:62a), a reference to God's personal name (see Exodus 3:14). That must have taken Caiaphas by surprise! Jesus had admitted who He was—the Christ, the Son of God.

Jesus did not then begin explaining about His death and resurrection, because religious people hate, and always have hated, the Cross. Rather, He warned Caiaphas, "Be careful, because the day is coming when *I* am going to be Judge. I will come again and you're going to see *Me* in the place of authority; and *you*, Caiaphas, will be judged *by Me*!" What happened next?

The High Priest, who was also acting as judge, jumped up. He'd heard enough. **"Then the high priest tore his clothes, saying, "He has spoken blasphemy! What further need do we have of witnesses? Look, now you have heard His blasphemy!""** (Matthew 26:65).

Caiaphas was extremely frustrated, shocked and angry. He assumed Jesus' claim to be a blasphemous lie. He started pulling at his clothes. "That's enough! From His own mouth He's condemned!" he announced. Do you see what Caiaphas was saying? "We're a court of law and, because Jesus has said this, we don't need any witnesses." How terrible! That was totally contrary to Jewish law yet again.[6] Have you read this verse without a smile coming to your face in view of the irony of it? It was a case under law, so of course the 'court' needed witnesses! However, it was a convenient idea, since no two witnesses could agree.

I think the heart of Jesus must have broken at this point: to be accused of blasphemy—Jesus, the very Son of God! He who had said, **"My food is to do the will of Him who sent Me, and to finish His work"** (John 4:34), was now being accused of blasphemy—by the very High Priest of God's people, Israel. It was Jesus who, in the Garden of Gethsemane, had sweat beads of blood from His forehead and said, **"O My Father, if this cup cannot pass away from Me unless I drink it, Your will be done"** (Matthew 26:42b). Can you imagine it? Blasphemy is a denial of God; it is slandering God, insulting God, showing contempt for God, cursing God, profaning God's holy name. Jesus' heart was aching to do His Father's will, yet He had to stand and listen to this ungodly hypocrite in front of Him accuse Him of blasphemy. How tragic. Can you also imagine what it must have done to the heart of the Father?—the Father who had said of Jesus, **"This is My beloved Son, in whom I am well pleased"** (Matthew 3:17b). It is appalling when you think of it.

After saying, **"Look, now you have heard His blasphemy!"** (Matthew 26:65b), Caiaphas then turned around to his 'cronies' in the Sanhedrin, and asked, **"What do you think?"** (verse 66a). But Caiaphas was the 'beloved' son-in-law of Annas, a ruthless man who exercised great power in Israel. Therefore, when Caiaphas asked, "What do you think?", they really didn't have much option but to agree. They knew full well that, had they disagreed, they might go home to find their houses burnt down, their wives

---

[6] It was illegal in a Jewish trial to use words from the mouth of the person being tried as evidence against him. Therefore, any words that Jesus said were not valid as evidence. Jesus referred to this principle when he said, "If I **bear witness of Myself, My witness is not true** [valid as testimony]" (John 5:31). Two or three (independent) witnesses were necessary to establish any matter.

murdered, or their children kidnapped.[7] If our two beloved brethren, Nicodemus and Joseph of Arimathea, had been there, however, *they* might have spoken out. But the rest were intimidated or in collusion with Caiaphas and Annas. Therefore, "**They answered and said, "He deserves death"**" (verse 66b).

Thus, during the night, on the same day as the trial, without any true witnesses, the religious leaders of Israel agreed with Caiaphas that Jesus was guilty and that His sentence should be death! Under the Law, if Jesus had committed blasphemy, then death was indeed the correct sentence (see Leviticus 24:10-16). They were right on that. But there was no proof of blasphemy. There was no evidence. There were no witnesses. If just one witness testified of a genuine crime, a matter was not established. That was what the Law said. Yet Caiaphas, with no witnesses at all, said, "Because of what you have said Yourself, Jesus, You are worthy of death!" However, Jesus' words in His trial could not be admitted as evidence.[8]

In verse 67 we come to the violence in the courtroom. This is our beloved Jesus. "**Then they spat in His face and beat Him**" (verse 67a). This suggests that they repeatedly spat, probably queuing up to spit in His face one after the other. The word for "beat" means 'punched'—with a closed fist. It seems that the members of the Sanhedrin walked past Jesus, spat on Him, and punched Him in the face and around His body with their fists. They were beginning to pass their sentence already.

---

[7] Jesus was first brought before Annas, the father-in-law of the High Priest Caiaphas (John 18:13). Annas was the corrupt head of a corrupt family, that had great influence in the Sanhedrin and throughout the land. He was probably the equivalent of a Mafia-type leader or the type of gangster found in America during the 1920s and 1930s. He controlled gangster-like operations in the desert at the time of Jesus.

Annas had been High Priest from AD 6 to 15, but remained the effective head of the chief priests in Jerusalem as long as he lived. At the time of Jesus, the High Priest was appointed and deposed by the Roman governors at whim. After being removed from office, Annas's influence remained so great that five of his sons, his son-in-law Caiaphas and a grandson all became High Priests. Thus, even after Annas left office, he was still popularly considered to be High Priest (Acts 4:6). Hence, according to Luke 3:2, both Annas and Caiaphas were called High Priests. Caiaphas held the office officially, but Annas was in control, behind the scenes. The fact that Annas retained such control and the fact that Caiaphas remained in office for about 18 years, from AD 18, indicate just how shrewd, corrupt and adaptable to Rome they were.

[8] Jesus had now claimed to be the great Son of Man, so a further case could now be brought against Him in which two or three of those who had heard His claim could testify of His supposed blasphemy! However, most people claiming to be the Messiah would usually be considered deceived or mad. Jesus' words were true and His claim to be the great Son of Man was not a lie! Therefore, no blasphemy had been committed.

Have you ever seen paintings of Jesus hanging on the Cross, showing Him lily-white and with one or two small cuts or marks on His body? That was not how it was at all. Isaiah prophesied, "**Just as many were appalled at You, so His visage was marred more than any man, and His form more than the sons of men**" (Isaiah 52:14).

People were appalled when they looked at Jesus. As He walked to the Cross, He appeared scarcely human; that is what this verse means. Jesus' face had been so punched that, when people saw Him, they were absolutely astonished. I believe they had never seen another prisoner so tortured and beaten up. And it was the religious leaders who had been first to do it; the soldiers then continued.[9] It was no wonder Jesus struggled to carry His Cross. He had been beaten within an inch of His life. I frankly cannot look seriously at any picture of Jesus hanging on the Cross which portrays Him with a frail, lily-white body, when the Bible definitely declares that His face and His body were so damaged that He was barely recognizable as human.

"**And others struck Him with the palms of their hands, saying, "Prophesy to us, Christ! Who is the one who struck You?"**" (Matthew 26:67b-68). Jesus' eyes were probably so puffed up that He could hardly see out of them. Those who held Jesus mocked Him and blindfolded Him (Luke 22:63-64). They went up and slapped Him around the face and taunted, "Come on, You're supposed to be a prophet. What's my name? Who hit You?" But not a word or a cry or a scream came out of Jesus' mouth. He endured His suffering in silence.

How could a man take such torture? How could anyone stand there and endure such illegal trials, be beaten up, and then be mocked in this fashion? The only answer is that He had you in mind! Jesus knew that unless He went to that Cross and died, there could be no salvation for you or for me. It was His *love for us* that caused Him to stand there and take all of the punishment. That's how much He loves you. He endured this bogus judgment because He was so occupied with you. He knew that if He died on the Cross, many would accept Him and become God's beloved children. "**For the joy that was set before Him [He] endured the Cross**" (Hebrews 12:2b).

---

[9] I think they were incited by Satan to do this. Satan, who hates Jesus, wanted to inflict as much pain and suffering on Jesus as he could, to destroy Him. He was possibly trying to kill Jesus before He could reach the Cross because, if he could stop Him reaching the Cross, he would prevent fulfilment of the Scriptures, 'breaking' the Word of God. However, at this point it seems Satan did not fully understand the implications of Jesus dying on the Cross and the scale of the victory that Jesus would win.

That was just part of one of the trials: a totally illegal affair. But let us stand in awe, because God is not mocked. After Jesus suffered and died, He then rose from the dead, exactly as He had predicted—to our eternal benefit. Hallelujah! He *did* rise from the dead!

Jesus' Final Trial before Pontius Pilate

We will now look at another of the trials, Jesus' final trial before Pontius Pilate. We will stay in Matthew's account, although it is also reported in the other gospels.[10] Jesus was led to Pilate, now accused of sedition (Luke 23:1-2).

Pontius Pilate, the Roman governor of Judea, had headquarters in Jerusalem called the Praetorium. This was quite a large building, with two or three, or perhaps four storeys. About halfway up it had a balcony which overlooked a beautiful square, or courtyard. Down below, in the basement, were the barracks of the soldiers, who lived there so that the Praetorium could quickly be protected if there was an uprising. The governor was therefore quite safe, no matter what happened.[11]

The balcony was set above the courtyard because, on certain days, the Jews could not enter the Praetorium itself. Jews considered themselves to be unclean (ceremonially defiled) if they entered a Gentile's house, so they certainly would not have wanted to enter the Praetorium on a feast day, for example. Any business that Pilate had to conduct on such a day thus had to be done with the Jews remaining outside. Therefore, he could walk out on to his balcony and conduct his business from there with the Jews, who would gather in the courtyard below. It was a clever mutual arrangement. On the day of Jesus' trial, this procedure was adopted in view of the Passover (John 18:28-29).

"Now at the feast the governor was accustomed to releasing to the multitude one prisoner whom they wished" (Matthew 27:15). At Passover, as a special peacekeeping gesture to the Jews, the Roman governor used to release a prisoner. Usually, he would let *them* select the prisoner. This was not because the Romans liked the Jews, but was

---

[10] We learn from Luke's Gospel (chapter 23) that Jesus was brought briefly before Pilate, who then sent Him to Herod. Herod then returned Him to Pilate.

[11] The Jews in Israel were allowed a degree of liberty and self-government under the Romans. The Sanhedrin, for example, had various judicial functions. However, it could not carry out a death penalty without approval from the Roman governor. Roman citizens had various rights and protections under Roman law, but the Roman governor held almost total power over the non-Roman population.

designed to help pacify the Jews and keep them from causing too much trouble. Passover was the feast which looked back to the Exodus, when the children of Israel had been released from bondage in Egypt, so this gesture was deemed appropriate.

The time was now early morning (John 18:28). Pilate was in the Praetorium and about to come out on to his balcony to speak to the Jews; Jesus was under guard inside the Praetorium; and crowds were milling about down in the square below. There were probably Gentiles among the crowds, as well as Jews, and they had all come to see two things. They had come first of all to see Jesus; and they had also come to see whom Pontius Pilate would release to them as his 'gift' this year.

"And they had then a notorious prisoner called Barabbas" (verse 16). Mark's Gospel tells us more about Barabbas: **"And there was one named Barabbas, who was chained with his fellow insurrectionists; they had committed murder in the insurrection"** (Mark 15:7). Barabbas was a known murderer and insurrectionist. Whether his name was really Barabbas we can't be sure, because many men who wanted to lead a revolt against the Romans would give themselves a messianic-type name such as Barabbas—which meant 'son of (the) father'.

"Therefore, when they had gathered together, Pilate said to them, "Whom do you want me to release to you? Barabbas, or Jesus who is called Christ?"" (Matthew 27:17). In other words, Pilate said to those gathered, "The choice is up to you! Do you want Barabbas, a known murderer and insurrectionist, or do you want Jesus, the 'Messiah'?" This was clever. Notice why Pilate said it: **"For he knew that because of envy they had delivered Him"** (verse 18).

Israel's religious leaders had put Jesus on trial to get rid of Him—because of envy. Pilate knew it was unjust. There was no real case for Jesus to answer. Pilate could have gone along with the chief priests and elders immediately and released Barabbas, but he probably wanted to make them squirm a bit! He therefore turned to the crowd and said, "Right, you people choose! Who is it going to be? Barabbas or Jesus?" That way, he could enjoy watching the religious leaders become enraged if the crowd chose to release Jesus; and they wouldn't be able to blame him. Also, he wouldn't have to feel guilty if Jesus was condemned—the crowd would be to blame.

Now we learn a bit of Pilate's family history. **"While he was sitting on the judgment seat, his wife sent to him, saying, "Have nothing to do with that just Man, for I have suffered many things today in a dream because of Him""** (verse 19). The word "just" means 'righteous' or 'upright'. Pilate had handed the choice over to the crowds, and was now sitting on the judgment seat waiting for their decision. However, his wife was distraught; she'd had a terrible dream concerning Jesus. Therefore, she sent Pilate a warning, "He's an innocent man; He's a righteous man. Have nothing to do with that Jesus." I think she was under the conviction of the Holy Spirit.[12]

"But the chief priests and elders persuaded the multitudes that they should ask for Barabbas and destroy Jesus" (verse 20). The chief opponents of Jesus were the religious leaders of the land, the very ones who were supposed to represent God. They actually swung the crowd in favour of Barabbas. They preferred to have a murderer released rather than to have the perfect, sinless, Son of God. It was so evil. The crowd might have chosen to release Jesus, but I imagine the leaders went wandering through the crowd, saying, "Pick Barabbas! That Jesus is just a false prophet. Trust us on this!"

If there is one characteristic of crowds, it is that they are fickle. A few days earlier, the crowds had been throwing palm leaves down as Jesus entered Jerusalem, shouting out, **"Hosanna to the son of David! Blessed is He who comes in the name of the LORD! Hosanna in the highest!"** (see Matthew 21:9). However, this time it would be an entirely different cry. They would not be shouting, "Hosanna!" (which means "Save now!").[13]

"The governor answered and said to them, "Which of the two do you want me to release to you?" They said, "Barabbas!"" (Matthew 27:21). The crowd started shouting, "Barabbas! Barabbas! We want Barabbas! Give us Barabbas!" **"Pilate said to them, "What then shall I do with Jesus who is called Christ?""** (verse 22a).

Notice what it says next: **"They all said to him, "Let Him be crucified!""** (verse 22b). They *all* shouted, "Crucify Him!" **"Then the governor said, "Why, what evil has He done?" But they cried out all the more, saying, "Let Him be crucified!""** (verse 23). This was the only defence Jesus had, and it came from the Roman governor! However, the religious leaders had

---

[12] We don't know whether Pilate became a saved man; but his wife must have been very close to salvation at this point. Historians report that Pilate died violently, possibly by suicide, several years later. Historians describe Pilate as a vile, brutal, cruel and calculating man, with little concern for truth or justice.

[13] Hosanna means 'Save now' or 'Help us now', in other words 'Save us we pray!' or 'Save us, please!' It became a common acclamation and wish, meaning 'Save and prosper!' They had almost certainly shouted, "Hosanna!" a few days before because they believed or hoped that Jesus was their awaited Messiah who would deliver them from the Romans. However, they failed to see that it was principally their own sins that Jesus was going to deliver them from.

now stirred up the crowd into a frenzy. They were shouting and it was getting louder and louder. No answer was given to Pilate's question; they just shouted, "Crucify Him, crucify Him!" That was all they were now interested in.

"When Pilate saw that he could not prevail at all, but rather that a tumult was rising..." (verse 24a). Pilate could not afford to have a riot on his hands, because the emperor would want to know why it had been allowed to occur; so he was now in a predicament. He preferred to release Jesus, because he hated the Jews and he knew Jesus didn't deserve to die. However, the crowds might then get out of control and begin to attack the Praetorium. Therefore, **"...he took water and washed his hands before the multitude, saying, "I am innocent of the blood of this just Person. You see to it""** (verse 24b). In the ancient world, when you washed your hands publicly you were saying, "I'm having nothing more to do with the matter. I disagree with all of you, but carry on as you want!" Pilate could have acted forcefully, being the governor, but instead he said, "Do as you please. I'm not responsible!"

The crowd's answer is one of the most terrifying verses in the whole Bible: **"And all the people answered and said, "His blood be on us and on our children""** (verse 25). Thus, standing in front of the Praetorium in the square, the whole crowd was in effect declaring, "Let responsibility for the blood of Jesus Christ be on us and on our children!"

History tells us what happened. In AD 62, just 29 years later, in that same square, a later governor crucified 3600 Jewish nobles on that very spot—the place where these people had shouted, "We take full responsibility!" In that very square, 3600 crosses were established. When you think of it, it was almost certainly many of the same people, together with many of their children, who were crucified. Then, eight years after that, in AD 70, the whole square was awash with blood and with dead bodies as Roman soldiers under Titus swept into the city and killed every Jew in sight. More than a million Jews suffered and died at that time, and that square was filled with blood—of those who had accepted responsibility for the death of Jesus, and their children.

I consider this with awe and fear. Remember that the Bible says, **"The fear of the LORD is the beginning of wisdom"** (Proverbs 9:10). It is not for us to judge concerning these issues; rather it is for us to acknowledge the extreme awesomeness of these events and of our God.

This helps to explain why Jesus said certain words on His way to the Cross. Luke 23:27 tells us, **"And a great multitude of the people followed Him,**

and women who also mourned and lamented Him." Whenever something awful was happening, a group of women wailers used to come along and weep. (You could actually hire such a crowd.) Here, it seems, such wailers had come and joined the crowd that was following Jesus, which included some of Jesus' family and friends.[14]

"**But Jesus, turning to them, said, "Daughters of Jerusalem, do not weep for Me...**" (Luke 23:28a). Why did He say that? It was because He knew that, in just a few days, He was going to rise up from the grave! "Don't waste your tears on Me," He was saying, "I'm going to die; but I'm going to rise again. You should be giving thanks, because I'm going to win your salvation. Don't weep for Me!" "**...but weep for yourselves and for your children. For indeed the days are coming in which they will say, "Blessed are the barren, the wombs that never bore, and the breasts which never nursed!"**" (Luke 23:28b-29).

Jesus knew what was about to come upon the Jewish nation. As He stood before Pilate, He knew that thousands of Jewish noblemen would be crucified right below where He was standing, just 29 years later. He also knew that, just 37 years later, more than a million Jews would lie dead at the hands of the Roman army. And He knew that then, for almost 2000 years, the Jews would be scattered and persecuted right around the world. (He also knew, by the way, that the nation which blesses Israel will in turn be blessed by God.)[15]

The account of the trial ends: "**Then he [Pilate] released Barabbas to them; and when he had scourged Jesus, he delivered Him to be crucified**" (Matthew 27:26). Jesus was whipped with a whip which had metal or bone pieces at the end of each of its tails—to within an inch of His life. The whole garrison of Pilate's soldiers then mocked Jesus inside the Praetorium, clothing Him with a purple robe and twisting a crown of thorns upon His head. They then saluted Him, struck Him on the head with a reed, spat on Him and pretended to worship Him (verses 27-31). Satan was no doubt there, inciting them, trying to destroy Jesus.

---

[14] Such wailers were often hanging around. Sometimes, instead of having a grand funeral with a marvellous tombstone, some people would hire such women to come along and bewail their loss; and onlookers would say, "See how they loved him!" (This got them off the hook if they didn't love the person who had died terribly much.) Mary and Martha might have had a crowd of wailers after Lazarus died, but it is doubtful.

[15] See Genesis 12:1-3. God definitely warns that anyone who lays a hand on the nation of Israel is going to be cursed, but those who bless Israel are going to be blessed. This principle is explained more fully in Chapter 12. The Roman Empire was largely destroyed by AD 476. We who are Christians should bless Israel always; we must pray for Israel always. And we should pray for our own nations too, that they would take the right course regarding Israel.

CONCLUSION

This was the start of the judgment of Jesus. We haven't even reached the Cross itself yet. We have seen just some of the sufferings Jesus endured before He reached the Cross, none of which He deserved. It was all illegal, cruel and unjust.

The judgment of Jesus by the first five of the eight personalities or groups we are considering was a total travesty of truth and justice. However, Jesus loved us so much that He endured it all for us. How wonderful! May we all seek to serve the Lord with all our hearts, in truth—and selflessly, even as Jesus laid down His life for us. Amen.

7. WHEN CALVARY BLOSSOMED
The Righteous Judgment of Jesus in our place by God

Now we are going to deal with the remaining group of three responsible for the judgment of Jesus. So far we have seen the bogus trials of Jesus before men, when Jesus was tried illegally and unjustly. Now we are going to see Him approaching the Cross and on the Cross.

It is important to realize what a victory it was for Jesus even to arrive at the Cross. We talk so much about His victory *on* the Cross, and rightly so. However, we should also recognize the magnitude of His victory in just arriving at the Cross—of what it cost Him to get *to* the Cross.

JESUS HAD TO DIE BY CRUCIFIXION

About 1500 years before Jesus Christ came to the earth, Moses did something rather extraordinary out in the wilderness. He made a model of a serpent and he lifted it up on a pole. We know from John's gospel that this act represented how the Son of Man, God's Messiah, was going to die (see John 3:13-15). He was not going to die in just any manner; He was going to be lifted up above the earth. In fact, He was going to die on the 'tree' of Calvary, but the fact that He would be raised up to die between heaven and earth was revealed through Moses.[1]

Many other Hebrew prophets also spoke about the Messiah who would come, hundreds of years before Christ actually died on the Cross. They also revealed various facts about Christ's life, including aspects of His rejection, suffering and the manner of His death (see Luke 24:25-27). Some of them revealed that He was going to die a terrible death. He would be rejected (Psalm 118:22; Isaiah 53:3), deserted (Zechariah 13:7), betrayed by a friend (Psalm 41:9) and would die as a transgressor with the wicked (Isaiah 53:9, 12). He would be pierced (Zechariah 12:10), specifically in His hands

---

[1] This story is examined in the first series of Basic Bible Studies in BBS 5. See Numbers 21:4-9 and John 3:13-15.

and His feet (Zechariah 13:6; Psalm 22:16), but none of His bones would be broken (Psalm 34:20; Exodus 12:46).

It is important to realize that the prophets were referring to crucifixion right back then, hundreds of years before it arrived on the historical scene. Crucifixion was developed and then used widely by the Romans. However, before the Romans were even a 'twinkle in history's eye', Hebrew prophets were referring to how their Messiah would die by crucifixion! Thus, before the Roman Empire had arisen, its means of capital punishment had been outlined in the Bible![2]

Such prophecies certainly must have confused or stunned the Jews at the time—if they'd understood them—because their method of capital punishment was usually stoning. They used to pick up large stones and throw them at the person who was condemned. However, their prophets were saying that the Messiah was not going to die by stoning. His death would be entirely different.

The 'miracle' of Jesus reaching the Cross

As soon as some fact like that is revealed, Satan immediately sets out to thwart the plan of God. Satan therefore sought to destroy Jesus and to stop Him going to the Cross, right from the time He was born. If he could kill Jesus before He reached the Cross or ensure that Jesus would die by some other method, he would break God's word. God would be proved a liar, and he could go free! Do you see this important principle?

I believe that this explains why the elders, the chief priests, the scribes, the Sanhedrin, the soldiers and others were so cruel and violent towards the Lord. They were stirred up by Satan himself. If they had actually caused Jesus to die under their torture, Satan would have defeated the plan of God.

Therefore, when Jesus reached the Cross, what a victory it was! He nearly didn't make it. He was almost skinned alive by the leather scourging whip. After a few more minutes He might have died; but in God's perfect timing He survived. Then when Jesus began carrying His cross, He could hardly complete the journey from the Praetorium, where He'd been kept and tried, to Calvary. Imagine Jesus, dripping with blood, and the soldiers pointing at Him and the two thieves saying, "Right, you three, pick up your crosses!"

---

[2] The Romans may have borrowed the idea of crucifixion from the Phoenicians or Persians, but they developed it into a routine method of capital punishment. They especially used this agonizing method of execution for disobedient slaves, as well as thieves, assassins, insurrectionists and other rebellious provincials. It was very rarely used for Roman citizens.

The two thieves, taking their crosses on their backs, could cope; but Jesus, despite being a very strong man, probably struggled to lift His cross up to His shoulder and walk with it, after all of the violence inflicted upon Him.[3]

Soldiers would have encircled this little group of three men as they set off with their crosses from the Praetorium. Their centurion was probably leading them, trying to make the group walk quickly to get away from the following crowd. But when he shouted, "March!" and the soldiers and the two thieves started moving, Jesus struggled to keep up. I imagine Satan tried to oppress Jesus heavily at that time, as He set out in that procession to Calvary (see Isaiah 53:7).

Jesus had to get there; and He knew He had to get there. He must have been thinking, "I've got to make it, otherwise My beloved ones won't be saved. I must do all My Father's will." But Jesus, in His human body, was struggling. So what did God do? He called in reinforcements! The story is told in Mark chapter 15.

The role of Simon of Cyrene

"**Now they compelled a certain man, Simon a Cyrenian, the father of Alexander and Rufus, as he was coming out of the country and passing by, to bear His cross. And they brought Him to the place Golgotha, which is translated, Place of a Skull**" (Mark 15:21-22). They were aiming for Golgotha, the Place of a Skull. The skull comprises the bones of the head—and that was where Jesus was going to die. It was a picture. The Church had been planned long before all of this. And I believe the name 'Golgotha' was inspired by God, because His Son was going to die there as the 'Head' of the Body—His Church.

We can imagine Jesus stumbling along, and the centurion looking behind and realizing that Jesus could not keep up. The crowd would soon be upon them, and he wanted to get Jesus to the place of execution as quickly as possible. Ahead of them a man was coming. His name was Simon and he was from Cyrene, the chief city and Roman capital of North Africa. I always picture Simon as a rich businessman; I'm not sure why. In North Africa the people usually wear long white garments; so I always imagine that Simon was dressed in a long white garment, standing out clearly.

---

[3] You had to be extremely strong to pick up the moneylenders' tables in the Temple as Jesus had done (John 2:15; Matthew 21:12; Mark 11:15). Jesus had been a carpenter for a number of years before He began His ministry (Mark 6:3). These facts, as well as the distances He walked and the schedule He kept, according to the gospel accounts, suggest He was very strong and fit. Depending on the type of cross, it may have been the large wooden cross-bar that Jesus had to carry, but this is not certain.

Therefore, the centurion shouted, "Hey, you! Come here and carry this man's cross!"

Notice that Simon was "**passing by**". He was not part of the procession accompanying Jesus and the two thieves. He probably was not interested in the procession at all. It is likely he was one of the many Jews in Cyrene, and had come up to Jerusalem to keep the feasts. It was now the Feast of Passover and Unleavened Bread, and he probably intended to stay right through until Pentecost. What did *he*—a rich man, a visitor with his white robe on—have to do with two thieves and another Man who were on their way out of the city to be crucified? He was just "**coming out of the country and passing by**". He had probably just arrived and was hurrying into Jerusalem.[4]

Notice the word "**compelled**" in verse 21. Simon did not want to help. It was a great inconvenience, but he had to obey. He might have protested, "But look at my white robe. Look at that crude wooden cross. And look at the blood on it from this man's back. Do you expect me to pick it up? Don't you know I've got servants of my own?" But the Roman centurion would have ordered, "Do as I say!" Interestingly, the word translated "compelled" was derived from a Persian word meaning 'a courier', who waited on the king and pressed others into service for the king. That was exactly what Simon was going to do: serve the King of the Jews—the King of kings!

Simon obeyed. He got in amongst the two thieves and Jesus and he picked up Jesus' cross and marched with it up to Golgotha. And when the group arrived, I think the angels in heaven must have let up a cheer. "They're almost there!...Yes, they're now there! It's nearly done. Glory to God!"

Peter tells us that angels "**desire to look into**" the things we now understand about our salvation—the sufferings of Christ and the glories that follow (1 Peter 1:11-12). In the Greek this means that they look around to try and see what's happening; they are 'peering round the door'—or 'rubber-necking'! I believe that when Jesus arrived at Golgotha *all* the angels were looking down at that procession. Oh, the excitement that must have broken out!

Have you ever thought of God's remarkable providence in all this? The Romans 8:28 principle—have you thought of it? Simon had come up for the Passover feast, and he ended up carrying the very cross upon which the

---

[4]No Roman would help take the cross of a condemned criminal, and no Jew would do so willingly.

Messiah was going to be sacrificed for the sins of the whole world. I expect that he stayed and witnessed the death of the Lord—God's Passover Lamb. There is some evidence that Simon became a believer afterwards (cf. Mark 15:21; Romans 16:13; Acts 11:20). Oh, it was worth soiling his clothes. It was worth getting dirty and inconvenienced for this!

Jesus thus arrived at Calvary. Victory had been won in part. Now we come to the Cross itself, the Cross of Calvary, where the complete victory was secured forever. We need to see all the events surrounding the Cross in their correct order, with the emphasis God wants them to have.

How God was Responsible for the Judgment of Jesus on the Cross

We will now consider the remaining three of the eight who were responsible for the judgment of Jesus on the Cross: the three in fact who were *primarily* responsible for the Cross of Jesus and the death of Jesus. They are, as we have already noted, God the Father, the Son and the Holy Spirit. How amazing!

The Son of God's role

I want to consider the Son first of all, because I have not heard many people ever talk about how Jesus was Himself responsible for going to the Cross. But He was!

When you think about it carefully, it is quite obvious. Jesus could have said at any point, "No, I won't go to the Cross!" At any time He could have called upon legions of angels and they would have come to deliver Him (Matthew 26:53). A fiery chariot would have taken Him back to heaven if He'd asked for it, or He could have stepped down from the Cross instantly.

What kept Him on the Cross then? Why did He endure all that suffering? The answer is simple, yet wonderful! He was prepared to be "**obedient unto death, even the death of the Cross**" (Philippians 2:8b, AV) to fulfil His Father's will and because of His love for you and for me!

Here are seven scriptures which demonstrate the fact that Jesus willingly allowed His own death. He volunteered Himself.

1. John 10:17 records these words of Jesus: "**Therefore My Father loves Me, because I lay down My life that I may take it again. No one takes it from Me, but I lay it down of Myself. I have power to lay it down, and I have power to take it again. This command I have received from My**

Father." Jesus laid down His life. The Roman soldiers thought *they* were killing Jesus; but they could crucify Jesus only because He allowed them to do so.

2. In Ephesians 5:25 we find a beautiful picture of Christ and the Church, as a husband and wife. **"Husbands, love your wives, just as Christ also loved the church and gave Himself for it."** Christ gave Himself voluntarily and deliberately for the Church.

3. Galatians 2:20. **"I have been crucified with Christ; it is no longer I who live, but Christ lives in me; and the life which I now live in the flesh I live by faith in the Son of God, who loved me and gave Himself for me."** Paul was speaking as an individual. He did not say Christ gave Himself "for us", but rather **"for me"**. Can you say, "He died for *me*"? We should not have false humility and say, "But He died for everyone else as well." The truth is that He died for me and He died for you. He died for each one of us in particular.

4. Titus 2:14-15a. **"Who gave Himself for us, that He might redeem us from every lawless deed and purify for Himself His own special people, zealous for good works. Speak these things, exhort, and rebuke with all authority."** Christ gave Himself for us.

5. In Matthew 20:27-28, Jesus said, **"And whoever desires to be first among you, let him be your slave—just as the Son of Man did not come to be served, but to serve, and to give His life a ransom for many."** A slave has to remain at his master's home all of the time. He cannot go home when his hours are completed. God wants us to be His little bond-slaves, constrained by love, who do not want to leave His presence and who don't try to. That is a real challenge, isn't it? He came to serve others and give up His life for others.

6. 1 John 3:16. **"By this we know love, because He laid down His life for us..."** No one took Jesus' life from Him. He laid it down for us. **"And we also ought to lay down our lives for the brethren"**—just as Christ did.

7. 1 Timothy 2:5-6. **"For there is one God and one mediator between God and men, the Man Christ Jesus, who gave Himself a ransom for all, to be testified in due time"**.

Christ Himself was thus clearly responsible for His own death on the Cross. He could have stopped it at any time if He'd wanted to, but He chose not to. He had His eyes on you! He was so occupied with the love He has for you and for me that He was constrained to go through with it. Moreover, He wanted to fulfil His Father's will; and His Father's will was that He should go to the Cross and die there for us. This brings us on to consider the Father.

The Father in heaven's role

A picture of the Father's role is given in Genesis chapter 22, where Abraham was told by God to go and sacrifice his son Isaac. I love this story because it tells us how Abraham laid wood for the altar on Isaac, who had to carry it, just as Jesus began to carry His cross up to the place where He was going to be sacrificed.

Isaac asked a question: "We've got the fire and the wood; but where is the lamb, father?" And Abraham's telling reply was, **"My son, God will provide for Himself the lamb for a burnt offering"** (Genesis 22:8). Isaac must have thought, "Yes, *God* is going to provide the lamb". However, then his father took *him*, laid *him* on the altar, and was about to slit *his* throat with the sacrificial knife, when suddenly the Angel of the LORD called out to Abraham from heaven and told him to stop. Think of that. Then, just at that moment, behind them there was a ram caught in a thicket. God had indeed provided the sacrifice for Himself.

However, there was a picture in all of this. God was Himself going to provide the sacrificial Lamb for mankind. Do you remember John the Baptist's words when he saw Jesus coming? He said, **"Behold! The Lamb of God who takes away the sin of the world!"** (John 1:29; see also John 1:36). "Here is *the* Lamb!", he was saying, "This is the One whom *God* has provided to be a sacrifice for our sins!"

The love of the Father is shocking really, isn't it?—that He was prepared even to sacrifice His own Son for you? The Father's heart must have just broken to think of it; but He was determined to go through with it. Likewise, Jesus was determined to go through with it, because of His love for His Father and for us.

Romans 8:32 says, **"He who did not spare His own Son, but delivered Him up for us all, how shall He not with Him also freely give us all things?"** The Father delivered up His Son for us all. **"For God so loved the world that He gave His only begotten Son..."** (John 3:16a). God the Father gave His Son for us.

There was a world of difference, however, between the outcome for Abraham and Isaac compared with that of the Father and Jesus, because an Angel stopped the slaying of Isaac. There was no angel who could stop the slaying of Jesus at Calvary. The 'sacrificial knife' of the Father was truly plunged right into the very 'heart' of His Son on the Cross, and out of it flowed His love and His saving grace. The Father was not only *prepared to* do it; He actually did it.

The Holy Spirit's role

The Holy Spirit was involved too. The writer to the Hebrews argued, "**For if the blood of bulls and goats and the ashes of a heifer, sprinkling the unclean, sanctifies for the purifying of the flesh, how much more shall the blood of Christ, who through the eternal Spirit offered Himself without spot to God, purge your conscience from dead works to serve the living God?**" (Hebrews 9:13-14). Jesus offered Himself as a perfect sacrifice to God through the eternal Holy Spirit.

Therefore all three members of the Godhead were involved and were responsible for the judgment of Jesus on the Cross. It was the will of the Father; it was the will of the Son; and it was the will of the Holy Spirit.

God willed it

Consider this! If we had been there, and had said, "Father, look what's happening to Jesus! Is that your will?", then echoing from the cloisters of heaven would have come a resounding, "Yes! This *is* My will. I *want* My Son to die on the Cross, because I love you!" If we had tried to approach the Cross to help Jesus down, and had said, "Jesus, I won't let this happen to You!", then do you know what He would have said? He'd have said, "Go away! I came to the earth for this very reason, to die on this Cross for you. No one else can do this, so leave me to do My Father's will!" In fact, He probably would have used the same words He'd spoken earlier to Peter, "**Get behind me, Satan!**" (Matthew 16:23b). We might have pleaded, "Father, will You stop this?"; but He would have stopped us. He would have set Himself against us. For it was the will of the Father, of the Son and of the Holy Spirit for Jesus to die on that Cross.

I remember so clearly the day when I was shattered by a little phrase in Isaiah 53:10. I remember saying to God, "Lord, I just don't understand this scripture." The verse begins: "**Yet it pleased the LORD to bruise Him; He has put Him to grief**"—and "**the LORD**" here refers to the Father. It actually *pleased* the Father to bruise Jesus! The Father truly *does* love Jesus perfectly. The Father and Jesus *do* genuinely, deeply love one another. Yet the Father knew that only through His Son could salvation come to the lost people of this world, whom He loves so much too. Therefore, it pleased the Father to bruise His Son. He knew that Jesus would rise from the dead and bring many sons to glory (Hebrews 2:10). Hallelujah!

THE UNIQUENESS OF THE CROSS OF CHRIST

The Cross of Christ was completely unique. We do not need to qualify the word 'unique', in fact, because it means 'the only one'. The Cross was the only event of its kind and it happened once and for all.

We need to understand that thousands, or probably tens of thousands, of people died on crosses under the Romans. The Romans had been hanging people on crosses right from the establishment of their empire, decades before Jesus died; and many of their victims took several *days* to die, in agony. Many would also have been beaten terribly before they got to their crosses. Many would also have been unjustly judged and crucified despite being innocent of their alleged capital crimes. Jesus' death on the Cross was not unique in these respects.

What was it then that made the Cross of Jesus Christ unique? It was simply this: *the involvement and intervention of God*. Jesus Christ was God come in the flesh as a man; and God put the sins of the whole world on Jesus Christ on the Cross. Only God Himself could do this. No other man crucified ever had the sins of the whole world put on him.

Herod, though he was powerful, could not put the sins of the whole world on Jesus. Pontius Pilate, despite all his authority, could never put the sins of the whole world on Jesus. The Jews couldn't. The Gentiles couldn't. Satan couldn't. And note this: *you* cannot do it either. You can never put your own sins on Jesus. But the fact is *God did it*! The Father did it! The Holy Spirit did it. And Christ, the Son of God, allowed it to happen to Himself. **"And the LORD has laid on Him the iniquity of us all"** (Isaiah 53:6b).

That is why the Cross of Jesus Christ is unique. There was no one else good enough to die for the sins of the world. Many 'good' people might have said, "I'm so concerned for this world that I'm prepared to die for it." However, they never could accomplish what Christ did and bring salvation. Only Jesus could do it—the perfect, sinless Lamb of God—through the intervention of God.

The members of the Godhead were thus the three operators primarily responsible for the Cross of Jesus Christ. They were responsible for Jesus going to the Cross and for the sins of the whole world being put on Him. Therefore, they were responsible for our salvation. What a glorious mystery this is!

THE TIMETABLE OF THE CROSS

"Now it was the third hour, and they crucified Him" (Mark 15:25). Jesus hung on the Cross for some six hours, from the third hour (8 to 9 a.m.

in the morning) right through until the ninth hour (2 to 3 p.m. in the afternoon). The hours of the day were counted from 6 a.m.

When we look in the gospels we can see that the period of six hours was basically divided into two halves: "**Now when the sixth hour had come, there was darkness over the whole land until the ninth hour**" (Mark 15:33). Just before midday, about three hours after Jesus had been lifted up on the Cross, something happened. It was as if a shadow passed right over the land; and darkness fell—over perhaps the whole earth.

It is interesting that not only does the Bible tell us about this darkness; other people wrote about it as well. The historian Phlegon wrote about an event that occurred in the fourth year of the 202nd Olympiad. (In the Greek calendar, that means the year AD 33 or, more specifically, the whole of the Greek year spanning AD 32 and 33.)[5] He wrote this: *"In that year, there was a darkness more striking than any other on record, for it became night at the sixth hour so that the stars were visible in the heavens, and a great earthquake in Bithynia overthrew most of Nicea."* He assumed the event must have been an eclipse. However, he was certainly wrong about this. Jesus died on the Feast of Passover, when there was always a full moon. When the moon is full you cannot possibly have an eclipse of the sun, because the moon is on the opposite side of the earth to the sun. (Also, no total solar eclipse lasts for more than a few minutes.)

We also have the writings of a man called Tertullian who, about two hundred years after Christ, went to Rome to look up records. He found records of a great darkness that occurred around this time, that affected the Roman Empire in Europe.

When an eclipse of the sun does occur, daylight suddenly disappears, the stars come out and a hush descends. The birds stop singing, everything stops and there is a deathly quiet. We can therefore imagine the scene at the time of Jesus' crucifixion in Israel. Darkness and silence fell over the land. Something was about to happen.

For the first three hours on the Cross, Jesus was there as a burnt offering to God. Such an offering was voluntary and was pleasing to God. Jesus was effectively saying, "Father, I've done Your will. I want to please you!"

However, something terrible then happened at midday, and God was not prepared to have any sinful human eye look upon the scene. It was to be

---

[5] An Olympiad, the unit of Greek chronology dating back to 776 BC, comprised four years. There were thus 194 Olympiads to the year AD 1. The 195th Olympiad began in AD 1 and ended during AD 5. The 202nd Olympiad began during AD 29 and ended during AD 33.

something very private. Therefore, the sun was darkened. Suddenly Jesus, instead of being a burnt offering, became the sin offering for mankind. That is what I believe happened shortly before midday. God's righteous judgment was taking place. Darkness fell and the sins of the whole world were put on Jesus as He hung on the Cross.

Jesus became the Sin Offering for us All

During the sixth hour on that unique day in AD 33, every single one of your sins and mine were laid on Jesus on the Cross, and He became the sin offering for mankind. As if this wasn't enough for Him to endure, God the Father and the Holy Spirit then 'turned away'—it was as if they turned their back on Jesus. God's holiness required it. How incredible!

In 2 Corinthians 5:21, a well known verse, Paul said this: "**For He** [God the Father] **made Him** [Jesus] **who knew no sin to be sin for us, that we might become the righteousness of God in Him.**" The Father made His Son to be sin for us. Jesus didn't have any sin in Him. He had no experience of sin in Himself. Yet our sins were put on Him by the Father and He bore them for us all.

In Galatians 3:13 Paul said: "**Christ has redeemed us from the curse of the law, having become a curse for us (for it is written, "Cursed is everyone who hangs on a tree")**". Jesus was not cursed on His own account or because He deserved it. He became a curse for you and for me. It was entirely because Jesus loved us so much that He was willing to be put up on that tree.[6]

In John 3:14 Jesus said, "**And as Moses lifted up the serpent in the wilderness, even so must the Son of Man be lifted up.**" Martin Luther wrote that, on the Cross, Christ became the greatest sinner ever. That is almost blasphemous, if you don't understand what he was talking about. He didn't mean that Christ had committed any sins. Rather, all of our sins were *put on* Christ on the Cross. He took our sins, every one of them. He took on Himself the sins of the whole world—my sins and yours.

"**And at the ninth hour Jesus cried out with a loud voice, saying, "Eloi, Eloi, lama sabachthani?" which is translated, "My God, My God, why have You forsaken Me?"**" (Mark 15:34). Darkness and silence were over

---

[6]After executing a person for a capital crime, the Jews would sometimes hang the body on a tree prior to burial the same day. The body could not remain all night on the tree, lest the land be defiled, because the hanged person was cursed by God (Deuteronomy 21:22-23).

the land, but suddenly a loud cry came from the lips of Jesus.[7] He had endured all the torture in silence. He hadn't screamed; He hadn't cried out; He hadn't resisted. He had left all the taunts and all the gibes unanswered. All the torment from the crowds He had just let run over Him. However, when the crushing weight of our sins was put on Jesus, and He knew that His Beloved Ones had turned away from Him, He cried out into the darkness. I imagine that His cry echoed all around Jerusalem out of the dark silence.

For all eternity Jesus had enjoyed perfect fellowship with His Father and with the Holy Spirit. There had never been a time when they had not experienced each other's wonderful love flowing between them in perfect communion. But suddenly our sins cut Jesus off from His Beloved Ones. Oh, the cry of anguish; I can almost hear that roar of pain! He had never known sin or such a separation before, yet suddenly He was cut off from those who truly loved Him. Imagine that break of fellowship; Jesus had never known anything like it. I can hear the echoes of that scream, **"Eloi, Eloi, lama sabachthani?"**

Jesus had done nothing wrong, yet the LORD caused the iniquities of us all to fall on Him (Isaiah 53:6b). And it was the crushing weight of our sins coming down on Him that caused such intense anguish. The Father laid our sins on His Son. Then He gazed at His Son and said, "I cannot look upon You any longer!"—and He turned His back and effectively went away in the opposite direction. That's the Cross of Jesus. It's not just the physical pain that we should consider, but the spiritual pain that Jesus suffered in all of this. He was bruised for our iniquities (Isaiah 53:5b).

He loved us that much! He loved *you* that much! Sometimes people say, "I don't think He loves me," when they haven't had a revelation of what Jesus went through. If Jesus did not love us, He would not have endured all He went through. Nothing else could have caused Him to go through such agony. But He chose to go through it for you and for me. He knew that no one else could ever bring us salvation.

"Some of those who stood by, when they heard it, said, "Look, He is calling for Elijah!"" (Mark 15:35). The reason they thought this was because the word for God that Jesus used when quoting Psalm 22 (*Eloi* or *Eli*) sounded like *Elias* or *Eliyahu*, the Greek or Hebrew for Elijah. **"Then someone ran and filled a sponge full of sour wine, put it on a reed, and**

---

[7] The Hebrew word translated **"groaning"** in Psalm 22:1, the psalm Jesus quoted, implies that Jesus screamed or 'roared' on the Cross.

offered it to Him to drink, saying, "Let Him alone; let us see if Elijah will come to take Him down"'" (Mark 15:36).

In the first series of Basic Bible Studies I talked about how Jesus died spiritually and then physically on the Cross. By spiritual death I simply mean that He was cut off from living fellowship with His Father for those three hours, before He died physically and was cut off from the land of the living (Isaiah 53:8b).

The sin that Adam committed brought spiritual and physical death into the world. Adam died spiritually when he sinned; then physical death came to him later. Jesus therefore had to die for sin spiritually and then physically. He had to be cut off from His Father and then He had to die physically. Jesus was cut off because of our sin once and for all. The result is that our sins need never separate us from the Father again. Hallelujah! **"Believe on the Lord Jesus Christ, and you will be saved"** (Acts 16:31). Amen. Put your trust in the Lord Jesus and recognize that God has already dealt with all of your sins on the Cross.

"It is finished!"

After three hours as the sin offering for mankind on the Cross, Jesus knew it was enough. He had paid for every sin that had ever been or ever would be committed. And when His work was done, He died physically.

Notice what Jesus cried out just before He died: **"So when Jesus had received the sour wine, He said, "It is finished!"'"** (John 19:30a). "We've done it, Father," He was declaring, "the work is completed!" Praise God for this triumphant, joyous, glorious cry![8]

Then Jesus said, **"Father, 'into Your hands I commend My spirit'"** (Luke 23:46b). "Father, My work is all done, so now I'm coming home! I can't wait to get there!" **"And having said this, He breathed His last"** (Luke 23:46c).

Jesus would not have died if our sins had not been fully paid for. God knew about every sin; and Jesus only died when they were *all* paid for. Oh, how He loved the Father! How Jesus loved His Father and poured Himself out for His Father. It is so wonderful to consider this love which, in this crisis hour of His life, meant He was prepared to suffer so much. Don't ever

---

[8]The Greek word *tetelestai* translated "It is finished!" also meant 'the debt is paid in full'.

think that Jesus hasn't paid for your sins. He would not have breathed His last and died if that were the case.[9]

The Centurion by the Cross

"And Jesus cried out with a loud voice, and breathed His last. Then the veil of the temple was torn in two from top to bottom" (Mark 15:37-38). People usually read out Jesus' words on the Cross softly. I'm surprised. The Bible says He cried out with a *loud* voice! **"Now when the centurion, who stood opposite Him, saw that He cried out like this and breathed His last, he said, "Truly this Man was the Son of God!""** (verse 39). Why should he say that?

The centurion was standing near the foot of the Cross. He thought that *he* had put Jesus on the Cross. He thought that *he* was responsible for the death of Jesus. He'd been watching Jesus for six hours, he'd witnessed the strange darkness and he'd heard all of Jesus' words from the Cross. Suddenly, after six hours, he heard Jesus declare that His work was done and that now He was going to die; and immediately He *did* die.

Imagine being crucified, hanging on a cross, waiting to die. One of the dreadful things about it is that you cannot die, even though you want to. Your hands are held up, so you cannot stab yourself and bring your life to an end. You are probably higher than people can reach, so your friends cannot come and kill you. If they were to come with a long spear, soldiers would stop them. No one can put you out of your misery.

This centurion had probably watched hundreds of people being crucified. He would have seen the victims hanging for hours and even several days on crosses, in agony, desperate to die. I imagine that many of them had cried out, begging, "Kill me, please! I can't take this any more." Imagine it! However, it was not so with Jesus.

---

[9] The principle for the Christian is exactly the same: when your job is done you can die. Unless through very severe discipline you die prematurely, you will die when your work is done. Therefore if someone dies young, we can be sure his work was finished, and it was time for him to be face to face with the Lord. There need not be unending sorrow; that person has gone to a better place and we're going to join him soon. We are all heading home to be with the Lord forever; we do not need to hang around here once our work is completed. God so loves us that He doesn't want us here any longer than is necessary. When an ambassador's term of service is finished, he or she does not stay in the foreign country, but immediately goes home. I'm looking forward to my homecoming so much! It's gripping me more and more every day. I'm coming home, praise God, but not until my work is finished (cf. Isaiah 57:1).

This centurion was utterly amazed because, all of a sudden, Jesus said, **"Father, 'into Your hands I commend My spirit'"** (Luke 23:46b), then immediately He died. And no matter what he thought of Jesus before, that centurion suddenly understood. He thought *he'd* killed Jesus, but now he realized that *this Man* had His own life in His own hands. He realized that if anyone was responsible ultimately for Jesus being on that Cross, it was Jesus Himself, who had allowed it to happen. Oh, what glory is in that! The centurion suddenly recognized that Jesus had power over His own life. I believe that he was saved, I really do. I believe he was so stunned that he couldn't get over this. A Man had actually had His life removed from Him precisely when He wanted to die. This was Jesus; and this is what He meant when He said, **"No man takes it** [My life] **from me, but I lay it down of Myself"** (John 10:18a). Praise the Name of Jesus!

Sin has been Paid for Once and for All

I want to reiterate this: When Jesus died physically it was a sure sign that the sins of the whole world—those committed before He died and those to be committed after He died—had been paid for in full on the Cross. That means He has paid for all of the sins *you* have committed in your life up to now, as well as all the sins you will commit in the future. He would not have died otherwise.

"For Christ also suffered once for sins, the just for the unjust, that He might bring us to God, being put to death in the flesh but made alive by the Spirit" (1 Peter 3:18). Christ alone could pay the cost necessary to reconcile us to God, and He did it once and for all time on the Cross.

"For when we were still without strength, in due time Christ died for the ungodly. For scarcely for a righteous man will one die; yet perhaps for a good man someone would even dare to die. But God demonstrates His own love towards us, in that while we were still sinners, Christ died for us. Much more then, having now been justified by His blood, we shall be saved from wrath through Him. For if when we were enemies we were reconciled to God through the death of His Son, much more, having been reconciled, we shall be saved by His life. And not only that, but we also rejoice in God through our Lord Jesus Christ, through whom we have now received the reconciliation" (Romans 5:6-11).

If anyone does not know Christ, it is time to face up to the Cross. Jesus died for your sins and there is no other way to be saved. For there was none other good enough to suffer and die for the sins of the whole world.

When Calvary Blossomed

We were sinners and God's enemies when Christ died for us. Yet still He died for us, because He loved us so much.

Thus we can picture the dead body of Jesus hanging on the Cross. He had become a curse for us (Galatians 3:13). And I like to think that Calvary 'blossomed' at 3 o'clock in the afternoon. I imagine that the sun came out again, that every flower opened up and that every bird started singing—because Jesus' work had been finished!

Resurrection now lay ahead for Christ. However, He had some preaching to do down in Hades first. He had to go and proclaim His victory to the spirits in prison, who had been disobedient in the past (see 1 Peter 3:19-20); and He had to go to Paradise (or 'Abraham's Bosom') too. In Paradise He would proclaim His victory to all those people who had so far believed on Him. Then, in three days, He would take these 'spoils of war' up to heaven with Him: **"When He ascended on high, He led captivity captive..."** (Ephesians 4:8b).

He had these things to do; but His work of salvation was finished forever! Ahead for Him now was resurrection; ahead was ascension; ahead was glory with the Father once more! Ahead was wonderful, wonderful fellowship with the Father and the Holy Spirit. And ahead now was a wonderful bride, the Church—His redeemed—His precious, beautiful, beloved ones. Ahead for Christ was exaltation. He had completed His work to perfection. Praise His wonderful Name!

Jesus deserves all the honour we can give Him now, for He didn't balk at what was required of Him. He went through all the suffering and died for each one of us. Eight personalities or groups were responsible for the judgment of Jesus: five falsely, but three gloriously! And the three laid down their own desires—the love they have for One another—because of the love that they also have for you and for me.

You did not deserve to have Jesus lay down His life for you. You didn't deserve it. But He now does deserve to have you lay down your life for Him! He *does* deserve it. May we give Him all the honour, all the glory due to Him and all our obedience. For Jesus is now indeed seated at the right hand of the Father, exalted in the heavens, His name higher than any other name! At the name of Jesus, let us make sure that *our* knees bow today. Amen.

8. SELF-JUDGMENT OR CHASTENING?
The Importance of Self-Judgment for the Believer

This is the first of three chapters covering the judgment of believers. This chapter examines the importance of self-judgment for those of us who are believers. The next study then discusses the consequences of us *not* judging ourselves, namely chastening, or discipline, from God. Finally, we will look at the judgment of believers' works and consider the issue of our service and reward.

We first need to understand this very clearly: Our relationship with God has two aspects to it. The first aspect is what I call our *kindred relationship* with God. The second is what I call our *fellowship* with God, or our *walk* with God. The distinction between them is extremely important.

KINDRED RELATIONSHIP

The moment someone believes on the Lord Jesus Christ—that is, when he or she personally accepts the truth of the gospel and receives Jesus as Lord and Saviour—many important things happen. I'm not going to list them all in this study.[1]

One of the glorious things that happens when we believe on Christ—which should probably be number one on the list—is that we become children of God. We become part of God's family. That is what I mean by our *kindred* relationship. We see this in Galatians 3:26, where Paul said, "**For you are all sons of God through faith in Christ Jesus.**" God is now our Father, and we are His sons. This is 'automatic' at the very instant we first believe on the Lord. Isn't that wonderful to know!

Some of us would not have chosen the natural father we had if given a choice. We might feel that we were rather 'lumbered', and might like to have swapped our particular father. Some people, in contrast, think that

---

[1] The changes that accompany salvation are grouped in a list of 37 things in Basic Bible Study 102.

their father is the greatest dad in all the world! No matter how you feel about your father, however, there is nothing you can do about him. Whether he is good, bad or indifferent, he *is* your father. You might deny being his son or daughter but, nevertheless, you are. You might be the spitting image of your father and, because you loathe him so much, change your name or even your whole appearance, but you are still your father's child. That is what kindred relationship is all about. It is unchangeable.

The same is true concerning our relationship with our Father in heaven. It is a kindred relationship. Once you are born again, you are born into the family of God, and there is nothing that can ever get you out of the family. Praise God! God may not be very pleased with you at times, in view of certain sins or unsanctified aspects of your life; but He is still your Father, and He is always going to stick by you. You are in this kindred relationship with God for good. It is secure and nothing can ever change it.

FELLOWSHIP WITH GOD OUR FATHER

The same is not true of the second aspect of our relationship with God—the *fellowship* aspect. If we take the natural father-son analogy again, we can see this perfectly. You *are* your father's son, but you may not have had consistent 'fellowship' or 'communion' with him for the past few years. You may not be getting on so well. This is what I mean by the *fellowship* aspect of the relationship. It is your fellowship that has been broken if you are not getting on. And there will always be some particular cause for this—something that has come between you.

I remember that, when I was a child, there would sometimes be an argument at home if I was stopped from doing what I wanted to do. I would immediately storm out of the room and would sit upstairs—really regretting it, because the television was downstairs, the food was downstairs and the people I loved were downstairs! But there I was upstairs, too stubborn to budge! I was still part of the family, but our fellowship had been broken. It had nothing to do with whether I was still my father's son. I still was, of course—although sometimes my father was frustrated with me, undoubtedly. The kindred relationship was unchanged, but our fellowship had been interrupted.[2]

---

[2] For me, the saddest thing on the radio are SOS messages. It is amazing how we can listen to such messages and forget what they mean. Someone, somewhere has a father, say, whom he or she has not seen for several years. They haven't been in contact; and they no longer even have one another's addresses or any other means of making contact. This demonstrates what we are considering here. The kindred relationship remains, but fellowship has been broken.

Fellowship needs Continual Refreshing

As we come to consider God's judgment of the believer, it is essential to understand that it is our *fellowship* with God that we are concerned with, *not* our *kindred* relationship with God.

The difference between these two aspects can best be seen, I think, in John chapter 13—where we find Jesus and His disciples taking their last Passover meal together. We can picture the scene: they were all reclining on couches in the upper room, with their heads facing inwards and their feet pointing outwards. John describes how Jesus "**rose from supper and laid aside His garments, took a towel and girded Himself. After that, He poured water into a basin and began to wash the disciples' feet, and to wipe them with the towel with which He was girded**" (verses 4-5).

In ancient times, people used to take a bath before they went out, but, by the time they had walked in sandals through dusty streets to a friend's house, their feet would be dirty again. Therefore, they would always wash their feet or have their feet washed at some time during their visit, simply to get the dust off. Incredibly, we find the Lord Jesus Himself on this occasion—the Lord of glory, whose home was originally in heaven—picking up a bowl of water and beginning to wash His disciples' feet!

Have you ever washed someone else's feet? The thought is quite revolting. It is a humbling thing to do. However, the Lord so loved these men that He didn't mind serving them in this way at all. In fact, He was about to deal with something far more revolting than their feet and dust—He was going to deal with their *sin*. Compared with the Cross to come, this was nothing.

"**Then He came to Simon Peter. And Peter said to Him, "Lord, are You washing my feet?"**" (verse 6). We don't know for certain where He started, but Jesus eventually came to Simon Peter. Peter possibly withdrew his feet. "Lord, You're not going to wash my feet!" he said. This was a natural reaction, but it was not a right reaction.[3] "**Jesus answered and said to him, "What I am doing you do not understand now, but you will know after this"**" (verse 7). Jesus was saying, "Look, Peter, there's

---

[3] Some people react similarly today. They never expect to receive anything from God. But the Lord really does desire to wash our feet and to give to us, as well as to receive from us our love and worship. That is why, when we pour ourselves out to God—not to receive from Him, but to bless Him—we find that we always receive as much as we give and, in fact, much more. God is such a generous giver! There is nothing unspiritual about allowing Jesus to wash our feet. He wants to do it, because He loves us so much!

something of great importance in this, that you will know by experience later."

"Peter said to Him, "You shall never wash my feet!"" (verse 8a). This is a double negative in the Greek: "You are not, not going to wash my feet!" Peter was emphatic about it. But **"Jesus answered Him, "If I do not wash you, you have no part with Me""** (verse 8b).

"Simon Peter said to Him, "Lord, not my feet only, but also my hands and my head!"" (John 13:9). Dear Peter was so impetuous! Notice how in verse 6 he resisted Jesus, saying, "Lord, washing my feet is too much!" but now in verse 9 he said, "Washing my feet is not enough!" That is an impetuous man![4]

"Jesus said to him, "He who is bathed needs only to wash his feet, but is completely clean; and you are clean..."" (John 13:10a). This was an amazing truth. Jesus was referring to *salvation*. To be saved we need to be washed by the Holy Spirit. To be clean, the Holy Spirit has got to take us and wash us.[5] Notice how Jesus said, **"He who is bathed..."**, which is passive. The moment we believe on the Lord Jesus Christ we are washed *by God*. We are then completely clean; we do not need to bathe ourselves or be bathed again. We are perfectly, absolutely clean. We are washed once and for all. But our feet still need to be washed—only the feet.

Once established, our kindred relationship with God is sure. We do not have to be saved again after we have been saved once! However, our fellowship, represented by the feet, needs constant washing. Our *walk* with God *does* need washing and re-washing continually. This is the tremendous truth Jesus was explaining. Peter didn't understand it yet; but he was going to know it by experience later. He was going to be out-of-fellowship many times, but he would learn to walk in the Spirit and would learn what this principle is all about!

---

[4] Impetuosity can be a good thing in the world, but it's a bad thing for Christians. It leads to a lot of problems. You learn to regret impetuosity after a while. It makes you say and do things and take decisions that you regret later, as Peter found out. If you are an impetuous person, however, do read up on Peter, and don't give up hope. Go to the Book of Acts and see what Peter became. If you are an impetuous person, God can really use you once He's gained control of your impetuosity. When you read the letters Peter wrote at the end of his life, what a tremendous man he was. He had learned so much during his long life.

[5] We find salvation referred to as a washing in Titus 3:4-5. "But when the kindness and the love of God our Saviour towards man appeared, not by works of righteousness which we have done, but according to His mercy He saved us, through the washing of regeneration and renewing of the Holy Spirit." The word "regeneration" means 'rebirth'.

Jesus continued: **"...but not all of you"** (verse 10b). He was saying, "Eleven of you are clean. You have believed on Me and are clean—you are in a kindred relationship with Me. However, one among you who is not clean." It was Judas Iscariot whom Jesus had in mind, of course. Jesus was thus explaining the gospel message to Peter. But I think He was also being tremendously gracious and preaching the gospel to Judas one more time—He never gave up on that man. He was also saying it for every person who might hear or later read this message: "Perhaps you will let Me wash you—then you'll be saved, you'll receive eternal life, you'll become a member of My Body—or perhaps you won't, in which case the prospect of judgment remains." **"For He knew who would betray Him; therefore He said, "You are not all clean""** (verse 11).

"So when He had washed their feet, taken His garments, and sat down again, He said to them, "Do you know what I have done to you? You call Me Teacher and Lord, and you say well, for so I am. If I then, your Lord and Teacher, have washed your feet, you also ought to wash one another's feet. For I have given you an example, that you should do as I have done to you. Most assuredly, I say to you, a servant is not greater than his master; nor is he who is sent greater than he who sent him. If you know these things, happy are you if you do them"" (John 13:12-17).[6]

Isn't it a tragedy that, in the Body of Christ today, we don't spend more time washing one another's feet? Instead, we often look at each other's blemishes. We gaze at everything that's wrong, effectively saying, "If I had feet like that I'd do something about it!" But the Lord didn't do that. He went around washing His disciples' feet. And if *He* did it, then we should do it. It is our responsibility. The Lord comes and blesses us when we don't deserve it. He does not hold back because of our faults. He pours out countless blessings. When we see someone else being blessed we are tempted to say, "Lord, they should never be blessed." And it's true! But *by grace* the Lord is blessing them anyway, just as He is blessing us. He comes and He washes our feet; and He does so again and again.

Hebrews 10:24 is a wonderful verse. It is one of those gems hidden away in the Bible. "**And let us consider one another in order to stir up love and good works**". I cannot get past the word "**stir up**"—or "**provoke**" as the AV translates it. When we talk about provoking someone, we mean deliberately niggling them, inciting them—deliberately getting under their

---

[6]It is interesting how Jesus reversed the order of "Teacher and Lord" to stress to His apostles that He was first of all their Lord and, second, their Teacher.

skin. The writer was thus saying, "If you're going to provoke others, then provoke them to love!"[7]

Paul wrote, "**Fathers, do not provoke your children to wrath**" (Ephesians 6:4). Rather, provoke them to *love*! That is a very good thing to do.

NO JUDGMENT FOR BELIEVERS IN RELATION TO THE KINDRED RELATIONSHIP

The point we need to understand is this. Our fellowship with the Lord can be broken by our sin. Our walk can be interrupted. It needs constant washing, constant refreshing, constant renewing by the Holy Spirit. But the kindred relationship can never be broken. Our sins were paid for on the Cross; and the moment we believed on the Lord Jesus, recognizing that He died for our sins, we became children of God—forever.

On the Cross Jesus bore our sins. He paid the penalty for them in full. That means they do not ever have to paid for again. *We* cannot pay for them— we don't need to and we never could pay for them ourselves. If we are talking about our kindred relationship with God, there is therefore no judgment remaining—absolutely none. No believer will ever be judged for his or her sins. They have already been judged and paid for in full by Jesus on the Cross, 2000 years ago. The following three passages confirm this.

1. "**There is therefore now no condemnation** [judgment] **to those who are in Christ Jesus**" (Romans 8:1a).

2. "**He who believes in Him** [the Son of God] **is not condemned; but he who does not believe is condemned already, because he has not believed in the name of the only begotten Son of God**" (John 3:18).

3. "**Most assuredly, I say to you, he who hears My word and believes in Him who sent Me has everlasting life, and shall not come into judgment, but has passed from death into life**" (John 5:24). This is the

---

[7] *We all have one effect or another on those around us. What is it that you provoke? Is it envy, jealousy or criticism? It should be love! You should walk into a room and your very presence should get under people's skin so that they can't help but love. That is what the writer to the Hebrews meant. The Lord Jesus did this; and it is what we should do too.*

Others provoke certain responses in us too. Sometimes, for example, we might go to someone and find it very difficult not to start gossiping. We didn't intend to gossip; it just seemed to come out once we were with them. They provoked it in us.

Our aim should be to manifest the fruit of the Holy Spirit so much that we provoke the same fruit in others. Everywhere we go people should be provoked to say, "I just love the Lord more and I love you and others more, since I met you. You provoked me!"

verse I love more than any other on this subject. Jesus began with the words "Amen, amen…," meaning "This is absolutely true, fixed, certain, faithful…". If you have believed on the Lord Jesus Christ, you will *not* be judged for your sins. They have already been judged. Therefore, no judgment remains outstanding, even after death.

This explains the matter of judgment in relation to our relationship with God. Jesus died for our sins and paid the penalty for them in full. Therefore, because *He* has paid for them, we are free. Glory to Jesus! However, the second aspect of our relationship with God is different. When we come to the *fellowship* aspect, we see that there *is* still judgment for the believer as far as this is concerned.

Judgment in Relation to our Fellowship with God

We should walk with God in obedience, every day. The result is a continuous, unhindered relationship. By 'fellowship' I mean this day-to-day relationship with the Father—our walk with God. There *is* judgment associated with our fellowship, or walk; and it does not take place in the future, after death. Rather, it takes place right now, during our lives here on the earth, before we die. Thus, there is judgment *now* for us who are believers. That's the 'bad' news!

However, let us see the good news too, in 1 Corinthians chapter 11—a passage we will refer to regularly during the rest of this chapter: "**For if we would judge ourselves, we would not be judged. But when we are judged, we are chastened by the Lord, that we may not be condemned with the world**" (verses 31-32). These verses do not refer to future judgment. They refer to judgment now, when our fellowship with God has been broken. They refer to judgment of the believer in this life—and they show the importance of *self*-judgment.

The Importance of Self-Judgment

Notice that these verses come towards the end of a lengthy letter. If you know anything about the Corinthian church, you will know that there is probably not a church quite like it anywhere today. If you think of the worst types of behaviour, then the Corinthians were almost certainly doing such things! Therefore Paul, with much sadness and trepidation, decided to write this 'scorcher' of a letter to them.

Starting in chapter 1 verse 10, Paul began to go through a whole catalogue of sins they were committing and matters they had misunderstood. He wrote: "I plead with you....I warn you....I urge you....It is actually reported that....Do you not know that?....I say this to your shame....Why do you not rather?....Now in giving these instructions I do not praise you...I hear that....and in part I believe it...."

By chapter 11 Paul was coming to the end of the list, and was explaining why some among them were experiencing God's severe judgment. He ended the section, in which he must have felt he was tearing them apart, on this marvellous note: "**For if we would judge ourselves, we would not be judged**" (verse 31). "You should be judging yourselves!" he was saying. They had *not* been judging themselves. They had not faced up to the stark reality of their sins. They were doing evil in God's sight, yet they were not acknowledging their behaviour as sinful. Instead, they were explaining away their sins and carrying on exactly as they pleased.

Note that it was the need for *self*-judgment that Paul was emphasizing—not judgment of one another. We have got to pay attention to our own lives first of all (Matthew 7:1-5). This leads me to make this important point: *you have got to be harsher with yourself than with anyone else, as far as sin is concerned*. Don't allow *any* sin in your life that isn't judged; don't put up with it! Other people may not know about it, but *God* knows about it. As soon as we see it there, we should acknowledge it as sin and begin, with God's help, to get it sorted out.

It is thus our responsibility to judge ourselves, so we need to know how to do it. We therefore need to have a fresh look at a familiar verse—which is perhaps used rather too glibly sometimes—namely, 1 John 1:9.

THE NEED TO CONFESS OUR SINS TO GOD

The apostle John wrote, "**If we confess our sins, He is faithful and just to forgive us our sins and to cleanse us from all unrighteousness**" (1 John 1:9). There should be no 'if' about it, really. We *must* confess our sins. If we do not, then there are consequences, as we shall see.

The word translated "**confess**" is the Greek word *homologeo*, which means 'to say the same thing' as someone else. What it means in this context is to agree with God about our sins. God loathes sin, so when we recognize a sin in our lives, we should say, "God, I agree with You and I loathe that sin too. Lord, I confess it is a sin. I acknowledge that what You say about it is true." We also need to understand the implications of sin in our lives and recognize that our sins do damage—not only to us, but to others. Moreover, our sins also cause great grief to our loving, wonderful, holy God.

Therefore, we should abhor sin even as He does. Confessing our sins thus means 'coming into line' and saying the same thing as God does.

Note that the tense used here is present and is continuous. In every believer there needs to be a heart eager for the Holy Spirit to reveal what is wrong. And I mean *eager*, I really do. We should not be afraid of God's Holy Spirit shining in. We should be ever eager to say, "Lord, please forgive me, cleanse me and deal with this sin. Yes, Lord, it's wrong."

If we are stricter with ourselves than anyone else can be, then we will never come across someone who trips us up. If someone comes and says, "Brother, I think this is wrong in your life," then you will be able to say, "I know. I've been confessing that sin for months. Will you pray with me and ask God to deal with it?" Hallelujah! It is continual confession that John had in mind. It does not matter if we have to confess the same sin again and again. John's emphasis was simply, "Do it! Confess your sins and make sure you stay in fellowship with God." However, confession should not become a flippant thing. It should involve seeking God's help to deal with the sin in our lives. That is judging ourselves.

There is actually only one practical way to deal with sin in our lives. There is only one way by which the power of sin can be neutralized—and that is by an every-second reliance upon the Holy Spirit. We need to be in fellowship with God to such a degree that we will not tolerate our love relationship with Him being interrupted.

I can speak from personal experience about this. I fought and fought against certain sins in my life for years. But then *I fell in love with Jesus*! Oh, this did what *I* could never do in my own strength, because I began to enjoy my fellowship with the Lord so much that I could not bear for it to be shattered by my sin. I was so desperate: "Lord, get me back in fellowship quickly. I confess that sin." We have to do this continually, every day, don't we? I do, and all of us do. The old sin nature is still present within us.

Look again at what Paul said: "**For if we would judge ourselves, we would not be judged**" (1 Corinthians 11:31). This is good news, isn't it? It is in our hands. If *we* will judge ourselves, *God* will not judge us. He will forgive us and wipe our slate clean. "**...He is faithful and just to forgive us our sins and to cleanse us from all unrighteousness**" (1 John 1:9b).

In Amos 3:3, God asked, "**Can two walk together, unless they are agreed?**" Of course they cannot! Agreement is essential. Therefore, God cannot walk with a believer who is practising sins in his or her life, without confessing them, because "**God is light and in Him is no darkness at all**" (1 John 1:5b). If you are trying to walk in the dark, you *cannot* also be walking with God. Your fellowship with God is broken. God cannot have unhindered fellowship with any believer who is calling white "black", and black "white". It is only when we come into line with God and say, "All right, Lord, I accept what You say," that our fellowship is restored. Then we can walk in the light with God once again (1 John 1:7).

"The sacrifices of God are a broken spirit, a broken and a contrite heart—These, O God, You will not despise" (Psalm 51:17). We should not have a proud heart—a heart that is self-righteously vindicating itself—but a heart which says, "God, everything You say about me is true. I'm sorry, Lord. I don't want to be like this. Please, by Your Spirit, enable me to walk with You and not to walk in sin." That is a broken and a contrite heart. You will never find a believer with such a heart criticizing others for their sins. Such broken people are too conscious of their own sins.[8]

The Purpose of Chastening by the Father

If you do not confess your sins, what then? Say you decide, "I'm not going to judge myself." What if there are certain things you will not accept as being sins and you refuse to bow the knee? We need to go back to 1 Corinthians 11, and read on. This is a serious, even fearsome subject that we are now broaching.

"For if we would judge ourselves, we would not be judged. But when we are judged, we are chastened by the Lord, that we may not be condemned with the world" (verses 31-32). It seems that the whole Corinthian church had not judged itself. But this applies to us too. If we do not judge ourselves, then God will have to judge us—and such judgment is God chastening, or disciplining, His children.

Our Father in heaven is the best disciplinarian in the world. He has given some rules in the Bible on how to bring up children and discipline them—and they are pretty tough rules! But God designed children, and He knows exactly how to bring them up. And being a perfect Father, that's precisely how He is going to discipline us also, when we get out of fellowship. We have got to get in line with what the Word of God says, no matter what our education or the world may have taught us—because it gives us God's righteous viewpoint and He is the perfect Father.

---

[8]Occasionally you might have to point out something to a brother or sister if you can see that he or she is out of line. However, it should break you up inside to have to do it, because you know that "There, but for the grace of God, go I".

I find that some Christians who claim to be really "moving in the Spirit" do not like talking about God's discipline much. They often like to over-spiritualize everything, instead of facing up to the nitty-gritty of what sin is and getting sin dealt with in their lives. But God *does* discipline us—as the Bible states very clearly. Whether we like to talk about it or not, God does talk about it and His discipline is a fact. Therefore, we have got to face up to it and even rejoice in it. God *is* our Father, and sometimes we *are* "**chastened by the Lord**".

The verb translated "**chastened**" means 'to discipline', 'to correct' or 'to train' as children. It does not mean simply 'to punish', though it might involve punishment at times. This is important to understand: *The chastening of the Lord is to train us, not to punish us for our sins.* Jesus has already been punished for all of our sins. Therefore, what God wants to do through chastening us is to train us to walk with Him in obedience and freedom, so that we will confess our sins, stay in fellowship with Him and grow to reach maturity in Christ.

CHASTENING IS A FAMILY MATTER—ZECHARIAH CHAPTER 3

When God disciplines us, it is a family affair. It is a matter of Father and son, or Father and daughter. Zechariah chapter 3 is my favourite passage on this subject.

The passage is set in a 'courtroom', probably somewhere in heaven, at the time when the Jews had come back to the land of Israel after the Babylonian captivity. They had been away for 70 years, but now they were back; and they had recently completed the rebuilding of the Temple.

Satan had opposed the rebuilding of the Temple (as the Book of Nehemiah shows), but God had enabled the Jews to complete it. Satan had lost that battle. Now he was thinking to himself, "They've managed to finish the Temple, so now I must make sure that they cannot use it." Having lost one battle, Satan thus decided to start a second battle, and he chose to target Israel's High Priest. The High Priest was a man called Joshua, while Zerubbabel was the political leader, or governor, in Judea. The Temple needed a High Priest, so the major attack Satan chose to make was to accuse God's High Priest of being unworthy to serve. "How can this man serve you, God, when he is a sinner?" Satan asked. The answer we should know. The answer was grace. *By grace* he *could* serve God!

None of us ever deserves to serve the Lord. Do you think that any of us could ever be so good that God could say to us, "Because you've done so many good works, now you *deserve* to serve Me"? Not at all! It is simply by grace. None of us should ever get proud about our ministries or anything else that we do. It is all by grace. We can never earn the right to serve God. We have got to remain humble before God—always.

"Then he showed me Joshua the high priest standing before the Angel of the LORD, and Satan standing at his right hand to oppose him" (Zechariah 3:1). Who is the Angel of the LORD? It is the Son of God, the Lord Jesus. We call such appearances of Christ in the Old Testament "Christophanies" or "Theophanies".[9]

The Lord Jesus was thus the judge during this incident. Satan also was standing there, opposing Joshua. He was effectively the prosecution; and he had a full dossier on all the sins he knew Joshua had committed. (In fact, Joshua had committed *many more* sins than Satan knew about, and *Jesus* knew about all of them already. He was going to die for them, some 500 years later!) Satan had come to do what he has always done: oppose, or resist, the people of God. Satan usually does this by accusing us before God.[10]

Who would defend Joshua? We should know this by now. The defence lawyer was the One who was also the judge, the Lord Jesus Christ! This courtroom was thus a little 'biased'—but in a good way![11]

"And the Lord [Jesus] **said to Satan, "The LORD rebuke you, Satan! The LORD who has chosen Jerusalem rebuke you! Is this not a brand plucked from the fire?""** (verse 2). Thus, the first thing that happened was that the judge rebuked the prosecution. Jesus was saying, "God the Father rebuke you, Satan!" (This is evidence of the Trinity.) The judge effectively dismissed Satan's case immediately, and Satan did not speak again. Hallelujah!

---

[9] See Appendix 3 in the book "Salvation" by Roger Price for an explanation of how Christ, the Son of God, appeared in the Old Testament.

[10] The phrase translated **"to oppose him"** (literally "to be an opponent to him") contains the word satan in Hebrew—from which we get the proper name Satan.

[11] John, when he was an old man, wrote: "My little children, these things I write to you, so that you may not sin. And if anyone sins, we have an Advocate with the Father, Jesus Christ the righteous" (1 John 2:1). An "Advocate" here means a 'defence lawyer'. In heaven today, the Lord Jesus is sitting at the right hand of God, representing us before God. That means that we do not have to defend ourselves. I have found a position of such deep peace since I stopped trying to defend myself. I can trust the Lord to defend me against all of Satan's accusations.

The Holy Spirit is in effect the defence lawyer for God, representing Him on this earth. When non-Christians blaspheme God, I believe the Holy Spirit comes, saying, "No! He's lovely. You need to know Him. You need salvation. You need Christ in your life!"

Notice what Jesus said about Joshua: he was a brand plucked out of the fire. That was grace. The Lord was saying, "I've rescued Joshua. *I* did it. His sin is therefore a family matter now. So what are you doing here, Satan?"

Wouldn't it be ridiculous in the normal course of events if, when your four-year old did something wrong, you called in the police and had a trial? Similarly, God deals with His own children Himself; their sins are nothing to do with Satan.[12]

"Now Joshua was clothed with filthy garments, and was standing before the Angel" (verse 3). The filthy garments represented Joshua's sins. The word "**filthy**" actually means 'vomit-filled' or 'excrement-filled'. Imagine such soiled garments. That is what sin is like to God.

"Then He [the Angel, Christ] **answered and spoke to those who stood before Him, saying, "Take away the filthy garments from him." And to him** [Joshua] **He said, "See, I have removed your iniquity from you, and I will clothe you with rich robes"'"** (verse 4). How wonderful.

Zechariah then began speaking. He knew what this meant. "**And I said, "Let them put a clean turban on his head." So they put a clean turban on his head, and they put the clothes on him. And the Angel of the LORD stood by**" (verse 5). The High Priest's turban was a blue mitre, to which a gold 'crown', or band, was fastened. On the plate of the crown was written "Holiness to the LORD" (see Exodus 28:36-37; 39:30), meaning "Set apart unto the LORD". Joshua had relied on the Lord for his defence, effectively admitting his sin. And the Lord, by grace, removed his iniquity and clothed him with rich garments and this lovely clean turban. The words "**stood by**" imply that the Angel approved of everything that was happening.

The important principle here is that discipline is a *family matter*. When we are talking about our fellowship with God being interrupted by our sin, the Father moves in, seeking to restore us, cleanse us and encourage us in our ministry. Our sin is entirely a family matter, between us and God. If Satan accuses us, Jesus will defend us. But God will discipline us if we do not acknowledge our sin—definitely.

---

[12] Paul said that, because we belong to the family of God, we must never take one another to court. We would be out of fellowship immediately and under God's discipline if we did. Our sins are a family matter. Anyone who does take a brother to court does not understand grace and does not understand selflessness. Above all, he or she does not understand the marvellous principle of the family of God. Nevertheless, the Corinthians were doing such a thing (see 1 Corinthians 6:1-8)!

God Gives Grace, then Disciplines Appropriately

When we have committed some sin, there is often a period of time during which God graciously is waiting for us to confess that sin. Some believers think that, because God is waiting, He has not seen the sin or has forgotten about it. I hope that none of us ever thinks like that! Rather, our Father is waiting for us to confess our sin—to judge ourselves. However, *if we do not, then He will soon start to discipline us*, to get us to that place of continual confession.

If God does need to discipline us and we do not listen, then the discipline will gradually get harder. It is important to realize this. If we continually refuse to get back in fellowship, by not judging ourselves and not confessing our sins, then our Father will be constrained to discipline us more. We can justify ourselves all we want—it will make absolutely no difference.

The Corinthians' Sin

One specific sin for which the Corinthians were being judged involved how they were taking communion, or the Lord's table (1 Corinthians 11:27-30). To me, the communion is the most sacred of all the things that we do. I cannot articulate adequately the position that the communion service holds; it is *very* important. However, the Corinthian believers had been treating it very casually, even coming in drunk sometimes.

"Therefore whoever eats this bread or drinks this cup of the Lord in an unworthy manner will be guilty of the body and blood of the Lord. But let a man examine himself, and so let him eat of that bread and drink of that cup. For he who eats and drinks in an unworthy manner eats and drinks judgment to himself, not discerning the Lord's body. For this reason many are weak and sick among you, and many sleep" (verses 27-30).

We should stand in awe and the fear of the Lord as we consider this. Many of the believers were weak, many of them were sick and many even had died. There *is* a sin which is 'mortal', a sin unto death. Even death can result from constantly refusing to face up to sin that God is pointing out in our lives. It is here in Scripture, whether we want to believe it or not. It is easy to over-spiritualize sin, it really is. But God's discipline will come, and increase, until we face up to our sin. It is always better to judge ourselves first.

The vast majority of believers die only when their task is finished. But there is this exception, for those who constantly choose to live in darkness, and wilfully refuse to get back in fellowship with God.[13]

Conclusions

We must face up to every sin. We need to ask the Lord to search our hearts, by the Holy Spirit, and convict us of every sin. Get before the Lord and ask Him to search your heart.

We need to be willing for God to teach us what He thinks about everything, because it is so important for our fellowship with Him to be unhindered. There is no area of our lives that this should not touch. We should not just think of the overt sins, such as losing our temper or lying, and so on. They are easy to identify. What about the hidden mental sins, such as pride, for example? How often do you confess pride in your life? Self-righteousness, criticism, maligning, and so on; these are all sins that God wants dealt with in our lives. We have got to ask God to reveal them. We *need* His revelation as far as our sin is concerned. And we must be tough with ourselves.

This question of fellowship with God is vital. We need *always* to be in fellowship with Him. Through fellowship is joy, through fellowship is faith, through fellowship is love. Bitterness, criticism, harshness and unkindness are all signs of broken fellowship, of a heart that is *not* broken and of a lack of confession. We desperately need rich, intimate fellowship with God.

In the next chapter we will look more closely at how God disciplines His children, and will see how the Corinthian church responded to what Paul wrote to them. We will look at the pivotal passage on discipline—Hebrews chapter 12. May we seek after the holiness of the Lord.

---

[13] If we are seeking to obey God and to grow in our Christian lives, we should not be concerned about this. This type of discipline is extremely rare. Sickness is not usually God's discipline, and hence neither is death. God will make it very clear to us if it is.

9. REASONS FOR DISCIPLINE
Chastening: God's judgment of sin in His children

We have to live in a very sinful world, and God's command to us is that we keep ourselves unspotted by the world (see James 1:27). Sin in our lives obstructs our fellowship with God. We should keep ourselves as a special people, a holy people to Him (1 Peter 2:9).

THE IMPORTANCE OF CONFESSING SIN

Like any good Father, God corrects us. By disciplining us, God is not in any way making us pay for the sins we have committed; Christ has already paid the penalty for them all in full. Rather, God's discipline is to bring us into line and instruct us. It is to train us so that we will grow up to be mature sons. It is to lead us to confess our sins, to draw us back into fellowship. God wants to spare us from harm and suffering, which are the natural consequences of our sin, and to encourage us to enjoy life in all its abundance, which comes through obedience.

God has provided two wonderful ways by which we may know what needs confessing in our lives. The first is by the Word of God. If something is listed as a sin in the Bible and it is in your life, then something is wrong. You need to confess it to the Father. The other way is through the help of the Holy Spirit. If you are aware that the Holy Spirit is grieved in your life, then something is wrong and needs dealing with.

Confessing our sins is a simple matter of acknowledging our sins to the Lord, as we have seen. If we judge ourselves, we will not be judged, as 1 Corinthians 11:31 tell us. If we confess our sins, God will not need to chasten us. If every sin in our lives has been confessed to the Lord today, then He can bless us freely and abundantly, without hindrance. However, unconfessed sin causes a blockage between us and God.

It is important to realize one more thing. If you are a young Christian, you will not be disciplined in the same way as a mature believer. The same principle is true in natural families too, of course. You would not take a very small baby and smack him—that would be extreme cruelty. Similarly, our Father in heaven disciplines us appropriately. You *will* discipline your 12-year-old if you are wise. And if your 12-year-old is wise (as very few are!), he or she will say, "Thank you for doing that."

A wise father makes sure that his child quickly learns to tell the truth about what he or she has done. If a small child will not confess to having made a mess on the floor, for example, a wise father will ask his child to admit it. The principle of telling the truth is far more important than the fact that a mess has been made. This illustrates how God does not want us to hide our sins. He wants them out in the open. *He* knows all about our sins already, of course, but He wants *us* to know about them too and to understand that they don't please Him. He wants us to admit the truth about them, by confessing them before Him.

Beware of the Deceitfulness of our own Hearts

The one way we must *not* try to get back into fellowship is by listening to our own hearts. The Bible says "**The heart is deceitful above all things, and desperately wicked**" (Jeremiah 17:9a). This is the word of God. It has been written down for more than 2500 years, and it is true. Do you believe it? It is true of your heart.

I've heard so many Christians say, "Well, the Lord knows my heart!" And that is true, of course. He does! But the problem is that *we* do not know our own hearts. Sometimes we might think that we are doing fine; but our heart is like a ruler that is not straight and is completely inaccurate in its measurements. You therefore cannot use your own heart to judge your own sins, because it is desperately wicked; that is what this verse tells us. Jeremiah continued by asking, "**Who can know it?**" (verse 9b). Who is *able* to know what is inside your heart? *You* do not know it; you are *not able* to know it. Only God knows truly what is in your heart.

We need God to show us how deceitful our hearts are, so that we will not put any trust in ourselves. We need to consider whether we are willing for Him to show us the depth of wickedness in our own heart and, when He does, to receive what He says. The Lord knows our hearts through and through. "**I, the Lord, search the heart, I test the mind**" (verse 10a). The picture here is of God picking up a lantern, lighting it, and going into all the little dark corners where we cannot look.

The word translated "**mind**" here is the Hebrew word for 'kidneys' (the AV translates it "reins"; in Greek it would be 'bowels'). This may surprise you. The people at that time understood that the seat of the emotions was around the kidneys; they thought their emotions came up from the kidneys. Thus God was saying here that He tests our deeper emotions—our love and affections. I believe that, if we have not known God's dealings on the issue of our affections, then we are in great danger. The heart is so deceitful that any wrong affections, or wrongly aligned affections, can cause any Christian to stumble in his or her life.

Oh the agonies of some people! Sadly, I know some people who have been genuinely saved and gloriously used by the Lord but, inside their heart—although they did not know it, and others did not know it—were 'renegade' affections. They suddenly fell in love with non-Christians, for example, and the Lord was thrown out of their lives. They quickly went from being glorious, spontaneous, overflowing Christians to being some of the most unhappy people I have ever met in my life. What went wrong? The heart is deceitful and desperately wicked, but they had not realized it.

Jeremiah described such renegade affections in other terms as well. He talked about God's people, the people of Judah, as wandering off after other lovers. He described them as, "**A wild donkey used to the wilderness, that sniffs at the wind in her desire; in her time of mating, who can turn her away?**" (Jeremiah 2:24a). What a description! In other words, "You're wandering around looking for a lover. You're like an ass on heat!" Another description, which I like, is this: "**You are a swift dromedary breaking loose in her ways**" (verse 23b). I've heard this paraphrased as a "flighty filly-footed camel", zig-zagging across the desert looking desperately for freedom and fulfilment! A dromedary, with two humps, is a perfect picture of a Christian with uncrucified affections—in a desert land, zig-zagging around, not knowing where to go to for satisfaction. If you are like that, then you need to realize that you will never find a 'lover' to meet your needs, because you belong to the Lord; no one else can ever satisfy you. And such Christians certainly 'get the hump'! They are desperately unhappy, because of uncrucified affections inside that put them out of fellowship with God and prevent them from enjoying His love and all His blessings.

We need to ask God to show us the depth of wickedness within our own hearts. It is so easy to gloss over sin, so easy to explain it away; but we must not do so. David learned the lesson, as we see in Psalm 139. In verses 23 and 24, right at the end, he cried out, "**Search me, O God, and know my heart; try me, and know my anxieties; and see if there is any wicked way in me, and lead me in the way everlasting.**" This should be the cry of every believer who is pursuing the holiness of the Lord. We should always be willing to believe the best of everyone else, but should believe the worst as far as our own hearts are concerned. When God reveals some area of darkness in us, we should say, "Lord, I believe it. That's *my heart* that You've shown me; and it's evil. Thank you, Lord, for giving me a new heart. Help me not to live in the futility of my old ways any more."

David was saying, "Lord, *You* show me if there is any wicked way in me. I can't see or judge correctly, but *You* show me." And God did. In verse 1 of the same Psalm, David said, "**O LORD, You have searched me and known me.**" In verse 11 he said, "**If I say, "Surely the darkness shall fall on me," even the night shall be light about me.**" David realized that, even when he hoped that the LORD had not seen his sins, He *had* seen them. "**Indeed, the darkness shall not hide from You, but the night shines as the day; the darkness and the light are both alike to You. For You have formed my inward parts** [kidneys]" (verses 12-13a).

When our inward parts, the very seat of our emotions, are possessed by God, then we know what it is to be 'broken-in' children of God. Then we know the unspeakable joy and peace which pass all understanding, because then there is no more 'renegade' inside. God has got hold of our affections; we are truly His, and we can enjoy intimate fellowship with Him. "**I am my beloved's and my beloved is mine**" (Song 6:3a). David asked God to search him and know his heart. And we have got to do the same, if we are going to see the holiness of God and be led "**in the way everlasting**" (Psalm 139:24b).

THE SINS OF THE CORINTHIANS

Let us go back to the Corinthian believers. We read a lot about them in the previous chapter. Remember that, in his first letter to them, Paul brought a number of sins to their attention. What a list of sins it was! I have made a list of some of them below, which by no means includes them all. As we read them, we need to remember that one of the purposes of the Word of God is to show us the sins in our own lives. We therefore need to ask how many of these sins apply to us, and, if they do, we need to confess them. We need to ask God to deal with them and help us get rid of them from our lives:

> Divisions, Contentions, Party spirit, Envy, Strife, Fornication, Incest, Adultery, Homosexuality, Covetousness, Idolatry, Drunkenness, Extortion, Taking a brother to law, Stealing, Offending a brother's conscience, Defiling the communion table….

These were just some of the sins that the Corinthians' were committing or had done in the past. If you are a legalistic believer, then probably you will react by thinking that such sins were bad enough to make them lose their salvation. However, do you know what the apostle Paul, who knew all about what was going on in the church, wrote right at the beginning of his letter? I would probably have listed all their sins immediately and would have ripped them apart. But Paul did not write like that. He knew that, although they were badly out of fellowship, they were still the beloved children of God. Here is what he wrote: "**Paul, called to be an apostle of Jesus Christ through the will of God, and Sosthenes our brother, to the church of God which is at Corinth...**" (1 Corinthians 1:1-2a). The word "of" means 'belonging to'—in other words "to the church belonging to God which is at Corinth". He continued, "**To those who are sanctified in Christ Jesus...**" (verse 2b). The word "**sanctified**" means 'set apart' or 'holy'—that is, *different* in character from the world! But this was written to the *Corinthian* church! It might seem an amazing way for Paul to greet the church, but this is exactly what he wrote.

The moment we believe on the Lord Jesus Christ we are put "in Christ" and sanctified—that is, made holy or set apart—*in Him*. We have then got to work out this sanctification in our lives on this earth: that is what dealing with sin is all about. The Corinthian believers *were* sanctified in Christ. Their salvation was absolutely secure as far as God was concerned. Paul went on, "**Called to be saints, with all who in every place call on the name of Jesus Christ our Lord, both theirs and ours**" (verse 2c). Paul addressed them as "**saints**", meaning 'holy ones'—even the Corinthians!

Paul had not said a word about their sins yet. He was encouraging them with truth, building them up first. There should always be such edification before you confront anyone about his or her sins. Indeed, throughout 1 Corinthians, Paul reminded the believers in Corinth of many wonderful truths about who they were in Christ, at the same time as telling them the truth about themselves.

"**Grace to you and peace from God our Father and the Lord Jesus Christ**" (verse 3). Paul said, "**Grace to you**", and I would have added, "And how you need it!" He then said, "**I thank my God always concerning you for the grace of God which was given to you by Jesus Christ, that you were enriched in everything by Him in all utterance and all knowledge, even as the testimony of Christ was confirmed in you**" (verses 4-6). Paul continued with encouragement right down to verse 9. His confrontation and correction then began in verse 10, and actually did not end until chapter 14!

The major fault in the Corinthian church was not the specific sins that the believers were committing. Rather, their *principal* sin was that they had become proud and were *explaining away their sins*. Instead of facing up to what was wrong in the church they had 'over-spiritualized' the situation. They thought, "We're overflowing with spiritual gifts. We have so many prophecies, so many tongues, so many healings and miracles....therefore, we must be doing all right." However, they were deceived. They were condoning the most awful sins in their midst at the same time.

A gift tells you something about the giver, not about the person receiving it. Paul was reminding the Corinthians that, although they had all the gifts, they needed personal holiness in their lives also. Nevertheless, their kindred relationship with God was secure, despite what they had done. Praise God!

1 Corinthians chapter 5 gives an example of the type of awful thing that they were not only tolerating, but condoning in the midst. "**It is actually reported that there is sexual immorality among you, and such sexual immorality as is not even named among the Gentiles—that a man has his father's wife!**" (verse 1). Someone in the church, a genuinely born-again man, was actually having a sexual relationship with his step-mother. (It probably wasn't with his actual mother; the implication is that either his father had married again or that his father had more than one wife.) And this was being condoned by the church. Paul was saying, "You are behaving worse than unbelievers, you Christians!" He then went on to give the key to understanding their real problem: "**And you are puffed up, and have not rather mourned, that he who has done this deed might be taken away from among you**" (verse 2). In other words, *pride* was their major sin. Paul was saying, "This believer should have been disciplined by the church, but you have done nothing!" His lifestyle was a blot on the Body of Christ, yet the church was putting up with his behaviour because they were puffed up with pride.

The Scriptures Teach us to Recognize and Avoid Sins

In 1 Corinthians chapter 10 Paul made this important point: If a sin is named in the Bible, it is to show us what sin is all about. Sin is not described to condemn us; rather, it is described to help us recognize our own sins so that we can confess them and learn to live righteously. "**Moreover, brethren, I do not want you to be unaware that all our fathers were under the cloud, all passed through the sea, all were** baptized into Moses in the cloud and in the sea, all ate the same spiritual food, and all drank the same spiritual drink. For they drank of that spiritual Rock that followed them, and that Rock was Christ. But with most of them God was not well pleased**" (1 Corinthians 10: 1-5a). All the people of Israel who came out of Egypt were identified with Moses; but with most of them God was not well pleased. Actually that is a vast understatement! There were, in fact, only two men with whom God *was* well pleased—Joshua and Caleb. There were at least two million others with whom God was not pleased, in view of their disobedience, unbelief and rebellion. Even Moses himself did not qualify to enter the Promised Land at that time.

The people sinned and they were judged: "**...for their bodies were scattered in the wilderness**" (verse 5b). Verse 6 is very important: "**Now these things became our examples, to the intent that we should not lust after evil things as they also lusted.**" The point Paul was making was this: if you understand these stories, you should know what types of behaviour to banish from your own life. The list of sins is there so that you can learn to avoid the same sins. Confess each sin to God and say, "Father, please deal with this sin in my life. By the Holy Spirit, please drive this thing out of my life!" We can be free. We do not have to be enslaved by anything or anyone except Christ. The examples in the Bible are given so that we might correctly judge the sins in our own lives and avoid further sins. As we read both the Old and New Testaments we will find sins mentioned that we probably did not even know were sins; our minds may need to be renewed.

In verse 7 Paul referred to a specific incident: "**And do not become idolaters as were some of them. As it is written, "The people sat down to eat and drink, and rose up to play.**" This refers specifically to the golden calf that the Israelites made. However, idolatry includes worshipping anything or anyone other than God Himself, and includes covetousness and greed (see Ephesians 5:5). The Holy Spirit might convict you, "Is television a god in your life?" for example.

"**Nor let us commit sexual immorality, as some of them did, and in one day twenty-three thousand fell**" (verse 8). This is not written to condemn us but to *warn* us. Sexual immorality is a serious sin, and this verse reveals what God thinks about it. If He did not like it then, He still does not like it today; God has not changed. We have got to ask God to help us turn away from any such sin in our lives.

"**Nor let us tempt Christ, as some of them also tempted, and were destroyed by serpents**" (verse 9). The word "**tempt**" refers to testing God.

The Israelites effectively said to God, "We're sick to death of the manna You keep giving us! Why have you brought us out of Egypt to die in the wilderness?" (see Numbers 21:4-9). They were not thankful to God for what He had provided. They were complaining. This is a warning to us: Don't do the same! Such an attitude is sinful, and must be taken very seriously. Therefore, if we are not happy with our lot under God, we should ask God to deal with this wrong attitude in us. We should be content wherever we are, just as Paul was: "**I have learned in whatever state I am, to be content**" (Philippians 4:11b). Whatever situation we are in, we should acknowledge God in it. Ask Him about the situation, if you are finding it difficult. He might want to change it. But let us *not* test Christ as some of them tested Him.

"**Nor murmur, as some of them also murmured, and were destroyed by the destroyer**" (1 Corinthians 10:10). Murmuring means having your say to God. But God dislikes murmuring. He happens to be God; so who are we to 'put our oar in' with Him? It is a sin, and it needs to be confessed and dealt with. Probably, all of us have murmured against God at some time and said, "God, I can't stand this any more. What do You think You're doing?" We need to ask God to forgive us.

"**Now all these things happened to them as examples, and they were written for our admonition, on whom the ends of the ages have come**" (verse 11). I wonder what your attitude is as you read these verses? Do you think this passage is not relevant to you?—because it clearly *was* written for you.

"**Therefore let him who thinks he stands take heed lest he fall**" (verse 12). Self-righteousness is another serious sin. Every one of us should be in the position where we say every day, "Father, help me. Please deal with *me*, Lord!" We should not self-righteously think, "I'm so glad that so-and-so can hear this message." No! It is *you* that God wants to deal with. These verses are terribly important, but they are not meant to condemn us.

Be encouraged! "**No temptation has overtaken you except such as is common to man; but God is faithful, who will not allow you to be tempted beyond what you are able, but with the temptation will also make the way of escape, that you may be able to bear it**" (verse 13).

Once you recognize a sin in your life, simply confess it to God! Ask Him, by the Holy Spirit, to deal with it. If it appears again, then ask Him again. He will always forgive, because He is a faithful and a wonderful God. The sin will eventually be dealt with if you are willing to allow God to change you. However, if you refuse to judge yourself—if you dig your heels in and say, "God, I won't accept your viewpoint on this. I'm going to carry on just as I am!"—then, like any good father, your Father in heaven will discipline you.

GOD'S DISCIPLINE—HEBREWS CHAPTER 12

The principal passage on God's discipline in the New Testament is Hebrews chapter 12. The word translated "**discipline**" in this passage is the Greek word *paideia*. It means, as we mentioned in the previous chapter: 'chastening', 'training', 'instruction' or 'education', particularly in relation to bringing up children. It refers to educative discipline, or disciplinary correction. We have a Father in heaven who wants to train us and, because He loves us so much, He is *determined* to train us. It is important that we receive teaching on this subject, because the Word of God tells us that it is part of our relationship with the Father. It is therefore good for us to study this subject. It is profitable for equipping us (see 2 Timothy 3:16-17).

Unfortunately, because our Bibles are split up into chapters and many of us tend to read one chapter at a time, it is easy to miss the logic and flow of some passages. In Hebrews chapter 11, for example, the account of all the characters described gradually builds up and comes to a climax—but the climax is in chapter 12! Many readers are just getting to the climax when they close their Bibles, because chapter 11 is over. What a shame! The writer has been listing marvellous characters in the Old Testament, saying, "By faith he did this....By faith she did that...", and so on. Most of these 'heroes' were naturally weak people, such as Gideon. However, *by faith* they really 'went places' with God. That should encourage us tremendously! These people did lots of wonderful things by faith, and now the writer comes to the climax—in Hebrews 12:1—where he says, **"Therefore, since we also are surrounded by so great a cloud of witnesses, let us lay aside every weight, and the sin which so easily ensnares us, and let us run with endurance the race that is set before us"**.

LAY ASIDE WEIGHTS AND SIN

The picture here is of an amphitheatre, or sports stadium, in which there is row upon row of seats; and the seats are all full. We are down below on the running track, where we are all running a race—the 'race' of the Christian life. The crowd up above us is not there to cheer us on. Rather, the crowd comprises all those who have run the race before us—and we know about some of their lives. The cloud is not a little cloud that you can see in the distance. Rather, it is a huge bank of cloud with no apparent boundaries. The writer was saying, "The fact that we've got so many examples to point to and learn from should inspire us to press on and also 'go places' with God!"

Every time we look up and recognize someone, we should recall, "Oh yes, he tripped just around that corner, didn't he? I must make sure I don't trip at that same point." Then you might run on further, remember someone else and say, "He stopped running when he reached here, didn't he? I must be careful not to do that." The writer was saying, "You are surrounded with a *huge* cloud of witnesses all the way round; and it's to encourage you!"

Seeing that we are encompassed with this great cloud of witnesses, what should we do? We should "**lay aside every weight, and the sin which so easily ensnares us**". There are two things mentioned here: weights and sin. We will consider them in reverse order.

The "**sin which so easily ensnares us**" means the sin which so easily 'entangles us', 'clings to us' or 'gets in our way'. Sin hinders us from running by entangling us or clinging to us. If you just brush against sin you find that it comes along with you. Do you know those little seed pods, with burrs on, that children throw at one another? If one just touches you, it sticks to you. Sin clings like that. When Paul said, "**nor give place to the devil**" (in Ephesians 4:27), he was warning us not to give *any* opportunity at all for sin to cling to us.

What did the writer mean by weights? They are clearly different from sin. These weights are encumbrances. They represent things that can be good and, in normal life, often *are* very good; but when you are running a race they are no good at all. The great illustration of this is a toga: the long, loose, flowing robe that Romans used to wear. Togas were very good outer garments indeed and people liked to wear them: they looked good; they were stately; they were practical; and they were also very comfortable. However, if you had to run in a race, a toga was no good to you at all, because it would slow you down and might cause you to trip over.

The best way to find out what is a weight in your Christian life is simply to *start running with Jesus*. As soon as you start running, you will quickly discover the things that weigh you down. If you are an athlete, for example, you will know that a big meal or books, for example, when you start running, are not helpful at all.

Taking my own life as an example, I used to be a great concert-goer. There is nothing wrong in going to concerts three times a week, nothing at all.

But when I started running with Jesus, I found that going to concerts so often was a weight that had to be laid aside. Similarly, there is nothing wrong with television, in principle. But as you start running with Jesus, you will soon discover if it is a weight in your life. There is no specific verse commanding, "Do not watch television!", but do you see the point?

We all have weights in our own lives. Such weights are what I call "doubtful sins". They are things that are not actually defined as sin in the Bible. However, when you start running with Jesus, you will soon know whether you need to give them up. Paul wrote: "**All things are lawful for me, but all things are not helpful**" (1 Corinthians 6:12a). He knew this in his own experience.

Looking unto Jesus

As well as laying aside every weight, and the sin which so easily ensnares us, what must we do? "**And let us run with endurance the race that is set before us, looking unto Jesus...**" (Hebrews 12:1b-2a). This does not mean simply looking *at* Jesus; it means looking *away* unto Jesus. In other words, we should take our eyes off ourselves, off our sins and weights, and the affairs of this world—and look away unto Jesus. The surrounding witnesses should encourage us as we're running our race, but our eyes should be fixed on Jesus. He is our goal and example.

This means occupation with Christ. *There is no way to live a victorious Christian life other than by being occupied with Christ*. When we get up it should be Jesus Christ we look to; when we are working or studying it should be Christ we are looking to; when we have dinner it should be Christ; walking down the street, Christ; or, whatever else we do, it should be Christ we are occupied with. It is how we live every day and hour that counts. Meetings, even prayer meetings, are nothing in comparison. Occupation with Christ is what matters in running our race.

We should not look at one another, either. We will soon find faults in one another and become critical if we concentrate on those around us. We should not do it! Rather, we should be "**looking unto Jesus, the author and finisher of our faith, who for the joy that was set before Him endured the cross, despising the shame, and has sat down at the right hand of the throne of God**" (verse 2). The word "**author**" here means the 'chief' or 'leader', as well as the 'one who begins' or the 'originator'. Jesus is also the "**finisher**", the completer, the perfecter of our faith. He is the best example that there is. And He is now seated at the right hand of the throne of God.

"**For consider Him who endured such hostility from sinners against Himself, lest you become weary and discouraged in your souls**" (verse 3). Who opposed Jesus? The religious leaders did. The political leaders did. The devil did. Many in the crowds did. Even some of Jesus' own disciples did at times. Even a thief on the cross, a guilty criminal, opposed Him. Therefore, we should meditate on Jesus, and remember what He had to endure. To be occupied with Him will help us bear every circumstance that comes, with joy. Keep your eyes fixed on Jesus!

"**You have not yet resisted to bloodshed, striving against sin**" (verse 4). What is the point here? The point is that Jesus *did* resist sin to the extent of shedding His blood—but you almost certainly have not done so. The word translated "**resisted**" means 'stood against', while the word "**striving**" means 'agonizing with'. A tremendous battle is described here. "You have not yet stood against sin to the point of bloodshed, agonizing with it," the writing was saying, "But Christ has!"

GOD CHASTENS HIS SONS

Now we come to the issue of chastening. "**And you have forgotten the exhortation which speaks to you as to sons: "My son, do not despise the chastening of the LORD, nor be discouraged when you are rebuked by Him"**" (verse 5). To "**despise**" God's chastening means to have contempt for it, to ignore it or to explain it away. It is so easy to explain away the Lord's discipline; but don't do it. Take it very seriously. If you despise it, it will get worse. If children ignore the correction given them, then wise parents will increase the discipline until they eventually learn. With God, it is the same. However, if you take God's discipline seriously and learn from it, He will soon be able to remove it.

"**For whom the Lord loves He chastens, and scourges every son whom He receives**" (verse 6). Oh, hallelujah! It is *because He loves us*—because He longs for fellowship with us—that God chastens us. If sin is blocking that fellowship, God would rather discipline us to restore our fellowship than allow us to carry on in our own way, not walking in the light. Are you a received son? I am, *I know*, because every time I step out of line my Father makes sure that I learn a few lessons. And I thank Him always, because I change and become wiser through it.

"**If you endure chastening, God deals with you as with sons; for what son is there whom a father does not chasten? But if you are without chastening, of which all have become partakers, then you are illegitimate and not sons**" (verse 7-8). The fact that you are chastened certainly does not mean that you have lost your salvation or that God doesn't love you. On the contrary, it means you have *not* lost your salvation. Only if we had no loving father would we receive no discipline!

"Furthermore, we have had human fathers who corrected us, and we paid them respect. Shall we not much more readily be in subjection to the Father of spirits and live?" (verse 9). We have had earthly, natural fathers as correctors, and we respected them for disciplining us. Now we have a spiritual Father. Therefore, when He corrects us, we should readily respect Him and be corrected by His discipline. If we do, the writer says we shall "**live**"! By accepting God's discipline, we shall come into fullness of life.

Oh, the Christian life is *so* glorious and wonderful! But the chastised Christian life becomes so awful, it can hardly be described—as you probably know, and as I definitely know, having tried to live it. How wonderful fellowship with the Father is! It is worth all the discipline when you are trained by it; it really is. You come into marvellous pasture-land that you didn't know existed before, into verdant green pastures with bubbling springs. Suddenly you say, "Why did I stay out in that wilderness for so long? Oh Lord, forgive my pride and my self-righteousness."

"For they indeed for a few days chastened us as seemed best to them, but He for our profit, that we may be partakers of His holiness" (verse 10). God disciplines us for our good, *that we may partake of His holiness*. That is what I long for. I want His holiness to be manifested in me, so that, when I walk around, the holiness of Jesus will characterize me, because I've made it my own. It *is* possible to get there. It *is* possible, *by the Spirit*, to put to death the misdeeds of the body (Romans 8:13). It *is* possible, because to walk in the Spirit neutralizes the power of the old sin nature. It's true! It takes time to get there, but it is true. Every time you see a sin, confess it; and every time God disciplines you, accept it! Then you will know peace and joy, and maturity will surely come through. Who is glorified? *He* is glorified, which is what we want, isn't it? Only Him.

"Now no chastening seems to be joyful for the present, but grievous…" That is certainly true; "**…nevertheless, afterwards it yields the peaceable fruit of righteousness to those who have been trained by it**" (verse 11). Note that God's discipline only yields fruit for those trained by it. This is what chastening is all about. It is to train us. And it is worth it, every bit. Its purpose is to transform us—that the peaceable fruit of righteousness might be produced in each one of us.

"Therefore strengthen the hands which hang down, and the feeble knees" (verse 12). What does this mean? The word translated "**strengthen**" ("**lift up**" in the AV) means 'set upright' or 'set straight again'. It was a medical term meaning to 'put dislocated joints back into joint'.

If you have ever had a dislocated joint you will know that it is not only painful, but it hinders you from moving. If your elbow joint is out, you are quite unable to play tennis, for example. This is what *sin* does in your life: it inhibits you from *functioning* as a member in the Body of Christ. Sin causes you to be 'dislocated', like a weakened hand, hanging painfully down. And it is not just painful for *you*; it is painful for the people around you—especially if, instead of facing up to your sin, you blame everyone else for it. This verse says, "Get back into joint!" Confess all of your sins to God!

The term "**feeble knees**" means 'paralysed knees'—that cause you to hobble. Instead of walking in the Spirit, sin causes you to hobble. It paralyses you. You must get back in fellowship, or discipline will come. If you judge yourself, you will not be judged.

"**And make straight paths for your feet, so that what is lame may not be dislocated, but rather be healed**" (verse 13). The phrase "**straight paths**" means 'level paths', 'smooth paths'—paths that are not difficult. If you do not confess your sins, things will get worse. However, by facing up to your sins, and avoiding sin, your path will become smooth. Why not rather be healed? God does not want to chasten us. He does not like judging. His purpose is not that. He loves us and wants us to walk uprightly with Him. Praise God! This is a glorious and wonderful picture.

"**Pursue peace with all men, and holiness, without which no one will see the Lord**" (verse 14). To see the Lord manifested bodily in us *is* possible—but only through holiness. The Father wants His Son to be revealed in each person. That is what His purpose is and that is what His discipline is for. Holiness *is* possible.

Every church or fellowship group has got to start manifesting the holiness of Jesus through every member of the Body in its place. If someone is dislocated, that person has got to get back into joint, or else he or she will gradually become more and more deflected from walking along a straight path with God. And the chastening of God will surely come.

However, I want to emphasize this: *We should never join in God's discipline of another believer.* As soon as we do, we put ourselves out of fellowship and, soon, we will come under discipline too! God is quite able to discipline His own children. He does not need our interference or help!

The Corinthians got back into Fellowship with God

Sometimes we tend to dwell on the negative too much. Immediately following the letter called 1 Corinthians in the New Testament is the glorious book called 2 Corinthians. Something wonderful happened in Corinth as a result of the first letter that Paul wrote to the believers. Isn't it a shame that the Corinthian church is generally known as "the Carnal church", instead of the church that responded to Paul's message and got back into fellowship with God.

The passage we need to look at is in 2 Corinthians chapter 7. There are two similar Greek words used in the passage that we need to consider (both of which are translated "repent" in the AV). The first is *metamelomai*, which means to 'feel sorry', 'be emotionally upset', 'care for afterwards' or 'regret.' It does not mean to repent.

No one ever got to heaven by *metamelomai*. It is said of Judas Iscariot that he was remorseful (Matthew 27:3). He probably wept many tears. But he never truly repented. True repentance enables any person to be accepted in heaven, anyone at all, and it is the word *metanoeo*, which means 'to change (your) mind' about something.[1]

In 2 Corinthians 7:8-11 both these Greek words are used. There is emotional upset or regret, and there is true repentance. Paul said to the Corinthians, "**For even if I made you sorry with my letter, I do not regret it; though I did regret it**" (verse 8a)—and the word translated "**regret**" here is *metamelomai*, the first word. Paul's letter had hurt them a lot, and he had felt bad about it for a short time. "But I don't regret it now," he was saying, "though I did regret it." "**For I perceive that the same epistle made you sorry, though only for a while**" (verse 8b). The letter had also upset the Corinthian believers for a short time.

However, in verse 9a we find the second word, *metanoeo*, used: "**Now I rejoice, not that you were made sorry, but that your sorrow led to repentance**". Their sorrow had led to true repentance, a change of mind. Paul was saying, "I rejoice utterly now because, although my letter upset you emotionally, it led you to a change of mind about your sin." The Corinthians had put things right in the church. They had been so upset and grieved at what Paul wrote that they changed their attitude towards the things going on in the church. Paul now rejoiced that he had written his

---

[1] For more details on repentance and these two Greek words, see Chapters 10 and 12 of the book "Salvation" by Roger Price, which covers the first series of Basic Bible Studies (BBS 1 to 14).

first letter. **"For you were made sorry in a godly manner, that you might suffer loss from us in nothing"** (verse 9b). They had been sorry not out of self-pity, not for attention, not because of false spirituality; it was none of these things. Rather, they suddenly realized how they had grieved the Lord.

"For godly sorrow produces repentance..." (verse 10a). True tears bring about a change of attitude to sin. False tears of self-pity usually lead just to more self-pity. Tears about failure tend to lead to more tears about failure. But true godly tears lead us to re-think our condition before God—and to repentance. The whole Corinthian church had been so upset by Paul's rebuke that they changed their thinking. They confronted the man who had been having a sexual relationship with his father's wife. We don't know for certain whether the man actually confessed his sin, but we *do know* that *the church* repented and regarded his behaviour as a blot on the Body of Christ.

"For godly sorrow produces repentance to salvation, not to be regretted; but the sorrow of the world produces death" (verse 10). Godly sorrow produces repentance to salvation, without regret. It produces a life that is full of joy, full of good things and not full of tears of regret—which is what believers will and do experience if they remain out of fellowship with the Lord. I have counselled so many people who have wept and wept about their sins, but then, a month later, they are still doing the same things. All their tears were in vain. They did not come to a true change of mind and heart before the Lord. It is *metanoeo* that is needed—a change of thinking. Any other type of sorrowing or crying produces death inside.[2]

"For observe this very thing, that you sorrowed in a godly manner: What diligence it produced in you, what clearing of yourselves, what indignation, what fear, what vehement desire, what zeal, what vindication! In all things you proved yourselves to be clear in this

---

[2] Everyone involved in counselling needs to know this: tears can be very superficial. I can think of four main reasons why people cry, that we need to be aware of: (1) For sympathy, pity or attention. Many people cry when they are filled with self-pity. It is easy to mistake this for true repentance, but it is not; it is self-indulgence. (2) Because of failure. You might be filled with a sense of self-failure and so you weep tears of desolation, because nothing seems to have gone right in your life. (3) The shock of being found out. Some people burst into tears because God has revealed something in their lives that they did not want anyone to know, or which they had deceived themselves about. Finally, (4) False spirituality. Some people think that tears are somehow 'spiritual'. Their tears are deceptive.

The only tears that are genuine before God as far as sin is concerned are tears prompted by love, because you love Him so much and you regret that you have hurt Him through your sin. That is godly grief, and it is quite different from all the rest.

matter" (verse 11). What a glorious end! The Corinthian church, having been judged terribly by the Lord, suddenly returned to a place of blessing. Praise the Lord!

Conclusion

This is how we should remember the Corinthian church. This is the church I rejoice in. Holiness began to emerge in their midst and they saw the Lord high and lifted up in their very midst.

We can have the same experience. "**For if we would judge ourselves, we would not be judged**" (1 Corinthians 11:31). We should not wait for the chastening of the Lord to get our attitude to sin sorted out. Get right with God now! Find a new place with God where He so occupies your life that you cannot bear to hurt Him with your sin—because sin is like a knife wound into the very heart of God. *That* will cause repentance. *That* will cause a re-thinking on the things that are grieving the Holy Spirit.

Holiness is what we, as believers, have got to manifest in our lives. It is what we need to show this world, which is in bondage to sin and cannot escape. We should be able to declare, "We are free, because the Lord Jesus Christ died for our sins on the Cross. And you too can be free!" We should walk in a new way in Christ, telling others, "Believe on the Lord Jesus Christ and you will be saved!"

10. PALACES OR MUD-HUTS?
The Judgment of Believers' Works

The Believer: Sinner, Son and Servant

A believer can be viewed in three main ways: (1) as a Sinner; (2) as a Son; and (3) as a Servant. The fact that these all begin with an 'S' is a coincidence, but it is useful for remembering them. For every believer these three descriptions apply.

We are all sinners by nature and we all sin (Romans 3:23; 1 John 1:8). However, once we believe on the Lord Jesus Christ we become sons of God (Galatians 3:26). After we have believed on the Lord, we then have the opportunity to serve Him (1 Thessalonians 1:9; Hebrews 12:28).

All three of these aspects have judgment associated with them. We have dealt with the first two already, but will briefly review them now. Then we will concentrate on the third aspect and see the judgment associated with us as God's servants.

1. The Believer as a Sinner

The judgment of the believer as a sinner has already taken place in the *past*; there is no further judgment to come. The reason for this, as we know, is that the Lord Jesus Christ bore every sin that we have committed, are committing, or ever will commit. He suffered and died for all of them on the Cross. As sinners, we have therefore been judged in the past, in Christ; 2000 years ago, on the Cross, we were effectively judged for our sins and were found *guilty*. But it was Christ who bore the penalty for our sins and not us.

As we learnt in the first series of Basic Bible Studies, there is now only one sin that any person can ever commit that has not been paid for—the so-called "unforgivable sin". This is the sin of not ever believing on the Lord Jesus Christ. It is summed up by Jesus' words in John's Gospel: **"He who believes in Him is not condemned; but he who does not believe is condemned already, because he has not believed in the name of the**

only begotten Son of God" (John 3:18; see also John 16:8-9). By definition, a believer cannot commit this unforgivable sin. However, if you are not a believer, then you are in danger of committing it and of eternal judgment. The solution is simple: **"Believe on the Lord Jesus Christ, and you will be saved"** (Acts 16:31b).

2. The Believer as a Son

We have seen the judgment connected with being a son of God in the previous two chapters. This judgment is *present*, in our lives right now. The Bible is clear: **"For if we would judge ourselves, we would not be judged"** (1 Corinthians 11:31). Every single day of our lives we should be judging ourselves and confessing our sins to God. We are beloved sons, in a kindred relationship with God our Father, but we have to judge ourselves continually to maintain unhindered *fellowship* with Him. The essential scripture is of course 1 John 1:9, **"If we confess our sins, He is faithful and just to forgive us our sins and to cleanse us from all unrighteousness."** It is up to us; we have freewill. If we choose not to face up to our sins, then our Father in heaven will have to discipline us. He is a good parent, so He *will* correct us; and it is His right to do so.

We have considered these two aspects before. Therefore, we will now concentrate on the third aspect: God's judgment of us as His *servants*. This involves the judgment of *our works*, and this judgment is *future*.

3. The Believer as a Servant

After we believe on the Lord Jesus we have the opportunity and privilege of being able to serve God. We can begin to serve the living God. And if we grow up in a correct manner, as healthy children, we will start producing fruit for God in terms of our character and our works. What is the purpose of a servant except to wait on his master? This is our role as servants. However, we should always remember that we are not just servants, but God's beloved children; and we should serve the Lord because of our love for Him who first loved us. It is both our privilege and duty to produce fruit for Him.

When we are young babes in Christ, we might not produce quite as much fruit as we should. However, as we grow up in the Lord our production should increase and increase. Then, one day our production is going to be judged. We have been judged already as sinners and justified (that is, made righteous) forever in Christ. We are now judged in this life as God chastens us—as He trains us to walk righteously. However, *all the works we do for God will also be judged one day in the future*. Therefore, in this study, our subject is the judgment of believers' works.

THE JUDGMENT OF BELIEVERS' WORKS

When is this judgment going to happen? How is it going to happen? Who is going to carry it out? Where will we be? How are we going to be feeling while it is taking place? These are some of the questions that immediately spring to mind.

An illustration of this judgment is the quality control you get in most factories, where a team of people might be busy producing television screens, radios, ice-lollies, or some other type of product. There is usually another group of people called the "Quality Control" or "Quality Assurance" department. Their job is not to check up directly on the people who are busy doing the work. Rather, their job is to check up on *the quality of the work itself*.

When, for example, a radio comes along, it will be tested; and if it looks just as it should, gives good reception and so on, it will be passed. However, every tenth radio perhaps, or every hundredth one, or, if it's an excellent firm, every thousandth one, might not work when it is switched on; so it is rejected and put away.

This is what the judgment of believers' works is all about. It is *not* judgment of the believer directly; rather, it is judgment of his or her *works*. Every day we should be producing good works, and it is the quality of these that has to be judged.

THE PARABLE OF THE SOWER

A parable dealing with this subject is the Parable of the Sower (Luke 8: 5-15, for example). We looked at it in the first series of Basic Bible Studies. Jesus explained the parable, and it has to do with production. It poses the question, "How productive are we with God?"

A farming scene is in view, with bags of seed representing the word of God. A sower comes along and he sows the word, broadcasting it all over the field. The parable then deals with what happens to the seed after it falls on to the ground. The seed is all the same. What differs is the quality of the ground that it falls upon. Jesus described four categories of ground.

The first category is the "wayside", that is, the strip of ground by the side of the field that has been trodden down by the farmer. After many years it has become really hard. The seed therefore bounces off and lies on the surface there. The birds of the air then come along, swoop down, pick up the seed and eat it. This is a picture of an *un*believer, whose heart is hardened against the gospel. The word comes to his heart, but it bounces off again; and Satan comes along and removes the seed as quickly as possible, because he doesn't want it to enter the heart.

From then on, however, the production of *believers* is described. The seed enters their hearts and remains. First, there is some shallow soil, which represents a 'shallow believer'. The word of God comes along and is received. The seed sprouts forth quickly, exhibiting wonderful growth, but after the intense heat of the sun comes the plant starts withering because it has no deep root. Do you know believers like that? They receive the word of God and they seem to start off so well. Yet as soon as difficulties, trials or persecutions come along, they stop growing and quickly wither up—and they end up with zero production. There are going to be believers just like this, who will get to heaven but will have nothing to show at all.

A second type of believer is then described. In this case, the seed is sown among thorns. The thorns tangle around the growing shoot and choke it. This represents someone who receives the word of God, who is truly born again, but the cares of this world—perhaps a desire for riches or pleasure, or a concern for reputation—choke any growth. We might find that our friends do not like us now that we are Christians, so we tone down our commitment a bit; but soon it dwindles completely. The result is zero production again.

In the last category, however, the seed falls on to good ground. It falls into good soil and grows to maturity, producing thirty, sixty or even a hundredfold. Exactly how much is produced will again depend upon the quality of the ground.

What determines the Quality of our Works?

Some people doubt that hundredfold production is possible. It would mean that, for every one grain you put into the ground, a hundred more would be produced. Imagine the blessings if every believer was turning out produce one-hundredfold! In Genesis chapter 26 there is a lovely scripture: "**Then Isaac sowed in that land, and reaped in the same year a hundredfold; and the Lord blessed him**" (verse 12). This tells us that it *is* possible. If Isaac could experience such production, then so can we!

It *is* possible to produce a hundredfold for God; but what it depends upon is the *quality of the soil*. The point is this: the seed *is* top quality; but how receptive are you to God? If you are not top quality ground, then even top quality seed will not produce a hundredfold. It may only produce sixtyfold, or thirtyfold, or less. You may only produce one-fold perhaps, in which case you will just about duplicate yourself, and that's all.

Only the Holy Spirit can actually produce any good in us at all, and it is only as the Lord deals with our lives that the Holy Spirit can change our character and start flowing through us, enabling us to do good works for God. This is the only genuine production there is. The flesh can produce no good fruit or work at all; but the Holy Spirit can. Praise God! This is the main principle we need to understand.

We should be growing continuously and serving God. The Lord has chosen to use us as His co-workers! You might say, "But I'm not good enough," and indeed none of us are! But *He* is in us. Hallelujah! It is His work through us that counts, not our own goodness or strength.

WHEN IS THIS JUDGMENT OF OUR WORKS?

We will be judged shortly after the Rapture of the Church. The day is coming very soon when the Lord Jesus shall descend from heaven with a shout. And He is going to come for one reason—because He doesn't want His Church on this earth any more. If you are a believer and you die before that day arrives, you are going to rise up from the grave. Your body will be reconstituted and you will be given a resurrection body. Those who are alive will then be 'caught up' or 'snatched away' together with you, to meet the Lord in the air. Therefore, if you have got loved ones who have already gone on, they are going to rise shortly before you. Praise God!

The Rapture will take place *before* our works are judged, so we are not talking about a judgment that could stop us going to heaven. Our sins have already been judged, so nothing can prevent us from getting to heaven once we have believed on the Lord Jesus Christ—absolutely nothing. Nothing shall separate us from the love of God: not our biggest problem or our biggest fear (Romans 8:35-39). All believers shall be snatched away to heaven, because it does not depend on us; it depends on Christ and His work. Whether we have done hundreds of good works, or none at all, we shall always be with the Lord. Praise the name of Jesus!

This is what I mean by the Rapture of the Church. It is described in 1 Thessalonians 4:13-18. For some believers, this might disagree with their theology, but they are going to go all the same! We are going to be 'raptured' from the earth—that is, 'taken up' into the clouds to be with the Lord forever: **"For the Lord Himself will descend from heaven with a shout, with the voice of an archangel, and with the trumpet of God. And the dead in Christ will rise first. Then we who are alive and** remain shall be caught up together with them in the clouds to meet the Lord in the air. And thus we shall always be with the Lord. Therefore comfort one another with these words" (1 Thessalonians 4:16-18).

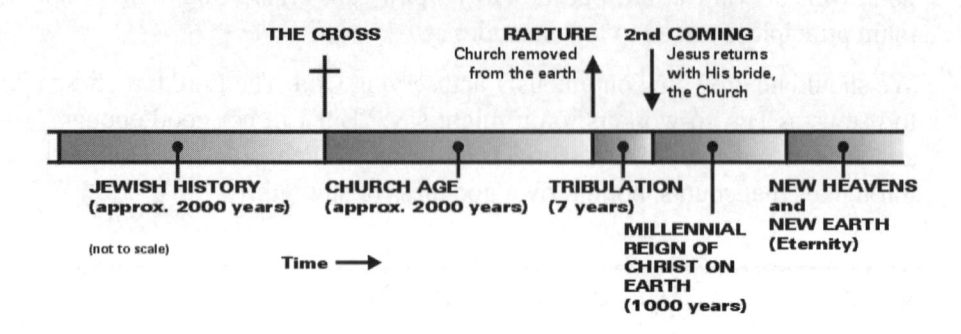

```
                    THE CROSS        RAPTURE      2nd COMING
                                  Church removed  Jesus returns
                                  from the earth  with His bride,
                                                  the Church

  JEWISH HISTORY      CHURCH AGE         TRIBULATION    NEW HEAVENS
  (approx. 2000 years) (approx. 2000 years) (7 years)    and
                                                         NEW EARTH
  (not to scale)                          MILLENNIAL    (Eternity)
                      Time →              REIGN OF
                                          CHRIST ON
                                          EARTH
                                          (1000 years)
```

The Church will thus be removed, so I always put an arrow going up when I draw this. Then, following the Rapture, there will be seven years of tribulation on the earth—or The Tribulation.

With the Church gone, God will use the Jews once again to preach the gospel. We know from Revelation chapter 7 that 144,000 Jews will be used to evangelize the whole world; and they will reap a large harvest—*more* than a hundredfold. Praise God! Under the most terrible conditions on the earth they are going to be very productive. (We have got some of the best conditions on the earth today, so we need to ask ourselves, "Are we being productive?" I hope we are. We will know one day, because our works are going to be judged.)

At the end of the Tribulation will be the Second Advent, or Second Coming, of Jesus Christ. The seven years of the Tribulation will terminate with the reappearance of the Lord Jesus—coming with us! We are coming back with Him, as His bride! We will go up at the Rapture; but seven years later we will come down again when Christ returns.

When will the judgment of our works take place then? It will be after the Rapture and before we return with Christ, during the time when the earth is experiencing tribulation. Let me emphasize again: it is not *us* who will be judged, but our *works* are going to be judged.

Judgment at the 'Bema' seat of Christ

The judgment of believers' works is often referred to as the "Judgment Seat of Christ". It is described in 2 Corinthians chapter 5. Once we are up in heaven, the judgment seat of Christ will come into view. I imagine all of us arriving in heaven with a bag, which contains our works. *We* will not be judged; but our 'bag of' works will be judged.

"We are confident, yes, well pleased rather to be absent from the body and to be present with the Lord" (2 Corinthians 5:8). Isn't that true of us all? We would rather be with the Lord than in the body. While we remain in the body, God still has a purpose for our lives here; but we'd rather be with the Lord.

"Therefore we make it our aim, whether present or absent, to be well pleasing to Him. For we must all appear before the judgment seat of Christ, that each one may receive the things done in the body, according to what he has done, whether good or bad" (verses 9-10). Each one of us—every single believer—has got to appear before the judgment seat of Christ.

The word translated "**judgment seat**" is the word *bema* in Greek. A *bema* was a raised platform on which a judge used to sit as he judged a particular case. It was usually quite small—although the one in Athens was 10 feet (3 m) tall, in view of the large crowds! We don't know how big the Lord's *bema* seat is going to be; I imagine it might be vast. Each one of us will appear before this judgment seat with our own bag of works.

The purpose of this judgment is "**that each one may receive the things done in the body**" (verse 10b). The Greek actually says "*through* the body". It is not sin that is in view here, but rather our *production*—the things we have done while in our present bodies on earth. And we shall receive accordingly.

Our works fall into two categories. They are either 'good' works, carried out in the power of the Holy Spirit (produced by His inspiration, motivation and energy), or they are works produced by our flesh, in which case they are bad and worthless. This is an awesome thing, isn't it? It means that, for all of us who are Christians, some of our works originate from the flesh, while others are from the Spirit. They will all be mixed up in our 'bags'.

Unfortunately, we are often more impressed by works done in the flesh. We might think, "Aren't I good? Look what *I've* done. *I* did this!" But God is not impressed at all, because anything of the flesh is absolutely worthless and evil to Him, fit only to be thrown on to the rubbish heap. Only by the working of the Holy Spirit through us can we produce anything good. Oh, how we need to have a revelation of this![1]

The difference between our good and bad works is that our good works are eternal, while all other works are not. Whatever *we* produce in our own strength is temporary and probably will not even outlast us. However, whatever we allow *God* to produce *through* us will last for all eternity—and we will receive a reward for it!

PALACES OR MUD-HUTS? (1 CORINTHIANS 3:11-16)

1 Corinthians chapter 3 contains the major passage dealing with the judgment of believers' works.

Paul wrote: **"For no other foundation can anyone lay than that which is laid, which is Jesus Christ"** (verse 11). Jesus Christ is the *only* foundation that is going to last. He is the only One who has done eternal work for us to build upon. The Greek word for "other" used here (*allos*) means 'another of the same kind'. No one can ever lay another foundation equal to Christ, or alongside Christ. We therefore need to beware of any person who comes along and bases anything on someone or something other than the Lord Himself. *Everything* must be based on Jesus: on who He is, and on the fact that He died, rose from the dead, ascended and is now seated at the right hand of God the Father, interceding for us. It is all Christ! What we believe and how we live must be based, beginning to end, on Jesus Christ.

The Mormons believe in some of what the Bible says about Christ, but they have another foundation too—the Book of Mormon. However, the Bible tells us that there can be no other foundation except one, and it is Christ. Any other foundation is no good at all. Even God the Father is not the foundation, but only Christ.

---

[1] In Isaiah chapter 40 there is a description of works of the flesh. Isaiah heard a voice. **"The voice said, "Cry out!" And he said, "What shall I cry?""** (verse 6a). This meant "Shout out!" It meant he had to go to the street corners and holler at the top of his voice! Isaiah was willing to shout, but he wanted to know what he should shout. That was obedience. This is what he had to shout: **"All flesh is grass, and all its loveliness is like the flower of the field"** (verse 6b). Many Israelites thought that, by doing lots of works in their own strength, they were pleasing God. Therefore, God wanted Isaiah to tell them, "All flesh: grass!" (the verb is omitted to emphasize the point). **"The grass withers, the flower fades, because the breath of the LORD blows upon it; surely the people are grass. The grass withers, the flower fades, but the word of our God stands for ever"** (verses 7-8). "That's all you're fit for," God was saying; "there's nothing enduring in you whatsoever!"

I once went to hear a vicar speaking about communism. He was a member of the Communist Party, and his subject was "Christianity and Communism: Paradox or Tautology?" He was trying to argue that communism *is* modern day Christianity. During his talk, he said that God raised up Jesus to start a social revolution, but Jesus failed. Therefore, God raised up Karl Marx instead! What an incredible thing for a so-called Christian to say! No other foundation can be laid than that which is laid, which is Jesus Christ. Karl Marx is nothing in comparison. As we know from the first series of Basic Bible Studies, Karl Marx was a slave to sin, just like the rest of us, so he could not possibly buy anyone else out of the slave-market of sin.

The marvellous glory of the grace of God is this: *every single believer has the privilege of building (and the ability to build) on the true foundation of Jesus Christ*. If *I* was a master builder and had built a perfect foundation, I don't think I would let children come and start building on my foundation. But God does! Every believer can start building on the foundation God has laid. What a tremendous privilege this is.

The building materials are described in verse 12: "**Now if anyone builds on this foundation with gold, silver, precious stones, wood, hay, straw...**". We find two categories of material here. We can build either with gold, silver and jewels, or we build with the others, wood, hay and straw. And you couldn't get two more contrasting sets of material. Gold, silver and precious stones are all enduring. They last and they last. However, the others—wood, hay and straw—have no enduring quality whatsoever.

If you were to lose a gold ring in the garden and 1000 years later someone was to dig it up, it would still be shiny gold—after a quick clean! That is the nature of gold. It will not decay and it combines with almost no other chemicals.[2] If it had been an iron ring, however, there might be just a brown stain left in the garden after 100 years, or the decomposed ring would disintegrate when touched. Wood, hay and straw would simply have decayed and disappeared long before, after just a few years. Gold, silver and precious stones endure; that is the point.

There is another point to note as well, however. Gold, silver and precious stones are the type of material one would use in building a palace or temple. But the others—wood, hay and straw—they are the type of

---

[2] There is only one liquid I know of that will actually dissolve gold, and it is called *aqua regia*. It comprises one part concentrated nitric acid and three parts concentrated hydrochloric acid. It is extremely potent stuff!

material one would use in constructing a mud-hut. Therefore, the question we need to ask ourselves is this: "What am I building through my life? Am I building a palace for God or a mud-hut?"—based on the solid foundation that God has laid, Jesus Christ.

Will what you are building endure? Are you building a palace, through the power of the Holy Spirit, in obedience to God? Or are *you* busy building, in your own strength, a little mud-hut on the foundation that God has laid? There is no other foundation than Jesus Christ, but there *is* a choice of building materials that we can use on top. All the energy of the flesh will not last; but all the energy of the Holy Spirit *shall* last forever. All the works of the Holy Spirit *shall* endure.

In verse 13 we come to the actual day of the judgment seat of Christ. First I want to say this, however: Some people are afraid of this day. They think that God is going to hold up their works for everyone to see, because in the next verse Paul says, "**Each one's work will become manifest**" (verse 13a). Our work *is* going to be clearly shown for what it is, so they think, "Oh dear, everyone is going to see exactly what my works add up to." But notice what Paul said next: "**For the Day will declare it, because it will be revealed by fire; and the fire will test each one's work, of what sort it is**" (verse 13b).

If we picture a believer coming along with his or her bag of works, the Lord simply sets fire to the whole lot. The works of the flesh will start burning; so I do not imagine that they will remain for anyone to look at afterwards. Praise God! The things that were done by the Spirit throughout our lives will remain, however. Each of us will thus end up with a pile of ashes and with a pile of gold, silver and precious stones.

This might be bad news for some Christians—the "holier-than-thou" variety. They probably just cannot wait to get to heaven to say to others, "I knew you were working in the flesh. I told you so!" I do not believe that they will ever get the opportunity to say such a thing because, before any of us can stand and criticize others, everyone's 'dead' works of the flesh are going to be burnt up. Praise the name of Jesus! All that will come into view will be the gold, silver and precious stones—the jewels left behind after the fire. What a glorious day!

Some people are going to go before the judgment seat of Christ with a huge bag. However, when the flame is added to the bottom of their bag, there might be only one gold ring left, or a little diamond or an earring. Why? Because such people were dashing about in their own zeal, with their own enthusiasm, in their own strength—not doing the works of God through faith, in the power of the Holy Spirit. Many people say that they are working for God, when it is not for God at all; it is for self. Really, it is their own works that they are doing. That day is going to declare it.

I believe that when we get to heaven we will be in for one or two shocks. There are going to be some who were noted for their ministries, who had their names 'in lights', who will have a huge bag on that day; but what they end up with will be very different. In contrast, there might be a woman whom you would ignore in a crowd, who perhaps never spoke in any meeting at all and whom you wouldn't even notice in your church or fellowship; but she has been faithfully and quietly serving the Lord for years. She is going to come away from the judgment seat of Christ with only a tiny pile of ashes, while almost her whole bag of works will remain intact.

This makes me stand in awe, because it is not a man's reputation, personality, ability to talk, knowledge or anything else that count. None of these truly count for anything. Rather, it is how much the *Holy Spirit is doing through* your life and mine that really counts. We are all equal when it comes to this judgment. You might be intelligent, while someone else might not be quite so gifted. But both of you have the Holy Spirit inside, so you both can produce the fruit of the Spirit and good works for God. Glory to Jesus! *The Holy Spirit is thus the great equalizer*; don't ever believe that death is—it is not. There *is* heaven and there *is* eternal judgment after death. Death is no equalizer at all. Rather, the Holy Spirit is the marvellous equalizer. He turns fools into great and wise men of God. He takes the weak and the foolish, and He transforms them into towers of strength. That is the Lord. Hallelujah! It is the power of the Holy Spirit that counts.

"**If anyone's work which he has built on it endures, he will receive a reward**" (verse 14). The Greek implies "If anyone's work endures, and it will".[3] Some of our works *are* going to endure. If at any time on this earth you have allowed the Holy Spirit to move through you to produce works by His power, you will receive a reward for them. It is the grace of God.

"**If anyone's work is burned, he will suffer loss...**" (verse 15a). The Greek again implies "If, and it is true". Some people really will suffer loss. They will suffer loss of reward.

---

[3] See Appendix 1 in the book "Salvation" by Roger Price for an explanation of how the original New Testament Greek often reveals more meaning in a conditional sentence than comes across in English translations.

"**But he himself will be saved, yet so as through fire**" (verse 15b). This does not refer to Purgatory. It refers to a man who has a huge bag of works; but they are all dead works—they are all fleshly works. God cannot bear those fleshly works in His presence, so they have got to be burnt to ashes. However, the man himself will still be saved, "**yet so as through fire**". This is a tragic man. He might even be someone who preached thousands of sermons, gave Bible studies galore, wrote books, and so on. He might have led numerous meetings, and dashed all around the country or even the world. However, when he gets to the judgment seat of Christ and his works are tested, he finds that all his works amounted to nothing. Nothing that he did was of eternal quality. He did not do anything in the power of the Holy Spirit at all; He always worked in the power of his flesh. Oh, what a tragic man! He will enter heaven with not one jewel to show for all his work. Yet he spent his whole life working for God, so he thought. There are going to be plenty of such people when we get to that place. It is absolutely tragic, when you think of it.

The surest way to have gold is leading people to the Lord. I believe it must be so, because salvation is eternal. Fire is not going to burn up anyone's eternal salvation. So if you bring one person to know the Lord, then definitely you have at least one piece of gold already. That work is going to last through the fire, because nothing can ever separate a believer from the love of God.

"**Do you not know that you are the temple of God and that the Spirit of God dwells in you?**" (verse 16). Believers are the temple of God. That is the point. The Holy Spirit dwells in us. Therefore, we already have all the ability we need and all the power we need to carry out the work of God in our lives. I am so glad Paul ended with this particular truth, because it shows that every Christian has the ability to produce for God thirty, sixty and even a hundredfold, by the power of the Holy Spirit within us. And all of our good works—those done in the power of the Holy Spirit—are going to last straight through into eternity. Glory to Jesus!

How to Produce Enduring Works

We therefore need to understand how to produce works that will endure, and how to guard against producing works that will be burnt up. There are two specific "Do nots!" given in Scripture that instruct us.

In Ephesians 4:30, Paul said, "**And do not grieve the Holy Spirit of God, by whom you were sealed for the day of redemption**". Don't cause the Holy Spirit to cry within you! I know many Christians who are weeping.

However, it is not because of their circumstances. Rather, it is because the Holy Spirit inside of them is weeping. It is our sin, primarily, that causes Him to weep. He is grieved when we refuse to walk in the light with God and try to live independently. If you are allowing sin in your life—sin that you know about, unconfessed sin—then you are grieving the Holy Spirit. And if He's crying within you, He cannot be producing through you. *Before we can produce good works for God, we have to be in fellowship with God*. No one ever produced works of eternal value while not walking in the light with the Lord. That is why the confession of our sins is so important.

The second "Do not" is found in 1 Thessalonians 5:19. Paul said, "**Do not quench the Spirit.**" The idea here is that the Holy Spirit is like a fire burning within us. To quench a fire means to smother it. I could paraphrase this verse, "Give up smothering the fire of the Holy Spirit!" Don't try to smother Him out! Many Christians try to hold the Holy Spirit back in their lives, when He wants to flow out in joy, in love, in various gifts, and so on. Many Christians sit thinking, "I'm too shy. I'm not good enough. What will people think of me?" and they never step out. Often this smothers the Holy Spirit inside. Let Him burn! He is burning with love for Jesus and He wants to burn in each one of us. As soon as He is allowed to work through us, we will begin to produce works of good quality—works that will last through God's judgment fire. And we shall receive a reward for such works. Praise the name of Jesus!

The Matter of Rewards

At the judgment of our works, the Lord Jesus will be sitting as judge, just as a judge used to sit at an athletics meeting. The athletics judge would sit there and assess how well each participant had done: the discus thrower, the javelin thrower, those running the mile, and so on. Then he would hand out the prizes.

What are the prizes that Jesus will hand out? They are *crowns*. Crowns will be given to faithful believers. Our piles of works which last through the fire are going to be replaced by crowns.

In the ancient world, athletes used to train for years and years. The crown they could win was a garland or wreath of foliage—often made from oak leaves—which fitted around the head. Sometimes it contained a bit of ivy, some roses, some violets, or even parsley! Amazingly, they struggled and struggled just to get that one prize. Can you imagine it? It was of no real value, except for the honour of the victory.

In 1 Corinthians chapter 9 there is a short phrase that compares our reward with that of an athlete: "**Now they do it to obtain a perishable crown, but we for an imperishable crown**" (verse 25b). The special crown that athletes won was a sign that they were "*victor ludorum*"—the winner at the games. It was the prize for their special achievement. They would strive and strain for years just to get that tangled mass of leaves, that would last only for a few days before it began to decay! However, we can gain a crown that is not corruptible—that will last forever! How much *more* therefore should we strive through the Spirit to do good works for God, and to live in victory over sin and all the power of the enemy!

I could say much more about the athletic games. There are many pictures that we could paint to show how Christians should behave, based on athletes in the ancient world. In 2 Timothy chapter 4, for example, Paul described himself as a wrestler. He also wrote this, knowing that he might die any day: "**For I am already being poured out as a drink offering, and the time of my departure is at hand. I have fought the good fight...**" (2 Timothy 4:6-7a). Consider Paul's assurance. The word translated "**fought**" here is *agonizomai*, from which we get the word 'agonize'. "I've agonized well," Paul was saying. And sometimes this is exactly how it is in the Spirit, as we press on in our walk with God. "**I have finished the race, I have kept the faith. Finally, there is laid up for me the crown of righteousness, which the Lord, the righteous Judge, will give to me on that day, and not only to me but also to all who have loved His appearing**" (verses 7b-8).

Paul, on 'death-row', soon to die, was confident of his reward. Notice how he mentioned those who love the Lord's appearing. These are people who can die very readily because they have spent their lives truly serving Christ. They are looking forward to dying; they are looking forward to the Lord's return. They haven't wasted a second.

Some Christians, if they knew they were going to die tomorrow, would say, "Lord, I'm not ready to go." But Paul said, "**I have fought the good fight**". He knew the One whom he'd believed (2 Timothy 1:12) and he knew the Word of God. He knew that ahead for him was a wonderful crown—not a perishable tangle of leaves, but an imperishable crown waiting in heaven just for him. Oh, hallelujah! I want that assurance myself; and I believe I have it. I believe I *am* ready to die, and can say, "I have fought the good fight." However, just as Paul wrote earlier in his life, I also know that there is much work to be done first (see Philippians 1:21-25).

I believe we *can* have this assurance, without being presumptuous—that the work we have done has glorified God and has been done for Him, in the power of the Holy Spirit. We can have the assurance that our reward is going to come forth. Let us have no *false* humility. Although it is good to work 'just to please the Lord', we need to realize that God *wants* to give us a crown. There is nothing wrong with looking forward to receiving our reward.

What is going to happen to the crowns that we receive? We see the answer in Revelation 4:10-11, which describes heaven opened, just before the Rapture of the Church. John was looking in, and he saw "**twenty-four elders**". These are probably leaders of the angelic hosts.

"**The twenty-four elders fall down before Him who sits on the throne and worship Him who lives for ever and ever, and cast their crowns before the throne, saying: "You are worthy, O Lord, to receive glory and honour and power; for You created all things, and by Your will they exist and were created**" (verses 10-11). Do you see the picture? Even these elders will take their crowns off and throw them down before the throne, at the feet of Jesus. I therefore believe that every one of us is going to do the same. We are going to enter the great throne room of God, take the crowns that we've been given and throw them down before the feet of Christ. Therefore, it cannot be wrong to desire a crown. I want Jesus to have the biggest and the best crowns. The more I can gain, the better. I don't want other people to notice. I just want to give Him my best. That is why we should be working for the Lord, serving Him faithfully. God is glorified by the Holy Spirit working through us; and we will glorify Him by casting our crowns before Him.

The judgment seat of Christ is coming. Consider it! There are going to be some people who thought they had spent their whole lives working for God, but they are going to enter the throne room of the One they tried to serve with nothing to give Him. Oh, may the Lord preserve us from this! However, on that day there will be no more sorrow and no more tears. Old things will have passed away. But right now, my desire is to give Him the best. I'm sure we all desire this.

Conclusion

The Church is the principal witness for God on the earth today. We who are believers are ambassadors of Christ. God wants us to be His witnesses. He desires to have vessels through whom He can work. Let us therefore say, "Here I am, Lord. Use me! Lord, I'm giving up *my* enthusiasm, I'm giving up *my* ambition. I want *Your* work to be done through me, I want *Your* Spirit to work through me. One day, Lord, I know I'm going to stand before Your judgment seat and my works are going to be judged. Lord, I want as many crowns as possible to cast before Your feet." Let us be servants of God, just as we are His sons.

I must end with a wonderful scripture: Hebrews 10:23-25. This is a word for all of us. "**Let us hold fast the confession of our hope without wavering, for He who promised is faithful**" (verse 23). God has promised us an eternal inheritance, a certain hope; and He is faithful.

"**And let us consider one another in order to stir up love and good works**" (verse 24). We considered earlier how we should provoke one another to love the Lord more. But we should also provoke one another to do good works. When we see other Christians who are walking with God we should be provoked to say: "Lord, I want to be used by You just like she is"; "I want to be full of the fruit of the Holy Spirit just like he is"; "Lord, I want that joy. I want that power. I want the stability that they've got!" We should be provoking one another to love and good works all the time.

"**Not forsaking the assembling of ourselves together, as is the manner of some, but exhorting one another, and so much the more as you see the Day approaching**" (verse 25). This still applies today. There are some who feel they can go it alone; but we need one another desperately. By ourselves we can never do the things that can be achieved when God is working through a body of believers. We need to be in fellowship with one another and submitted to one another. We need to exhort one another every time we meet, share experiences about the Lord and build one another up. Why? Because the Day of the Rapture is approaching and, after that Day, every work that we have produced is going to be judged. I want all that I do to redound to the glory of the Lord!

11. THE FIVE CYCLES OF DISCIPLINE
God's Chastening of Israel

We have mentioned very little ancient history so far; but in this study I am going to introduce us to four major empires that have affected the Jews. Apart from our brief look at Sodom and Gomorrah, and our discussion of the Flood, we have only covered judgment in relation to individuals: the judgment of Satan, the judgment of Jesus, the judgment of believers and their works. Now, as we broaden the scope, we are going to consider national and international judgments, because God also has a hand in the affairs of nations.

THE UNIQUENESS OF ISRAEL

Anyone who studies history and the Bible finds that God has a hand in the affairs of one nation in particular. All other nations fade into mists of time compared with this one nation—Israel. From this viewpoint, the history of any other nation, great or small, whether the USA, Russia or Britain etc., acts only as a backdrop to God's unfolding drama that is going on around His chosen people, the Jews.

When you look back through history you can see that the major empires or nations have ended up going either for or against the Jews. And if you follow history through, you can observe the results of a nation standing either *for* Israel or standing *against* her. That is how interested God is in His beloved people. He is predominantly concerned with this one special nation.

Did you know that the Jews have been around for about 4000 years? Numerous other empires and nations arose later, but have since been lost in the mists of time; but for 4000 years the Jews have been on this earth. It is no wonder that, when Frederick the Great of Prussia (1712-1786) asked his chaplain for a proof of the Bible's authenticity, he immediately replied, "The Jews, your Majesty!" This Bible-believing man said that more than 200 years ago. If the Jews were a proof of the Bible then, they are even more of a proof today!

Why should Israel occupy such a significant place in world history? It is simply this: *God sovereignly chose Abraham (and subsequently Isaac and Jacob), and made a covenant with him.* One of the promises God made to Abraham was that his descendants would be so numerous that they could never be counted (Genesis 13:16). At the same time, God promised to give Abraham and his descendants the land of Israel forever (Genesis 13:14-17). Therefore, for these promises to be fulfilled, some of Abraham's descendants must live on the earth for as long as the earth remains.

Have you ever wondered why there have always been people who have tried to destroy the Jews—why anti-Semitism has been a mark of every single generation for 4000 years? The major reason, I believe, is that *Satan has been trying to destroy the Jews.* Satan, as well as God, has been preoccupied with the Jews. But why should this be the case?

God made a promise to Satan after he rebelled against Him. God promised to humble him and crush him (see Genesis 3:14-15). God also revealed, throughout successive generations, how the One who would principally achieve this, His Messiah, would be a Jew—a descendant of Abraham.

If Satan can break one promise of God, he knows that he will have effectively broken every promise of God. Therefore, Satan wants desperately to destroy every single Jew, because then God's word to Abraham will have been broken. And if he could manage to break *that* word of God, he would get off 'scot-free' because God's promise to destroy him would also effectively be broken. This is the basic reason why the Jews have always been at the centre of persecution and hatred.[1]

We are not dealing, therefore, with just any nation when we consider Israel. We are dealing with things that are 'universe-shattering'. For if the Jews were to disappear from the face of this earth, Satan would escape his impending judgment, God's character would be maligned forever and Satan would have proven God to be a liar— unable to fulfil the promises He made to His people. Every Jew whom you meet should therefore put a smile on your face, because he or she reminds you that the promises of God *are* sure. Glory to God! Thus all history does, and will continue to, revolve around the Jews and the land of Israel.

---

[1] It is probable that Satan's main concern before Christ came was to prevent the Messiah from being born as a Jew. He failed of course! Now that Satan realizes that Jesus Christ, a Jew, triumphed over him through the Cross, he is seeking to enact revenge. Satan is now also trying to break other promises of God to the Jews, such as: they will always remain and be His people; they will be brought back to possess the land of Israel once again; and Jesus will return to Jerusalem and be welcomed as their King. God's faithfulness and His power to keep His promises are thus the real issues at stake.

Do you think, for example, that Russia is so important? Russia *is* important to God and he loves the people there, but Russia is important *as a nation* principally because one day she is going to affect the Jews, either for good or for ill. In the case of Russia, the Bible tells us which it is—and it's for ill.[2] The same principle applies to every other nation.

Israel is a very remarkable nation. The Jews have been just a little group of people at times, and a vast multitude at other times, but as a nation they stand in a unique position with God. If the Jews had remained in fellowship with God, they would have been blessed by Him at all times, and Israel would have stood out and represented clearly the blessings of God, as well as the faithful, covenant-keeping nature of God, to the nations all around. People would always have looked at the Jews and said, "Their God really loves them. Their God really cares for them and looks after them. Who is this God of Israel?" The Jews have always had this unique opportunity of being able to represent their loving, wonderful God and Saviour to the peoples all around—*as a nation*. (We now have a similar opportunity, of course, as members of the Church—the Body of Christ on the earth today.)

Sadly, as we know from the Bible, time and again Israel turned away from her God and rebelled against Him. The people rejected God, went their own way and even turned to idols. As a Father, God always disciplined Israel, just as He disciplines His individual children who get out of fellowship today; and He continues to discipline Israel today. Whatever the type of judgment, God always gives grace first, as we have seen. We are therefore now going to look at how God *graciously* disciplines Israel, in this chapter which I've entitled "The Five Cycles of Discipline".

THE FIVE CYCLES OF DISCIPLINE

God's grace always precedes His judgment. How then was grace given to Israel prior to God's judgment? We have already glimpsed one major way: wonderful men of God were sent—the prophets. There were also many other ways, of course.

The prophets were marvellous, obedient men of God, whom God sent into the midst preaching the message, "Repent! God loves you. Remember His promises to us, His people. Turn back to Him and He will forgive your sins!" They warned the Jews that God would judge the nation if they continued going their own way and would not change their behaviour.

---

[2] See Ezekiel chapters 38 and 39, which are explained in Basic Bible Study 59 entitled "Does Russia have a Future?"

They pleaded with the people to be faithful to God, to turn away from their false gods and wrong aims. If the people of Israel repented, then they quickly experienced God's blessings again. But if they refused to repent, then they experienced God's hand of judgment.

As we know, the prophets were cruelly treated and despised. In most cases, the people refused to hear God's word and chose to carry on in their own sinful ways. Finally God, in His marvellous grace, sent His only begotten Son to Israel, saying, "You are going along the wrong path! Here I am, your King. Serve Me! Love Me!" Now that was grace. However Israel, as a nation, would have nothing to do with Him.

However, God's grace went beyond appealing to the Jews and reminding them of His goodness. It tempered His actual judgment as well. When Israel stepped out of line and refused to heed His word, God did not just intervene and smash them down—as I would have done, and you probably would have done. Rather, He did something wonderful: He disciplined them *gradually*. At first God punished them only a little and, then, if they ignored that, He punished them a bit more. Then, if they still continued to ignore His warnings, He punished them more, and a bit more, until, finally, the discipline became very serious indeed. Because He is gracious, God even told Israel beforehand about each of these stages of discipline in the Law. He then sent the prophets to remind the people of the warnings God had given. This was grace upon grace.

The stages of God's discipline were clearly outlined in the Law—in Leviticus and in Deuteronomy. Thus, as soon as the first stage came into operation the Jews should have thought, "We're under God's discipline, just as the Law describes. We must be out of fellowship, so let's repent!" God would have returned blessing upon them immediately, if they had begun to obey Him again. Five stages, or 'cycles', of discipline were described in the Law. They represent stages of judgment but, clearly, they are another example of grace before judgment too.

BLESSINGS AND JUDGMENTS: LEVITICUS CHAPTER 26

In Leviticus chapter 26 we find the five cycles of discipline listed. However, because there is always grace before judgment, the chapter begins with what would happen if Israel stayed in fellowship with God. It is a wonderful picture; take it in as you read it. God first warned the Jews not to have any idols, and reminded them to keep His Sabbaths and reverence His sanctuary—because He is the LORD their God. Wonderful promises then follow.

"**If you walk in My statutes and keep My commandments, and perform them, then I will give you rain in its season, the land shall yield its produce, and the trees of the field shall yield their fruit. Your threshing shall last till the time of vintage, and the vintage shall last till the time of sowing; you shall eat your bread to the full, and dwell in your land safely**" (verses 3-5). Imagine that! If they would just walk in obedience to God, then they would receive rain just when their crops needed it—because God happens to be in charge of the meteorology department up in heaven! They would always have enough to eat and drink—more than enough to satisfy—*and* they would have safety on every side.

"**I will give peace in the land, and you shall lie down, and none will make you afraid; I will rid the land of evil beasts, and the sword will not go through your land. You will chase your enemies, and they shall fall by the sword before you**" (verse 6-7). How wonderful! They would have no fear. There were wild beasts in the land, but they would be gone. Israel's enemies would just be chased away and defeated.

"**Five of you shall chase a hundred, and a hundred of you shall put ten thousand to flight; your enemies shall fall by the sword before you. For I will look on you favourably and make you fruitful, multiply you and confirm My covenant with you. You shall eat the old harvest, and clear out the old because of the new**" (verses 8-10). There might have been only five of them, but they would be able to chase off a hundred. Ten thousand enemies would say, "Look, here come a hundred Israelites. Let's run!" What a blessing! And each new harvest would be so large and come in so rapidly that they would have to eat the old quickly or dispose of it to make room for the new. How marvellous!

"**I will set My tabernacle among you, and My soul shall not abhor you. I will walk among you and be your God, and you shall be My people. I am the LORD your God, who brought you out of the land of Egypt, that you should not be their slaves; I have broken the bands of your yoke and made you walk upright**" (verses 11-13). This was the greatest promise of all. God would be their God and would walk among them. He had redeemed them from Egypt so that they might enjoy liberty and walk righteously with Him. He wanted a people among whom He could dwell. This was God's purpose.

All this was what God was offering the Jews if they would walk in His statutes and keep His commandments (verse 3)—if they would stay in fellowship with Him. Notice that there were not five cycles of blessing. Rather, they would have *all* of these blessings at once and continuously if they simply remained in a right relationship with their God—by obeying Him. That was the positive side.

"But if you do not obey Me, and do not observe all these commandments, and if you despise My statutes, or if your soul abhors My judgments, so that you do not perform all My commandments, but break My covenant, I also will do this to you..." (verses 14-16a). Now we come to the stages of discipline that Israel would come under, and indeed still comes under today, because of disobedience. However, we can see the grace of God, even on the negative side: for there wouldn't be just *one* great judgment, as was the case with God's blessing. Rather, God's discipline, because He is gracious, would come in stages; and they would receive *all* of the blessings again if they simply repented at any stage.

The Israelites would be dwelling in safety and peace when, all of a sudden, they would notice something: things were starting to go wrong. The description in verses 16b-17 then summarizes the order in which things would go wrong. This was the first cycle, or stage, of God's discipline.

The First Cycle of Discipline

"I will even appoint terror over you..." (Leviticus 26:16b). They were going to experience fear. They had no fear when under God's blessing, but, now that they were out of fellowship, they would start worrying about the situation around them.

"Wasting disease and fever, which shall consume the eyes and cause sorrow of heart" (verse 16c). This refers to terrible disease breaking out in the land. Such epidemics should have prompted the Jews to say, "The Book of Leviticus warns us about this. We must be out of fellowship." They would thus have opportunity to consider these things and to repent.

"And you shall sow your seed in vain, for your enemies shall eat it" (verse 16d). Householders would be asleep in bed when the Moabites, the Edomites, or some other nation would come into the land and plunder the fields. The harvest would be stolen, so they would not get to enjoy it themselves. But it would not be the Edomites or Moabites principally behind this; it would be *God*. He would be saying to Israel: "You're out of fellowship!" It would be His judgment, but it would be His gracious warning also—grace before further judgment.

"I will set My face against you, and you shall be defeated by your enemies. Those who hate you shall reign over you, and you shall flee when no one pursues you" (verse 17). God was warning Israel, "You're going to start losing battles. You'll have to do what your enemies tell you!"

Do you know Christians who are on the run from dangers that might never happen? They are busy building up reserves now, just in case what they fear comes true. If this starts happening to you, immediately get on your knees, confess your sins and get back in fellowship with God.

Israel would thus be given a marvellous opportunity to turn back to God. If the people would not listen, He would simply proceed with a second cycle of discipline: "**And after all this, if you do not obey Me, then I will punish you seven times more for your sins**" (verse 18). This warning meant, "I will punish you more severely." All the successive cycles are preceded by a phrase similar to this.

The Second Cycle of Discipline

The characteristics of the next stage of discipline are given in verses 19 and 20. Things would now start to get worse.

"**I will break the pride of your power**" (Leviticus 26:19a). National pride would dissipate. Instead of being proud to belong to Israel, the people would become afraid and ashamed to mention that they were Jewish.

Next, "**I will make your heavens like iron and your earth like bronze**" (verse 19b). There would be no rain. The people would look up into the sky and, although it might look grey, not a drop of rain would start falling. The ground would become very hard through lack of rain.

"**And your strength shall be spent in vain; for your land shall not yield its produce, nor shall the trees of the land yield their fruit**" (verse 20). The people would work hard, but there would be no reward. "**Then, if you walk contrary to Me, and are not willing to obey Me, I will bring on you seven times more plagues, according to your sins**" (Leviticus 26:21). "Are you going to repent now?" God would be asking, "If you do, then you will immediately enjoy all My blessings again. But if you don't, cycle three of My discipline will begin!" There would thus be another opportunity to repent. God would still be showing grace before judgment.

The Third Cycle of Discipline

"**I will also send wild beasts among you, which shall rob you of your children, destroy your livestock, and make you few in number**" (Leviticus 26:22a). Children would be killed and property destroyed; "**...and your highways shall be desolate**" (verse 22b). No one would walk along the streets because of fear of being attacked.

These warnings were given principally to Israel, of course. But I believe we can also observe similar patterns in other nations, in the past as well as today. I think that, in our day, "wild beasts" is equivalent to 'wild men'; so for us this could represent terrorism, or gangsterism, breaking out in the land. If I were to apply these cycles to Britain, I believe we would now be under cycle three of God's discipline.[3] Our national pride has been broken; gangsterism has broken out; children are being murdered; and people are afraid of being attacked. I believe this nation needs urgently to repent and turn back to God—and I am convinced that God graciously has given us these warning signs. The characteristics of cycles one, two and three are evident for those of us who are looking. The fact that we need to import huge amounts of food and other goods is another example. We are certainly under God's discipline. So far, cycles four and five haven't happened to us—but they might if we do not repent.

The message of all the cycles of discipline was, "There's still time to repent! But if you harden your hearts, God's judgment will become more severe." The Jews could even read what was going to happen to them next if they did not repent. Wasn't that gracious of the Lord? God could have sent just one mighty judgment and wiped them out. But no! He is so loving and gracious. His aim was to bring them to repentance.

God treats other nations, and those of us who are Christians, in a similar way. He does not come and immediately smash us down. Rather, He gives us a little discipline at first and, if we ignore it, He makes it worse. He always disciplines us appropriately.[4]

The Fourth Cycle of Discipline

"And if by these things you are not reformed by Me, but walk contrary to Me, then I also will walk contrary to you, and I will punish you yet seven times for your sins" (Leviticus 26:23-24). This confirms that God's desire was that His discipline should reform His people. It was to change the way in which they were walking.

"And I will bring a sword against you that will execute the vengeance of My covenant" (verse 25a). Notice how God said, **"And I will..."**. *He* was the One who was going to judge Israel—no one else was responsible. Nations were going to rise up and start fighting against Israel; but it would be *God* allowing them to come. It would be His fourth cycle of discipline.

---

[3] This study was recorded in 1976. The same is still true.

[4] There is also the principle that, from those who are given much, much will be required (cf. Luke 12:48b, James 3:1, etc.).

"**When you are gathered together within your cities I will send pestilence among you; and you shall be delivered into the hand of the enemy**" (verse 25b). The people lived in strongly defended cities, with huge walls and large doors that could be shut tight. When they heard that an enemy was coming, they would retreat inside the city walls and lock themselves inside. "But just when you think you are secure inside," God was saying, "diseases will break out in the midst of the city." That meant the enemy would soon be able to defeat them.

"**When I have cut off your supply of bread, ten women shall bake your bread in one oven...**" (verse 26 a). There would be so little wheat that it would take just one oven to bake for ten families. In other words, the food supply would drop to one tenth of normal. Famine would thus break out in the land: "**...and they shall bring back to you your bread by weight, and you shall eat and not be satisfied**" (verse 26b).

The Jews would thus come under the control of an outside force under cycle number four; and there would be famine. Nevertheless, "Repent!" was still God's message. It was still not too late to reverse the decline.

The Fifth Cycle of Discipline

"**And after all this, if you do not obey Me, but walk contrary to Me, then I also will walk contrary to you in fury; and I, even I, will chastise you seven times for your sins**" (Leviticus 26:27-28). God was stressing again, "*I am* the One chastising you. Don't blame your enemies. *I* am responsible." The judgment would now become much more severe—even shocking.

"**You shall eat the flesh of your sons, and you shall eat the flesh of your daughters**" (verse 29). Food would become so scarce that cannibalism would break out. And history proves that this is exactly what happened. The Jews, who loved their own children, indeed did become so short of food on occasions that some actually reached the point of cannibalism within their cities (see for example 2 Kings 6:24-31).

"**I will destroy your high places, cut down your incense altars, and cast your carcasses on the lifeless forms of your idols; and My soul shall abhor you**" (verse 30). The high places were where idols were set up. Tragically, many Jews indeed practised idolatry at those times when they stubbornly refused to repent; and idolatry would become another reason why God would judge them so severely.

"**I will lay your cities waste and bring your sanctuaries to desolation, and I will not smell the fragrance of your sweet aromas. I will bring** the land to desolation, and your enemies who dwell in it shall be astonished at it"** (verse 31-32). The outsiders living in the land would look around at the awful destruction and be shocked. They would say, "This is astonishing. What could these people have done to cause this?" But it would be *God* who had caused it.

Now we come to the main characteristic of the fifth cycle of discipline. **"I will scatter you among the nations and draw out a sword after you; your land shall be desolate and your cities waste. Then the land shall enjoy its sabbaths as long as it lies desolate and you are in your enemies' land; then the land shall rest and enjoy its sabbaths. As long as it lies desolate it shall rest—for the time it did not rest on your sabbaths when you dwelt in it"** (verses 33-35). Not only would the Jews have other nations controlling them in their own land, but they would now be taken away into other countries. The land of Israel would thus lie desolate—untended and fallow.

"And as for those of you who are left, I will send faintness into their hearts in the lands of their enemies; the sound of a shaken leaf shall cause them to flee; they shall flee as though fleeing from a sword, and they shall fall when no one pursues" (verse 36). Those who survived and went into exile would know great fear. They would simply be walking down a street when the sound of a tree rustling in the wind would make them run in terror. **"They shall stumble over one another, as it were before a sword, when no one pursues"** (verse 37a). They would run in such panic that they would fall over one another, even trampling one another to death, when there was no real danger. That is how afraid they would be. This was severe judgment; and it really happened to the Jews.

"And you shall have no power to stand before your enemies. You shall perish among the nations, and the land of your enemies shall eat you up. And those of you who are left shall waste away in their iniquity in your enemies' lands; also in their fathers' iniquities, which are with them, they shall waste away" (verses 37b-39). God would give His people over to perish in their iniquity.

GRACE IS ALWAYS AVAILABLE

This would be God's judgment, because His people had ignored His grace again and again, continually refusing to turn back to Him and repent. Nevertheless, look what God then said, right at the end of the fifth cycle of discipline. **"But if they confess their iniquity and the iniquity of their fathers, with their unfaithfulness in which they were unfaithful to Me,** and that they also have walked contrary to Me, and that I also have walked contrary to them and have brought them into the land of their enemies; if their uncircumcised hearts are humbled, and they accept their guilt—then I will remember My covenant with Jacob, and My covenant with Isaac and My covenant with Abraham I will remember; I will remember the land**" (Leviticus 26:40-42).

Oh, hallelujah! "It is still not too late!", God was saying. This was grace again. "**Yet for all that, when they are in the land of their enemies, I will not cast them away, nor shall I abhor them, to utterly destroy them and break My covenant with them; for I am the LORD their God**" (verse 44).

God would still be offering grace and blessing to Israel, even under His most severe judgment. Under the first cycle of discipline, they could repent. If the second cycle came in, they could repent. Under the third cycle, they could repent, and so on, right down to the fifth cycle. God would *never* break His covenant with Israel. He will *always* be their God. Israel will never be utterly destroyed.

THE FOURTH AND FIFTH CYCLES IN DEUTERONOMY

We find the five cycles of discipline described again in Deuteronomy chapter 28. The blessings that Israel would experience if they obeyed God are described first again, in verses 1 to 14. Then, the curses that would come as a result of not obeying God are outlined, starting in verse 15. The difference between Deuteronomy 28 and Leviticus 26, the passage we have just looked at, is that Deuteronomy does not list the cycles in order. Also, the description of the curses that would come as part of the fourth and fifth cycles is much more detailed in Deuteronomy. In fact, be warned! The picture is horrific.

"**Moreover all these curses shall come upon you and pursue and overtake you, until you are destroyed...**" (Deuteronomy 28:45a). In other words, "Wherever you try to escape, these curses are going to follow you." Why? "**...Because you did not obey the voice of the LORD your God, to keep His commandments and His statutes which He commanded you. And they shall be upon you for a sign and a wonder, and on your descendants for ever. Because you did not serve the LORD your God with joy and gladness of heart, for the abundance of all things**" (verses 45b-47). These curses would be a sign to Israel that they had not served God with joy and gratitude, as they should have.

177

From verse 48, the fourth and fifth cycles of God's discipline are described vividly. "**Therefore you shall serve your enemies, whom the LORD will send against you, in hunger, in thirst, in nakedness, and in need of all things; and he will put a yoke of iron on your neck until he has destroyed you. The LORD will bring a nation against you from afar, from the end of the earth, as swift as the eagle flies, a nation whose language you will not understand**" (verses 48-49). A foreign nation would come in and take over the land of Israel, and the Jews would have to serve their enemies. For the Jews, who were usually proud of their nation, this was a terrible prospect—they served no one!

Next, God described the type of foreign nation they would serve—and this was a description of the Assyrians in particular: "**A nation of fierce countenance, which does not respect the elderly nor show favour to the young. And they shall eat the increase of your livestock and the produce of your land, until you are destroyed; they shall not leave you grain or new wine or oil, or the increase of your cattle or the offspring of your flocks, until they have destroyed you. They shall besiege you at all your gates until your high and fortified walls, in which you trust, come down throughout all your land; and they shall besiege you at all your gates throughout all your land which the LORD your God has given you**" (verses 50-52). As God had said in Leviticus, Israel's cities would be besieged, the food supply would be plundered and cut off, and the result would be famine.

The next few verses describe the cannibalism that would result. If you want to know just how terrible this could be, I suggest you read Josephus's account of the Jewish-Roman War of AD 66-73, in which he went into detail about the cannibalism that actually took place. When people are desperately hungry they will indeed think very differently to normal and some *will* actually turn to cannibalism.[5]

---

[5] See Josephus's "Wars of the Jews". The terrible famine is described in Book V: Chapter X: Section 3, for example. In VI:III:4, Josephus refers to a Jewish mother, Mary, who killed and roasted her infant son. The other Jews were horrified. There were also instances of cannibalism during the extreme famine that occurred when Jerusalem was besieged by Babylon, hundreds of years earlier in 588-586 BC (see Lamentations 4:4-10). There is also an example of cannibalism recorded in 2 Kings 6:24-31, which took place when Syria besieged Samaria.

There was a case, some time ago, where a plane came down in the Andes Mountains in South America, and the survivors began eating human flesh just to keep themselves alive. The survivors were asked afterwards, "How could you do it?", but they were so hungry they simply had to do it.

"You shall eat the fruit of your own body, the flesh of your sons and your daughters whom the LORD your God has given you, in the siege and desperate straits in which your enemy shall distress you" (verse 53). As you read this, remember that the people are in desperate straits—they truly are starving. They probably have already eaten all of their shoes and all of the bits of leather in their houses just to try to get some sustenance. All they would have to do to avoid this degrading level of cannibalism is repent, and God would remove the curse from the land. The Bible does not mask its language. It was all a warning from God. He wanted Israel to avoid this situation. If you are of a weak constitution, I suggest you don't read on!

"The man among you who is sensitive and very refined will be hostile towards his brother, towards the wife of his bosom, and towards the rest of his children whom he leaves behind" (verse 54). This describes a man who was a very nice man in normal life. He was very refined. Even that man—the most gracious man you had ever met, probably a connoisseur of fine foods—would consider his own brother, wife and children as his enemies.

That would be bad enough; but the next verse reveals why: **"So that he will not give any of them the flesh of his children whom he will eat, because he has nothing left in the siege and desperate straits in which your enemy shall distress you at all your gates"** (verses 55). Even this refined man would eat some of his children, possibly after killing them himself. However, he would refuse to give any flesh to his brother, wife or remaining children to eat. It seems he would rather have them starve to death so that he could eat them as well. That is cannibalism of the worst order. It is appalling even to consider it.

The women would behave just as shockingly: **"The tender and delicate woman among you, who would not venture to set the sole of her foot on the ground because of her delicateness and sensitivity, will refuse to the husband of her bosom, and to her son and her daughter, her placenta which comes out from between her feet, and her children whom she bears; for she will eat them secretly for lack of all things in the siege and desperate straits in which your enemy shall distress you at all your gates"** (verse 56-57).

We need to remember that this fifth cycle of discipline would only occur a long time after God's discipline had started. It would come only as the result of prolonged, deliberate rebellion. God was warning Israel very clearly what could happen; and I believe He described it so vividly in order that the Jews would never want to get to this fifth cycle. It was the graciousness of God again. However, as history proves, the people ignored God's warnings. They chose to believe that God did not mean what He said in His Word, despite every indication to the contrary.

"If you do not carefully observe all the words of this law that are written in this book, that you may fear this glorious and awesome name, THE LORD YOUR GOD, then the LORD will bring upon you and your descendants extraordinary plagues—great and prolonged plagues—and serious and prolonged sicknesses. Moreover He will bring back on you all the diseases of Egypt, of which you were afraid, and they shall cling to you" (verses 58-60). God would make their plagues and sicknesses absolutely appalling. Some would be like those with which God afflicted Egypt. Other nations would probably look at Israel and say, "How could they have fallen to this level?"

"And you shall be plucked from off the land which you go to possess. Then the LORD will scatter you among all peoples, from one end of the earth to the other, and there you shall serve other gods, which neither you nor your fathers have known—wood and stone. And among those nations you shall find no rest, nor shall the sole of your foot have a resting place; but there the LORD will give you a trembling heart, failing eyes, and anguish of soul. Your life shall hang in doubt before you; you shall fear day and night, and have no assurance of life. In the morning you shall say, "Oh, that it were evening!" And at evening you shall say, "Oh, that it were morning!" because of the fear which terrifies your heart, and because of the sight which your eyes see" (verses 63b-67). The people would be scattered from their own land, have to worship idols and would experience unremitting restlessness. They would wish their lives away because of their terrible fear.

"And the LORD will take you back to Egypt in ships, by the way of which I said to you, "You shall never see it again." And there you shall be offered for sale to your enemies as male and female slaves, but no one will buy you" (verse 68). Egypt typifies a land of bondage. "You'll be taken back into bondage, just like in Egypt," God was saying, "but no one will want to buy you, in view of your bad condition!"

This is the fifth cycle of discipline. Let me emphasize that—the *fifth*. The fourth cycle would see enemies coming into the land and conquering it; but the Jews would still be allowed to stay in their land. They would just have to pay a tribute or tax to the enemy that controlled them. However, the fifth cycle was when their enemies would actually take the Jews back home with them and scatter them. It would come only after prolonged rebellion, if the Jews insisted on going their own way and serving other gods.

The Jews would be taken to Assyria and scattered, or to Babylon and scattered. Or, as has been the case for the past 1900 years, they would be scattered all around the world. God was warning them clearly, "If you won't listen to Me when your enemy is in the land, then the day will come when they'll take you away—and you'll *have to* serve their idols then!"

Examples from Israel's History

It is tragic that, on many occasions, Israel did not heed God's warnings. As history proceeded, the Jews refused to listen to God and refused to obey Him time and again. And several times Israel even experienced the fifth cycle of discipline.

I am now going to outline four occasions on which Israel got to the fourth stage of God's discipline. On three of these occasions they still refused to repent, and the fifth cycle of discipline came in. However, on one occasion they did listen to God, and we will see the dramatic consequence.

1. Israel taken away by the Assyrians (c. 721 BC)

The Assyrians, under Tiglath-Pileser III and then Shalmaneser V, came into the land and began attacking the northern kingdom of Israel, because the children of Israel had sinned and committed idolatry (2 Kings 17:1-23). God raised up wonderful prophets, such as Amos and Hosea, who preached the word of God to Israel and warned, "Look! We are under God's judgment. Turn from your evil ways! The northern kingdom will come to an end—if we don't repent!" But the people refused to listen.

"**Now it came to pass in the fourth year of King Hezekiah, which was the seventh year of Hoshea the son of Elah, king of Israel...**" (2 Kings 18:9a). Hoshea was the last king of Israel. Hezekiah was meanwhile king of the southern kingdom of Judah. The reference to Hezekiah was to provide a cross-check on the date. Thus it was in the seventh year of Hoshea's reign (c. 724 BC) "**...that Shalmaneser king of Assyria came up against Samaria and besieged it**" (verse 9b). Samaria was the capital of Israel and was now the only remaining part of Israel yet to be defeated. The Israelites retreated inside the city and secured all the gates; and Shalmaneser put his army all around the outside.

"**And at the end of three years they took it**" (verse 10a). The Assyrians were very patient. They just sat there, while the Jews inside used up all of their food and water. The Assyrians probably made a few warning noises from time to time, to make the Jews really afraid! But do you see God's grace here? Israel had three years to repent, stuck inside the city. That was grace. If you were stuck inside your town for three years, don't you think you would begin to consider, "How can I get out of this?" I expect there were prophets inside Samaria too, saying, "Repent! That's all you've got to do. Just repent!" But the people ignored God's word. The result was that, at the end of three years (c. 721 BC), the Assyrians took the city: "**In the sixth year of Hezekiah, that is, the ninth year of Hoshea king of Israel, Samaria was taken**" (verse 10b).

The fifth cycle of discipline then came: "**Then the king of Assyria carried Israel away captive to Assyria, and put them in Halah and by the Habor, the river of Gozan, and in the cities of the Medes**" (verse 11). Why was this? "**Because they did not obey the voice of the LORD their God, but transgressed His covenant and all that Moses the servant of the LORD had commanded; and they would neither hear nor do them**" (verse 12). Because the people refused to listen to God and obey Him, the fifth cycle of discipline came upon Israel. The northern kingdom was thus destroyed. Tens of thousands of Jews were taken captive and deported.

2. The Assyrians withdraw from Jerusalem at the time of Hezekiah (c. 701 BC)

The second example follows on, beginning in verse 13, and involves events just a few years later in the southern kingdom of Judah. This is our example of a 'success', and it involves King Hezekiah.

Hezekiah had refused to serve the Assyrians (2 Kings 18:7). Israel had just been taken out of the land by Assyria—and in fact did not come back again. Now we come on to Judah. "**And in the fourteenth year of King Hezekiah, Sennacherib king of Assyria came up against all the fortified cities of Judah and took them**" (2 Kings 18:13). The Assyrians soon headed south into Judah and began to be victorious there. Assyria's attack was so successful in fact that Sennacherib, king of Assyria, claimed the capture of 46 strong, walled cities. In the end, only Jerusalem and one or two other cities were not conquered. Hezekiah was in Jerusalem.

Hezekiah offered to pay Sennacherib to go away, but he sent a great army against Jerusalem (verses 14-17) and told Hezekiah to give in. What was Hezekiah's reaction? "**And so it was, when King Hezekiah heard it, that he tore his clothes, covered himself with sackcloth, and went into the house of the LORD**" (2 Kings 19:1). Hallelujah! That was a different reaction altogether. "**Then he sent Eliakim, who was over the household, Shebna the scribe, and the elders of the priests, covered with sackcloth, to Isaiah the prophet, the son of Amoz**" (verse 2). Hezekiah had a wonderful prophet with him—Isaiah. I cannot think of a better person to have with you in such a crisis than him! Hezekiah was going to turn to the LORD. He was admitting, "LORD, I can't do anything. We need to repent." The sackcloth was a sign of repentance.

What did God do? Did He say, "I'll gradually take the Assyrians away soon"? Not at all! Rather, God caused the king of Assyria to hear a rumour of an enemy coming against him, so he went away (see 2 Kings 19:6-8).

However, the king of Assyria again sent messengers to Hezekiah, threatening to return and take the city (verses 9-14). When he received the letter, "**Hezekiah went up to the house of the LORD, and spread it before the LORD. Then Hezekiah prayed before the LORD...**" (verses 14b-15a). Hezekiah thus again turned to God for help. His prayer ended, "**Now therefore, O LORD our God, I pray, save us from his hand, that all the kingdoms of the earth may know that You are the LORD God, You alone**" (verse 19).

Immediately, Isaiah sent a wonderful message to Hezekiah. "**Then Isaiah the son of Amoz sent to Hezekiah, saying, "Thus says the LORD God of Israel: 'That which you have prayed to Me against Sennacherib king of Assyria I have heard.' This is the word which the LORD has spoken concerning him...**'" (verses 20-21a). It was quite a long message. It ended like this: "**Therefore thus says the LORD concerning the king of Assyria: 'He shall not come into this city...'** " (verse 32a). This was against all reason. Assyria had just destroyed 46 cities. The Jews had almost no army in Jerusalem, and the Assyrians were all the way around. Yet Isaiah was saying, "Don't worry! God has heard your prayer. They won't enter the city!"

The news got even better: " '**...nor shoot an arrow there, nor come before it with shield, nor build a siege-mound against it'** " (verse 32b). Isaiah was saying that there wouldn't even be a fight. The Assyrians would not even try battering the doors down or building a siege-mound.[6] "'**By the way that he came, by the same shall he return; and he shall not come into this city,' says the LORD. 'For I will defend this city, to save it for My own sake and for My servant David's sake'**" (verses 33-34).

Why would this happen? Simply because Hezekiah had turned back to God. Oh, that the Jews had repented more often! Then, they would have

---

[6] A siege-mound was the system whereby an army would dump large quantities of rocks, earth or sand in front of the wall of the city it was trying to conquer. It would thus make a ramp up to the top of the wall, so that the soldiers could charge up this runway, pass over the wall and enter the city.

been a glorious nation continuously, living in peace with no one attacking them, enjoying and exhibiting God's wonderful blessings all of the time.

Now we see the manner in which God did it. "**And it came to pass on a certain night that the angel of the LORD went out, and killed in the camp of the Assyrians one hundred and eighty-five thousand; and when people arose early in the morning, there were the corpses—all dead**" (verse 35). What an incredible event: 185,000 Assyrians suddenly died in one night. Next day, when the Jews awoke and looked over the wall, the Assyrian army was no longer besieging their city, but lay dead. That's God! The Jews had not done anything—except repented!

"**So Sennacherib king of Assyria departed and went away, returned home, and remained at Nineveh**" (verse 36). If you read about all of Sennacherib's campaigns, on Assyrian tablets and in other inscriptions, there is a place where Sennacherib boasted of how he came against Hezekiah; but the history ends there![7] Then it records how he was killed later by two of his sons (as verse 37 tells us). All of Sennacherib's great victories were described in detail; but the Assyrians didn't like recording defeats. It was *God* who had defeated them!

That was a success: Judah repented and God miraculously delivered the Jews. What a shame it was, however, that Judah did not learn from this. For it was only 100 years later that we come to the third example and, tragically, it was another failure.

3. Judah taken away to Babylon by Nebuchadnezzar (c. 606 to 586 BC)

Several decades later, Egypt deposed the king of Judah and forced Judah to pay a tribute (2 Kings 23:31-37). Then, in 606 BC the Babylonians took over and came up against Jehoiakim, the new king of Judah, and he became Nebuchadnezzar's vassal for three years. Then King Jehoiakim rebelled and the LORD sent others against him too. This happened to Judah because of the sins of King Manasseh (2 Kings 24:1-4). Nebuchadnezzar spared Jehoiakim, but took away some of the Jews from the land, including some of the king's descendants and nobles (Daniel 1:3), and some of the articles from the Temple. It was the beginning of the fifth cycle of discipline.

---

[7] The famous inscription on the Taylor Prism reads, "As for Hezekiah the Judean [Jew]....like a caged bird within Jerusalem, his royal city, I shut [him] up." Sennacherib could not boast of capturing the city. Therefore, he made no mention of his army being defeated and just boasted of how he had besieged Jerusalem!

In 598 BC, Nebuchadnezzar returned and besieged Jerusalem. He made Jerusalem submit a second time and took 10,000 captives away (including the new king, Jehoiachin, members of the royal family and household, some 3000 nobles, the prophet Ezekiel and treasures from the Temple and the king's house).

When Zedekiah, the last king of Judah, was put on the throne, he rebelled against King Nebuchadnezzar. He turned to Egypt for help, but the Babylonian army still overran the land and took the cities. Judah's final downfall came in c. 588 to 586 BC, when Jerusalem was besieged for more than a year. It was finally destroyed in 586 BC, and the fifth cycle of discipline came in. This was only about 100 years after Hezekiah had repented with such a dramatic result; but now the people refused to repent. We will look at the account in Chronicles this time.

"**Zedekiah was twenty-one years old when he became king, and he reigned eleven years in Jerusalem. He also did evil in the sight of the LORD his God, and did not humble himself before Jeremiah the prophet, who spoke from the mouth of the LORD**" (2 Chronicles 36:11-12). Jeremiah had already been preaching for about 30 years when Zedekiah became king, saying, "Repent!"; but Zedekiah refused to listen. Jeremiah continued to prophesy throughout the final siege, saying that Judah's only hope now was to submit to Nebuchadnezzar. He had warned, "If you don't repent, then you know what's coming upon you—70 years of captivity!" He had even foretold the exact number of years (see Jeremiah 25:11-12; 29:10).

"**And he [Zedekiah] also rebelled against King Nebuchadnezzar, who had made him swear an oath by God; but he stiffened his neck and hardened his heart against turning to the LORD God of Israel. Moreover all the leaders of the priests and the people transgressed more and more, according to all the abominations of the nations, and defiled the house of the LORD which he had consecrated in Jerusalem**" (2 Chronicles 36:13-14). Zedekiah had taken an oath of loyalty to Nebuchadnezzar, but he broke it. He and all the leaders of Judah stubbornly refused to turn back to God. They were thus the ones primarily responsible for the fall of Judah (cf. Lamentations 4:12-13).

Here was the grace. "**And the LORD God of their fathers sent warnings to them by His messengers, rising up early and sending them...**" (2 Chronicles 36:15a). This refers to the prophets, whom God had sent time and again. The idiom "rising up early" implies 'regularly, time after time'. These messengers had come continually, saying, "You've got to repent!" The Jews should have remembered what had happened to Sennacherib.

But the king, and all the leaders of the priests and the people refused to bow the knee to the LORD. Note that God had sent His messengers **"because He had compassion on His people and on His dwelling-place"** (verse 15b)—because of His love for the Jews.

"But they mocked the messengers of God, despised His words, and scoffed at His prophets, until the wrath of the LORD arose against His people, till there was no remedy. Therefore He brought against them the king of the Chaldeans, who killed their young men with the sword in the house of their sanctuary, and had no compassion on young man or virgin, on the aged or the weak; He gave them all into his hand. And all the articles from the house of God, great and small, the treasures of the house of the LORD, and the treasures of the king and of his leaders, all these he took to Babylon" (verses 16-18). Nebuchadnezzar took away all the articles that were in the Temple and carted them off to Babylon. And the fifth cycle of discipline now came: **"And those who escaped from the sword he carried away to Babylon, where they became servants to him and his sons until the reign of the kingdom of Persia, to fulfil the word of the LORD by the mouth of Jeremiah, until the land had enjoyed her Sabbaths. As long as she lay desolate she kept Sabbath, to fulfil seventy years"** (verses 20-21).

4. Worldwide Dispersion after AD 135

The fourth example occurred much later, and relates to the time of Jesus Christ. The Romans were occupying the land, and it was the fourth cycle of discipline again. As Jesus made clear to the Jews in a number of parables, because they had not listened to the prophets whom God had sent, God had now sent His own Beloved Son to them. Would they listen to Him?

Jesus even told the Jews exactly what would happen if they would not repent. What grace! He said that armies would come against Jerusalem, many would be killed, Jerusalem would be taken over by Gentiles and the survivors would be led away captive to all nations (see Luke 21:20-24). Nevertheless, as a nation, the majority of Jews refused to repent and would not accept Jesus as their king and Messiah.

God gave still more grace to Israel, even after the death and resurrection of Jesus Christ. The unbelieving Jews were given more time to turn back to God. Now God spoke to them through the preaching and witness of the apostles and believers in the early Church.

Finally, 40 years after John the Baptist and Jesus Christ ministered in Israel, from AD 66 to 73, Roman soldiers came and took over the land fully, suppressing all opposition from the Jews. Jerusalem fell to the

Romans, under Titus, in AD 70. Then, following a further Jewish rebellion, most of the Jews in the land were scattered by AD 135.[8]

For some 1900 years, the Jews have remained scattered. However, now we are seeing them regathered into the land of Israel! For 1900 years they have been under the fifth cycle of discipline, and they are still under it in part at this present time. However, they are beginning to come out, as an increasing number turn to the Lord. Hallelujah! The nation of Israel has miraculously been 'reborn' and God is regathering Jews to the land from all corners of the world. We must pray regularly that Israel might continue to turn back to God and be saved.

LESSONS FOR THE GENTILES

If God so deals with Israel, then let those of us in other nations beware. For if He does not spare His beloved Israel from such discipline, what about nations like ourselves, that reject the Lord? The Jews are God's own special people, whom He has promised to preserve. If He has dealt with them so harshly at times, should we expect less harsh treatment?

To end, we need to look quickly at an important passage in Romans chapter 11, which describes the relationship between the Jewish people and the Church. The natural branches of God's cultivated olive tree refer to the Jews. It contains a warning for us in the Church.

"And if some of the branches [unbelieving Jews] **were broken off, and you** [believing Gentiles]**, being a wild olive tree, were grafted in among them, and with them became a partaker of the root and fatness of the olive tree, do not boast against the branches. But if you boast, remember that you do not support the root, but the root supports you. You will say then, "Branches were broken off that I might be grafted in." Well said..."** (verses 17-20a). Do you see the pride here? Some people in the Church will be tempted to think, "If the Jews were cut off and God has grafted *us* in, then we must be more important or more worthy than Israel." But that is a wrong conclusion. It is true that some of the natural branches have currently been broken off, but so what? Look at what Paul said next: **"...Because of unbelief they were broken off, and you**

---

[8]The Church was at first entirely Jewish. It comprised only Jewish believers, its apostles and prophets were Jewish and it was Jewish in understanding and influence. From Acts chapter 10 onwards, Gentiles began to hear the good news of Jesus Christ and were added to the Church, after they, too, had received the blessing of the promised Holy Spirit (Acts 10: 44-48).

stand by faith. Do not be haughty, but fear. For if God did not spare the natural branches, He may not spare you either" (verses 20b-21).[9]

Britain, France, Russia, China, the USA and any other nation can say what they like about Israel; but they are in greater danger than Israel ever could be. For Britain or France truly could be wiped off the face of the earth, never to exist again. However, Israel will never cease to exist. Russia, China or the USA could simply disappear from the face of the earth, if God's judgment comes in full upon them; but Israel will never disappear (see Jeremiah 31:35-37). The Jews will remain God's people forever.

Whatever country we live in, we need such humility before God that we will love Him and serve Him in obedience, with all our hearts and minds. Then indeed, just as God spared the Jews when they repented, He will also spare us.

This message is also for the Church. Let us beware of ever having pride, either about our position with the Lord or about the blessings that Israel forsook—that we might fully appreciate our position with the Lord and continue to enjoy His grace towards us. Let us walk in humility at all times. Amen.

---

[9] More details about the relationship between Israel and the Church, covering the key chapters Romans 9-11, are given in Special Topic Studies 91-92 entitled "The Truth about Israel". The Church has not replaced the Jews as God's chosen people, nor does it have a separate covenant with God, apart from Israel. Rather, Gentile believers have, in Christ, entered into the covenants and promises God made with Israel forever (Galatians 3:28-29). All of the promises God made to Israel will be fulfilled and, one day, all Israel will be saved (Romans 11:26). Israel's calling and gifts are irrevocable (Romans 11:29). Even the stumbling and hardening in part of Israel and the grafting in of the Gentiles through faith were revealed in the Old Testament scriptures. God's masterplan was that He might have mercy on all. The Church has come to receive mercy through Israel's disobedience, that Israel might receive mercy through the mercy shown to the Church (Romans 11:30-32). As Paul concluded, **"Oh, the depth of the riches both of the wisdom and knowledge of God! How unsearchable are His judgments and His ways past finding out!..."** (Romans 11:33ff).

12. HORNS AND CRAFTSMEN
The Judgment of Nations

We have seen how God used certain nations to chasten Israel, as part of His five cycles of discipline. Now I want to consider the different but related matter of how God deals with the Gentile nations—especially when they become anti-Semitic. Many of the nations God used to discipline the Jews fell into Satan's camp and moved into wilful persecution of the Jews.

As soon as that happened, God responded. This is an important matter for all nations today, because God still responds whenever anyone begins mistreating His beloved people, the Jews. He will react today if Britain or America starts opposing Israel. He will likewise respond if underlying hatred of Jews in Russia is allowed to prevail.

In this chapter we will discuss a passage in Zechariah which, I think, best describes God's mind as far as nations that judge the Jews is concerned. Before looking at it, however, we will look at the first promises God made to Abraham in Genesis chapter 12.

THE IMPORTANCE OF BLESSING ISRAEL

"**Now the LORD had said to Abram: "Get out of your country, from your kindred and from you father's house, to a land that I will show you. I will make you a great nation; I will bless you and make your name great; and you shall be a blessing. I will bless those who bless you, and I will curse him who curses you; and in you all the families of the earth shall be blessed**" (Genesis 12:1-3). This was the call of Abram, who later became Abraham. He was from Chaldea originally, but God called him out of that land.[1]

---

[1] Later, in Genesis 14:13, he is called "**Abram the Hebrew**". The word "Hebrew" probably means 'one who crossed over' or 'one from the other side'. Abram crossed over the River Euphrates (Joshua 24:3) to come out of Chaldea, and then he crossed over the River Jordan as he came into the Promised Land. It could mean 'son of Eber' (see Genesis 10:24-25; Luke 3:35), but the name Eber also comes from the verb 'to cross over'.

God's promise that He would bless all the families of the earth in Abraham was a reference not only to Abraham and the Jews, but to the Lord Jesus Christ—a descendant of Abraham. Through Him, all the families of the earth *are* blessed: because, any person from any nation can turn to the Lord Jesus and be saved, and receive a wonderful inheritance in Him.

It is essential for us to understand the promise, "**I will bless those who bless you, and I will curse him who curses you**" (verse 3a). God will bless any nation or group that blesses the Jews. It is true. What a tragedy it is, therefore, that our Government and most others do not realize it. God will, however, curse any person or nation that curses the Jews. That is also God's principle. And if we look through history at how nations that have influenced the Jews have, in so doing, influenced their own destiny, it is a most remarkable study.

Take, for example, the Spanish Empire. While the Spaniards looked after the Jews, their empire was great. But when they began to persecute the Jews, their empire soon came to an end. The Jews were then expelled from Spain. Many Jews came to Britain. The British took them in and looked after them—and the British Empire began to grow! That's history.

Any nation that has hated the Jews has fallen. When Hitler's Third Reich, for example, began mistreating the Jews, it was not many years before it collapsed. God will not stand for anti-Semitism among the nations, or allow it to go unpunished.

THE HORNS AND THE CRAFTSMEN

The passage we are going to look at in this chapter is Zechariah's famous vision of the horns and the craftsmen:

"**Then I raised my eyes and looked, and there were four horns. And I said to the angel who talked with me, "What are these?" So he answered me, "These are the horns that have scattered Judah, Israel, and Jerusalem." Then the LORD showed me four craftsmen. And I said, "What are these coming to do?" So he said, "These are the horns that scattered Judah, so that no one could lift up his head; but the craftsmen are coming to terrify them, to cast out the horns of the nations that lifted up their horn against the land of Judah to scatter it**" (Zechariah 1:18-21)

Can you see how this passage is divided into two halves? In verses 18 and 19 we have four horns mentioned; then in verses 20 and 21 we have four craftsmen. We therefore need first to answer the question: What does a horn stand for in the Bible? When God showed someone a horn or talked about a horn, what did He mean? This will help us identify those to whom the horns and craftsmen refer.[2]

THE MEANING OF HORNS

Remember the principle we have seen before, that the Bible is its own commentary. We can therefore look at where horns are mentioned elsewhere in the Bible, to find out what they represent.

In Daniel chapter 7, we have a vision described.[3] "**After this I saw in the night visions, and behold, a fourth beast, dreadful and terrible, exceedingly strong. It had huge iron teeth; it was devouring, breaking in pieces, and trampling the residue with its feet. It was different from all the beasts that were before it, and it had ten horns. I was considering the horns, and there was another horn, a little one, coming up among them, before whom three of the first horns were plucked out by the roots. And there, in this horn, were eyes like the eyes of a man, and a mouth speaking pompous words**" (Daniel 7:7-8). What does all this mean? Fortunately, this vision is interpreted in verses 23 and 24.

"**The fourth beast shall be a fourth kingdom on earth, which shall be different from all other kingdoms, and shall devour the whole earth, trample it and break it in pieces**" (verse 23). This actually refers to the Roman Empire—or the 'kingdom' of Rome. "**The ten horns are ten kings who shall arise from this kingdom. And another shall rise after them; he shall be different from the first ones, and shall subdue three kings**" (verse 24). Thus, here we have ten kings of this kingdom; an eleventh king then comes up who destroys three of the kings, so that eight remain.

What is a horn then? It represents a king. In more general terms, it represents *power and might on a national or international level*. We see the same again in Revelation chapter 17, which speaks about exactly the same empire. "**And the ten horns which you saw are ten kings**" (verse 12a).

---

[2] The implied meaning of the four craftsmen is 'horn-cutters' or 'horn-smashers'. They terrify and cast out the horns. The Hebrew word translated "craftsmen" means an 'artificer' or 'engraver', that is a skilled artisan or hammerer, of any material. It could thus mean a carpenter, mason or smith, depending on whether the material in view is wood, stone or metal. (The translation "carpenters" in the AV assumes that wood was in view.) The word was also sometimes used for a 'grave-cutter'—someone who dug out a grave from solid rock.

[3] The Book of Daniel is a very remarkable and wonderful book. It has similarities with, and can help us to understand, the Book of Revelation. Some background on why the Book of Daniel is so remarkable is given in Basic Bible Study 36, entitled "The Fall of Babylon (Part 2)".

This knowledge helps us to understand a number of other passages. We will look at two of them. In Jeremiah 48:25, God said, "**"The horn of Moab is cut off, and his arm is broken," says the LORD**". The horn refers to the king. Therefore, the king of Moab is killed; and his "arm"—that is, his might and power—is broken. Thus, the prophet's message was, "He is not going to be any more trouble!" The meaning is clear, once we understand the imagery of a horn.

In another passage, which I like very much, we find a wry humour in God's words—which is close to sarcasm. In Amos 6:13, the prophet gave a warning to the Jews—who were boasting. Israel had just conquered two cities between Samaria and Damascus, called Lo Debar and Karnaim. These were small cities, yet the Jews were proud about their victories. God said to them: "**You who rejoice over Lo Debar, who say, "Have we not taken Karnaim for ourselves by our own strength?"**" (verse 13). God was speaking sarcastically, because Lo Debar meant 'thing of nought' or 'nothingness', while Karnaim, the name of the second town, meant 'horns' or 'peaks'. It was a pun. God was thus reminding them that they had not really done so much; they had not won by their own strength! It was a clever way for God to get His message through. He went on, "**"But, behold, I will raise up a nation against you, O house of Israel," says the LORD God of hosts**" (verse 14a). "Watch out," God warned, "If you get proud, I'll send a nation against you that you *won't* be able to destroy!"

Let us go back and see what we find in Zechariah's vision. His account of it begins, "**Then I raised my eyes and looked, and there were four horns**" (Zechariah 1:18). To lift up the eyes means 'to concentrate on'. Zechariah was concentrating fully on what he saw. (What a tragedy it is that many in the Church do not concentrate on the important message of this vision as Zechariah did.) Four horns was what Zechariah saw before him—and we now know that these represented four kingdoms or empires, with their leaders.

THE FOUR HORNS

It is very helpful for us that Zechariah had an angel with him to interpret who these horns were. "**And I said to the angel who talked with me, "What are these?" So he answered me, "These are the horns that have scattered Judah, Israel, and Jerusalem"**" (verse 19). After the time of King Solomon, the Jews were split into two kingdoms in the land. To the north were ten tribes, called Israel, with their capital at Samaria. To the south was the southern kingdom of Judah, consisting of two tribes, with their capital at Jerusalem.

The four horns that Zechariah saw thus represented four kingdoms or empires that scattered Judah, Israel or Jerusalem. The horns particularly pointed to their leaders—their kings or emperors. Ancient history helps us now, because there were actually five great 'world' empires that impacted the Jews: Assyria, Babylon, Persia, Greece and Rome.

The four horns are therefore among these. But which are the four? Notice that the four horns *scattered* either Judah, Israel or Jerusalem. One of these five nations never did that. In fact, it was so kind to the Jews that it permitted them 200 years of peace—their second so-called "golden age"—and it is my favourite of all empires, Persia. The Persians never scattered the Jews but, rather, they helped them immensely.[4] We have therefore identified the four nations: Assyria, Babylon, Greece and Rome. Let us consider them each in turn, with their respective leaders.[5]

1. THE FIRST HORN: THE ASSYRIAN EMPIRE (C. 750 BC TO 612 BC)

For some time the northern kingdom of Israel progressively came under the fourth and fifth cycles of discipline. Assyria took over the land under Tiglath-Pileser III (c. 744-727 BC). By about 725 BC, Israel controlled only a very small area in the centre, consisting of the land around one of the mountains of Ephraim, with the capital, Samaria, on top. Tiglath-Pileser began deporting the Jews. God had warned the Israelites that He would scatter them, and He had raised up the Assyrians to do it.

In about 724 BC, the next king of Assyria, Shalmaneser V, came and besieged Samaria, as we saw in the previous chapter. We know from Assyrian history that he died during, or shortly after, the end of the siege, and King Sargon II replaced him. Shalmaneser V carried out the siege, but Sargon II claims to have finished the task. The city of Samaria fell in about 721 BC and many Jews from the northern kingdom were taken away into other parts of the Assyrian Empire (2 Kings 18:11). The king of

---

[4] Persia had a number of kings who were actually believers. We are going to talk about one a little later in this study—Cyrus the Great.

[5] Some people consider that Zechariah was shown four horns and four craftsmen because the number 'four' represented every enemy and every horn-cutter. 'Four' is sometimes used in Scripture to denote completeness in relation to geographical distance and direction (the "four corners of the earth" and the "four winds" for example). The implication would have been that, no matter who the enemy was and whatever direction he came from, God had a horn-cutter prepared to cut down all the enemies of Israel.

Assyria[6] then brought people from other provinces to settle in the land in place of the children of Israel—and they brought their idols with them (2 Kings 17:24-41). Assyria was therefore the first horn.[7]

2. THE SECOND HORN: THE BABYLONIAN EMPIRE (c. 612 BC TO 539 BC)

The second horn was Babylon, or Chaldea[8]—which we looked at briefly in the previous chapter. In c. 606 BC Nebuchadnezzar was riding along a ridge near Jerusalem, when he looked across, saw the beautiful city and decided to come against it. But it was God who actually called him in to attack the land (see Jeremiah 25:9). Jeremiah had preached and preached for 40 years, warning the people of Judah that they would be taken away into captivity. He had warned them, "Don't trust in Egypt! You might as well let the Babylonians in, since you won't repent!" And so Nebuchadnezzar came and took some of the people away into captivity, including princes and nobles such as Daniel and his friends (Daniel 1:3).

In 598 BC, Nebuchadnezzar returned to conquer Jerusalem, and took many more people away, including the king. Then, between 588 and 586 BC, he returned. This time, he destroyed Jerusalem. The Temple, royal palace and many houses were set on fire and the walls were broken down. He took all but the poorest Jews captive, executed many leaders and priests, confiscated all of the articles of silver and gold, and took them all away into exile in Babylon. Even more Jews were then deported from the land a few years later.[9]

---

[6] Sargon II was a focus of Bible critics last century. Because Isaiah mentioned him, critics ridiculed the Bible because they had no other evidence of Sargon's existence. However, Sargon's palace at Khorsabad was discovered and excavated in the AD 1840s, and many details of his battles were found described on tablets. Now there is more information available to us on Sargon II than on most other Assyrian kings. As usual, the Bible was proved entirely accurate!

[7] The intermarriage of these provincial colonists with the Israelites who remained in the land resulted in the 'hybrid' Samaritans who appear later in the Bible.

[8] An explanation of the terms "Babylon" and "Chaldea", and why they tend to be used interchangeably, is given in BBS 35, entitled "The Fall of Babylon (Part 1)".

[9] The Medo-Persian Empire (or just "Persian"), which was not a horn in Zechariah's vision, then succeeded the Babylonian Empire, after defeating it in 539 BC. It allowed the Jews to return from exile, to rebuild the Temple and to live in relative peace and prosperity. It continued until it was overcome by Alexander the Great as he expanded his Greek Empire as far east as India.

3. THE THIRD HORN: THE GREEK EMPIRE
(C. 331 BC TO 146 BC)

The man who made Greece great was Alexander the Great. He lived for less than 33 years, yet, by the time of his death in 323 BC, the Greco-Macedonian (or "Greek") Empire had conquered most of the known world. Under Alexander, the Jews were generally well treated. He liked the Jews and considered them to be excellent administrators. Therefore, he would take groups of Jews all over the world with him, to supervise the administration in every city that he conquered.

However, after Alexander the Great died (in Babylon, probably as a result of a fever), his vast empire fell into disarray and civil war, while several of Alexander's generals struggled for control. By 301 BC, the empire was divided between four generals, just as Daniel had prophesied (see Daniel 8:8, 21-22).

- Ptolemy I "Soter" obtained Egypt, beginning the Egyptian dynasty of the Ptolemies.[10] They later took over Cyprus, Palestine and parts of southern Asia Minor and Libya.

- Seleucus I "Nicator" soon obtained Babylonia, beginning the Seleucid dynasty, which later gained control of a vast empire stretching from present-day India and Pakistan to the Mediterranean. It included Syria, southern Asia Minor, Media and Persia.

- Lysimachus obtained Thrace and added northwestern Asia Minor. However, he was killed in battle and his kingdom was broken up.

- Cassander gained Macedonia after his father Antipater's death, but his territory was later taken over by Antigonus Gonatas.

Within a few decades, the Greek Empire was effectively in the hands of three ruling families: the Ptolemies (Egypt), the Seleucids (Syria/Asia) and the Antigonids (Macedonia and part of Greece).

Various Greek rulers struggled for control of the land of Israel. The Ptolemies prevailed and then fought hard to keep it. However, the Seleucids under Antiochus III ("the Great") took control of the land in

---

[10] The Ptolemies were thus Greeks originally. The famous Cleopatra, Queen of Egypt, was a Ptolemy. She was therefore a Greek and not truly an Egyptian! The Ptolemaic dynasty ruled Egypt until 30 BC, when Cleopatra committed suicide and Egypt came fully under Roman control. When Octavian gained control of Egypt from Cleopatra and Mark Anthony, he became ruler of the whole Roman world. This signalled the start of the Roman Empire, of which he became the first emperor, Augustus Caesar.

198 BC. Things continued well for the Jews for three decades, as they enjoyed considerable freedom and privileges. However, this all changed by about 170 BC, after the infamous Antiochus IV Epiphanes took over. He broke his father's promise to respect the Jews' religious autonomy and, soon, he was responsible for many atrocities against them.

In 170 BC, Antiochus invaded Egypt, but failed to take it. He withdrew to Jerusalem, where he subdued the 'rebellious' Jews and plundered the Temple. In 168 BC he returned to Egypt but had to retreat after a threat from Rome.[11] He came back to Israel, determined to overcome the Jews and to make Israel a buffer between Syria and Egypt (now protected by the Romans). He sent his general, Apollonius, with 22,000 men, to destroy Jerusalem. They forced their way into the Temple courts and desecrated them, killing the priests and offering them up as sacrifices.

Antiochus Epiphanes was determined to extinguish the Jewish religion. He introduced idolatry and forbade true worship, making it a capital crime to practise circumcision or to own the Scriptures. He killed an estimated 100,000 pious Jews. Inside the Temple, on the 25th day of the Jewish month Chislev in 167 BC, he slaughtered a pig (an unclean animal to the Jews) and sacrificed it to Zeus on a new altar set up on the altar of burnt offering, in the Holy Place. He then sprinkled its blood all around. The Jews were forced to make unclean sacrifices and to eat swine's flesh. Many Jews were scattered, while others fled from Antiochus because he was so evil. I won't go into more detail here, but this makes it clear that Greece, particularly under the Seleucid leader Antiochus Epiphanes, was one of the four horns.

4. THE FOURTH HORN: THE ROMANS (2ND CENTURY BC TO AD 476)

The Romans also mistreated the Jews. The Roman Empire controlled the land of Israel at the time of Jesus. Then, during the terrible Jewish-Roman War of AD 66 to 73, many Jews were killed. Titus's army captured Jerusalem in AD 70 and destroyed the magnificent Temple, just as Christ had prophesied. At the end of this war, the Jews, who were occupying a fortress on a high plateau at Masada, committed suicide rather than give in to the Romans.

---

[11]This was the famous incident involving the Roman legate Popillius Laenas, described at the end of Chapter 1.

Rome subdued the whole land, suppressing further Jewish revolts, until, by AD 135, the Jews had been scattered all over the world. After that time, there were only a few Jews left in the land of Israel.

God's Judgment on the Four Horns

These are the four horns. However, in this chapter, we are not primarily interested in how these horns scattered the Jews. Rather, we are interested in what happened to the four horns *after* they had scattered the Jews.

In each case, the "horns" became terribly anti-Semitic. Beyond being used by God to judge the Jews, each of the four kingdoms or empires began to despise the Jews and mistreat them.

As Genesis 12:3 tells us, God curses anyone who curses the Jews. The four horns—Assyria, Babylon, Greece and Rome—thus each came under the judgment of God themselves. That is what the next two verses in our passage in Zechariah are about, because now we find four craftsmen, or horn-cutters.

The four horns all became anti-Semitic; so God raised up a horn-cutter for each one of them, to cut them down to size. Imagine that! "You think you're so great, do you?" God was saying, "but I was the One who raised you up. And I've got a horn-cutter just for you Assyria, just for you Babylon, just for you Greece, and just for you Rome—because you've gone too far!" In the same way, some nations today are standing full of pride against Israel, but they do not realize that God has got a horn-cutter prepared just for them, to cut them down too.

"Then the LORD showed me four craftsmen. And I said [to the angel]**, "What are these coming to do?" So he said, "These are the horns that scattered Judah, so that no one could lift up his head; but the craftsmen are coming to terrify them, to cast out the horns of the nations that lifted up their horn against the land of Judah to scatter it"'** (Zechariah 1:20-21). Remember that Zechariah was looking up at what he saw. He had seen four horns, but now the LORD was showing him four horn-cutters.

THE FOUR CRAFTSMEN

How did the four horns fall? How did their empires come to an end? Who were the horn-cutters that destroyed them? We will now identify the four horn-cutters as well.

We should also recognize the graciousness of God to Zechariah, because he received this vision at the end of the Babylonian captivity. God showed him this wonderful principle of the horns and horn-cutters, and the whole of Israel's history was suddenly explained before him. It must have been such an encouragement to him, as he later sought, with Haggai, to encourage the people to continue rebuilding the Temple.

1. The First Horn-cutter: Babylon (Nabopolassar the Chaldean)

Let us consider the first kingdom, Assyria, and identify its horn-cutter. He was a very interesting man indeed, called Nabopolassar, the father of Nebuchadnezzar. At the time, Assyria was the greatest empire the world had ever seen. No one thought the Assyrians could be defeated. But *God could defeat them!*

Nabopolassar was a Chaldean, from the swamp area around the mouth of the River Euphrates.[12] He used to get tired of dwelling in the marshes and wanted to go up to the higher, drier land further north. Therefore, he began to lead rebellions against the Assyrians. He would carry out a skirmish sometimes, here or there, causing a little bit of friction with the Assyrians. However, I don't believe he ever dreamt that he could actually defeat Assyria.

I believe God arranged the timing of certain events, because just when Nabopolassar managed to unify the various groups of Chaldeans, two other nations agreed to fight against Assyria with him. The first group was the Scythians: the wild horsemen of Russia—and they were wild! Nahum talks about the horsemen coming in his Book, which is all about the fall of Assyria (see Nahum 3:1-3). The other nation was the Medes.

The Chaldeans, Scythians and Medes, who had all had enough of the Assyrians, thus joined forces and started fighting against their common enemy. In 614 BC, Assyria's sacred city of Ashur fell and, in 612 BC, the great capital city of Nineveh fell.

As is well known, the last king of Assyria (Sinshariskun-Sardanapalus), rather than be defeated, put all of his goods together in a huge pile in his palace, tied up all of his slaves, concubines and eunuchs at the side, put his throne on top and sat on it. He then told someone to set fire to the whole

---

[12] The life of Nabopolassar and the fall of Assyria are described in more detail in Basic Bible Study 35, entitled "The Fall of Babylon (Part 1)".

lot; and they all died in the biggest bonfire that history has ever known. The wealth of Assyria went up in smoke! And historians are amazed because, within just a few years, there was no trace of the Assyrians anywhere.

The Assyrians survived just a few more years with Egypt's help. The royal court fled from Nineveh to Haran, but the escapees were driven out and fell back to Carchemish. From 609 to 605 BC the Babylonians fought against the remaining Assyrian court and army in exile, but Nebuchadnezzar defeated them, together with the Egyptians, at Carchemish in 605 BC.

Never in the history of mankind has such a vast empire so completely collapsed, as did Assyria. Historians have no real explanation for it. The remains of Nineveh were not even recognized by the Greek historian Xenophon, as he led his 10,000 Greeks in retreat right past them in 401 BC, 200 years later. He told of how the travellers stopped to make camp, and there were great mounds visible on the horizon. He thought they were the remains of another city, Larissa. But a guide said, "That's all that is left of Nineveh." The magnificent city had become just huge 'rubbish heaps' on the horizon at that time.[13]

The Assyrians do not exist anywhere in the world today as an identifiable people group. (The nation of Syria does not come from Assyria; it is a different nation altogether.) The Assyrians were thus obliterated. Why? Because God sent a horn-cutter to cut them down! The first horn-cutter was therefore Nabopolassar, whose son Nebuchadnezzar was going to become so famous.

---

[13] Similarly, Alexander the Great fought the battle of Arbela in 331 BC near the mounds, unaware of their being the site of ancient Nineveh. There are other examples too of Nineveh going unrecognized throughout the centuries (by Strabo and Marco Polo for example).

Nahum and Zephaniah both prophesied about the downfall of Nineveh. Nahum predicted that Nineveh would meets its end with an "**overflowing flood**" (Nahum 1:8) and this is what happened. When the River Tigris overflowed its banks, the waters 'dissolved' parts of the walls, which had been constructed using sun-dried bricks. The besieging armies were able to invade through the breaches, plunder the city and set it on fire. The prophets also said that the city would be made desolate (Nahum 2:10), becoming a dry wilderness: a place for herds and beasts to lie down in (Zephaniah 2:13-15). Nahum said that Nineveh would be hidden (Nahum 3:11).

Nineveh lay undiscovered near Mosul, in the plains of Iraq, until the two great mounds there—Kouyunjik ('sheepfold') and Nebbi Yunnus ('Prophet Jonah')—were excavated and their relics identified by Austen Henry Layard (and others) during the 1840s—some 2500 years after Nineveh was destroyed! Assyrian cuneiform writing was deciphered during the 1850s.

2. The Second Horn-cutter: Medo-Persia (Cyrus the Great)

The neo-Babylonian Empire grew rapidly after 612 BC, after it defeated Nineveh under King Nabopolassar. Then, under King Nebuchadnezzar, it quickly became the dominant empire in the Near East from 605 BC.

The Chaldeans came into the land of Israel under Nebuchadnezzar. Then, as the Jews were scattered between 606 and 586 BC, the Babylonian Empire became the second horn. Now we come to the second horn-cutter, who came along and cut down the great Babylonian Empire. His name was Cyrus II, or Cyrus "the Great", king of Persia.

King Cyrus defeated the Medes around 500 BC and fused Persia and Media into one kingdom—the Medo-Persian Empire. He was a remarkable man. Long before he was born, God inspired Isaiah to write about him *by name*! And Cyrus became a believer in the LORD God of Israel—perhaps because he was shown how he fulfilled the very Word of God. What a dramatic thing![14]

God said, **"I am the LORD....who says of Cyrus, 'He is My shepherd, and he shall perform all My pleasure, even saying to Jerusalem, "You shall be built," and to the temple, "Your foundation shall be laid"'"** (Isaiah 44:24b, 28). Chapter 45 continues, **"Thus says the LORD to His anointed, to Cyrus, whose right hand I have held—to subdue nations before him and loose the armour of kings, to open before him the double doors, so that the gates will not be shut: 'I will go before you...'"** (verse 1-2a). Notice the mention of "double doors" here (or, as the AV says, "two leaved gates"). We will come across these again in a moment.

"'For Jacob My servant's sake, and Israel My elect, I have even called you by your name; I have named you, though you have not known Me'" (verse 4). It was because of God's love and faithfulness towards Israel that He called Cyrus by name, even before he was born. How wonderful!

By the time the Babylonian Empire was just 50 or so years old, it had become very anti-Semitic. The king of Babylon was then a man called Nabonidus, who launched a campaign into northern Arabia. He was keen on archaeology, and he preferred to stay at his headquarters at Tema in the

---

[14] Daniel possibly showed him this, after 539 BC, once Persia had conquered Babylon. The fact that Cyrus came to believe in the LORD God of Israel is shown by the decree he issued for the Jews to return to the land of Israel and rebuild the Temple in Jerusalem (2 Chronicles 36:22-23; Ezra 1:1-4).

desert. While he was away, digging up remains, he used to leave his son Belshazzar in charge at Babylon, as regent. Belshazzar hated the Jews very much, so God soon decided that the time had come to cut down the Babylonian Empire. We find the glorious account of the city of Babylon's final day in the Book of Daniel—the famous story of Belshazzar's Feast in Daniel chapter 5. Consequently, Belshazzar is now more famous than Nabonidus.

Belshazzar's Feast

The Babylonians were having a drunken party inside the great city of Babylon. The Persians were all around, besieging the city, but those inside were not at all worried; Babylon was vast, with massive fortifications, and there was sufficient food to last for many years—even decades. The Babylonians were therefore sure that they were perfectly safe; and they were calmly 'living it up' inside.

"**Belshazzar the king made a great feast for a thousand of his lords, and drank wine in the presence of the thousand**" (Daniel 5:1). Belshazzar was the regent, or acting king, at this time. Notice what he did next at the feast—which was blasphemous: "**While he tasted the wine, Belshazzar gave the command to bring the gold and silver vessels which his father** [grandfather] **Nebuchadnezzar had taken from the temple which had been in Jerusalem, that the king and his lords, his wives, and his concubines might drink from them. Then they brought the gold vessels that had been taken from the temple of the house of God which had been in Jerusalem; and the king and his lords, his wives, and his concubines drank from them**" (verses 2-3). Remember that all of these vessels had been made to represent the Lord Jesus and the work He would accomplish on the Cross. Many vessels were designed to carry blood, representing the blood of Christ. However, Belshazzar now decided to use them for his idolatrous party: "**They drank wine, and praised the gods of gold and silver, bronze and iron, wood and stone**" (verse 4).

Immediately we see the beginning of the judgment of God: "**In the same hour the fingers of a man's hand appeared and wrote opposite the lampstand on the plaster of the wall of the king's palace; and the king saw the part of the hand that wrote**" (verse 5).

Kings used to write lists of all their great accomplishments on the walls of their palaces. Then, during every party, they would position a candlestick in front of the account of their latest exploit, so that everyone could read about it and praise them! Here then was a wall of blank plaster, probably next to another wall covered with lists of Babylonian victories; and the king expected soon to fill up this blank wall as well. All of a sudden, near the candlestick which was illuminating the king's latest exploits, Belshazzar noticed a hand appear from nowhere and start writing on the plaster—where the next Babylonian victory was due to be recorded. The hand started writing, but the message was unlike any that had been written before. God had a special message for Babylon; and the candlestick meant that everybody could see it!

"**Then the king's countenance changed, and his thoughts troubled him, so that the joints of his hips were loosened and his knees knocked against each other**" (verse 6). Here we get the king's reaction: his knees started knocking—literally! He was quivering and shaking.

The account then tells us how Belshazzar brought in all the astrologers, soothsayers and wise men of Babylon to try to interpret the message; but they could not understand it. Finally, Daniel was brought in, at the suggestion of the queen, and he was offered a great reward if he could explain the writing. "**Then Daniel answered, and said before the king, "Let your gifts be for yourself, and give your rewards to another; yet I will read the writing to the king, and make known to him the interpretation"**" (verse 17). Daniel understood the writing, but was not interested in the king's reward.

Daniel said to him, "**O king, the Most High God gave Nebuchadnezzar your father** [grandfather] **a kingdom and majesty, glory and honour. And because of the majesty that He gave him, all peoples, nations, and languages trembled and feared before him. Whomever he wished, he executed; whomever he wished, he kept alive; whomever he wished, he set up; and whomever he wished, he put down**" (verses 18-19). Daniel was going to remind Belshazzar of some important truths before he interpreted the writing! It was *God* who had given Nebuchadnezzar all of these things and had allowed the Babylonian Empire to become so great!

"**But when his heart was lifted up, and his spirit was hardened in pride, he was deposed from his kingly throne, and they took his glory from him. Then he was driven from the sons of men, his heart was made like the beasts, and his dwelling was with the wild donkeys. They fed him with grass like oxen, and his body was wet with the dew of heaven, till he knew that the Most High God rules in the kingdom of men, and appoints over it whomever He chooses**" (verses 20-21). Nebuchadnezzar had been humbled by God and had become a believer. He had even published the first ever 'tract' afterwards—see Daniel chapter 4! Daniel now pronounced God's judgment and gave the reasons for it:

"But you his son, Belshazzar, have not humbled your heart, although you knew all this. And you have lifted yourself up against the Lord of heaven. They have brought the vessels of His house before you, and you and your lords, your wives and your concubines, have drunk wine from them. And you have praised the gods of silver and gold, bronze and iron, wood and stone, which do not see or hear or know; and the God who holds your breath in His hand and owns all your ways, you have not glorified. Then the fingers of the hand were sent from Him, and this writing was written. And this is the inscription that was written:

MENE, MENE, TEKEL, UPHARSIN.

This is the interpretation of each word. MENE: God has numbered your kingdom, and finished it; TEKEL: You have been weighed in the balances, and found wanting; PERES: Your kingdom has been divided, and given to the Medes and Persians"** (verses 22-28).

The writing on the wall and its interpretation involved a play on words. "MENE" was Aramaic for a maneh, or mina (50 or 60 shekels in weight or as coins), derived from the verb *mena*, to 'number' or 'count'. "TEKEL" meant a shekel, related to the verb to 'weigh'. "UPHARSIN" meant 'and half-manehs', related to the verb *peris*, to 'divide' or 'cut up'. Thus the writing meant literally, "Maneh, maneh, shekel and half-manehs", but Daniel interpreted the weights in terms of their related verbs as, "Numbered, numbered, weighed, and divides".[15]

Daniel thus informed Belshazzar that the Babylonian Empire had been judged and had come to an end. Incredibly, Belshazzar still insisted on giving Daniel his reward! **"Then Belshazzar gave the command, and they clothed Daniel with purple and put a chain of gold around his neck, and made a proclamation concerning him that he should be the third ruler in the kingdom"** (verse 29).

Babylon was shaped roughly like a square, with several sets of walls. The whole of 'Greater Babylon' was about 14 miles by 14 miles (22.5 km by 22.5 km)—56 miles (90 km) all around. The main central city had two huge series of walls around it, with many towers, surrounded by moats. Parts of the inner walls reached 300 feet (91 m) high! To stop people getting into the city via the River Euphrates, which ran right through the centre of the city, there were two huge sets of interlocking gates, one at the

---

[15] There was also a further play on words. Parsin was the plural of Peres, a 'half-maneh' weight (in verse 28), probably meaning 'two half-manehs'. This suggested division or judgment. It also suggested the associated word Paras, the word for Persia in Aramaic.

north where the river entered the city, and the other at the south, where the river flowed out. These gates (called the "double doors", or "two leaved gates" (AV), in Isaiah 45:1) were designed so that the river would keep them firmly closed. They had grilles in them so that the water could flow through, but they could not possibly be opened in view of the great force of the water. No one could get in.

Nevertheless, on the day that Daniel interpreted the writing, "**That very night Belshazzar, king of the Chaldeans, was slain. And Darius the Mede received the kingdom, being about sixty-two years old**" (verses 30-31). Darius the Mede was the uncle of Cyrus the Great. Later, he was left in charge of Babylon when Cyrus went off to conquer other places. Overnight the Persians and Medes managed to get into Babylon and conquer the city, without a 'shot' being fired. How did they do it?[16]

Cyrus was a strategic genius. He positioned part of his army around the city, mainly to the north and south near the interlocking gates; then he took the rest of his army further upstream, out of sight, and began to re-excavate a huge lake, that had been built years earlier to help prevent flooding in the city. Cyrus's army dug and dug, for several years, until the lake was large enough. Then, on the day of Belshazzar's Feast, when he knew that the Babylonians would be distracted, Cyrus instructed his army to dam the river, so that it started filling the basin they had dug out. Gradually, downstream in the city, the level of the River Euphrates began to fall, until soon the river was dry.

The attacking Persian soldiers then simply got down into the river bed (which conveniently had been lined with bricks!) at the north and south, opened the gates and walked right into the centre of the city. They thus entered the very capital of the Babylonian Empire unopposed; and, overnight, the whole city was taken without a major battle. That's a horn-cutter if ever I've seen a horn-cutter! Praise God.

The Babylonians thought that they were safe. But it doesn't matter how well fortified a city or nation is: if *God* has decided it is going to be cut down, it will be cut down. God will find a way. God had warned the Babylonians that their great capital was going to fall, and had even hinted at how Cyrus would achieve this.

There are numerous chapters in the Bible which deal with God's judgment of Babylon. For example, Isaiah prophesied, "**Come down and sit in the**

---

[16] More details on the city of Babylon and its remarkable fall are given in BBS 35 and 36, entitled "The Fall of Babylon".

dust, O virgin daughter of Babylon; sit on the ground without a throne, O daughter of the Chaldeans! For you shall no more be called tender and delicate. Take the millstones and grind meal. Remove your veil, take off the skirt, uncover the thigh, pass through the rivers. Your nakedness shall be uncovered, yes, your shame will be seen; I will take vengeance, and I will not arbitrate with a man" (Isaiah 47:1-3).

Jeremiah chapters 50 and 51 also deal with God's judgment of Babylon. Let's look at just a few verses, that I've chosen in particular because they also mention Assyria. Israel was under the fifth cycle of discipline at the time: "**'Israel is like scattered sheep; the lions have driven him away. First the king of Assyria devoured him; now at last this Nebuchadnezzar king of Babylon has broken his bones.' Therefore thus says the LORD of hosts, the God of Israel: "Behold, I will punish the king of Babylon and his land, as I have punished the king of Assyria. But I will bring back Israel to his habitation, and he shall feed on Carmel and Bashan; his soul shall be satisfied on Mount Ephraim and Gilead. In those days, and in that time," says the LORD, "The iniquity of Israel shall be sought, but there shall be none; and the sins of Judah, but they shall not be found; for I will pardon those whom I preserve"**" (Jeremiah 50:17-20). God was saying that He would judge Babylon, just as He had judged Assyria. However, the Jews—despite being scattered—would come back to the land and be forgiven. The land is Israel's habitation. God has given it to them.

3. THE THIRD HORN-CUTTER: THE ROMANS

After the fall of Babylon, the Medo-Persian Empire dominated the Near East from about 539 to 331 BC, and Israel enjoyed comparative peace and freedom as a 'satrapy', or province, of Persia.

The Greeks under Alexander the Great came to the land of Israel in 331 BC, and Alexander's successors and subsequent Greek rulers then dominated the land for most of the time until the Romans took over.[17] By

---

[17] The Maccabean family led the Jews in a successful revolt against the Seleucid Greeks, starting in 166 BC. The Temple was cleansed and rededicated in 164 BC, on 25 Chislev, exactly three years after its desecration by Antiochus IV Epiphanes. This marked the commencement of the Jewish Feast of Dedication or Lights (Hanukkah). The enraged Antiochus Epiphanes died shortly after. The Jews gained religious freedom in 163 BC, although still under Seleucid (Syrian) rule. They then struggled for political independence until 143 BC, after which they were able to set up an 'independent' Jewish state with Hasmonean priest-kings. From that time, the Jews had control over some or most of the land, under the so-called "Hasmonaean dynasty". This whole period is known as the "Maccabean period". The Maccabean state reached its peak in 103-76 BC under Alexander Jannaeus.

the time the Greeks began to mistreat the Jews terribly, God was already raising up the Romans who would judge them!

The Romans began gaining territory around the Western Mediterranean during the first few centuries BC. Then, during the 2nd and 1st centuries BC they gradually took over all the major parts of the Greek Empire in the east. In 146 BC the Romans destroyed Carthage, made Africa a Roman province, and then finally subdued Macedonia and Greece in the same year. By 133 BC, when Pergamum in Asia became theirs, they ruled most of the Mediterranean world.[18]

In 64 BC, the Roman general Pompey came to Damascus and took over Syria. Then he marched into Judea. In 63 BC, Pompey took Jerusalem and finally removed the Greeks from the land of Israel. He was the first Roman to come into the land and take over.

Thus, from 63 BC, the Romans controlled the land of Israel. And 63 years later, in obedience to a decree of the Roman Emperor Augustus (Luke 2:1), Joseph and Mary travelled to Bethlehem to be registered. Thus, Jesus Christ was born in Bethlehem, in obedience to the Romans—in fulfilment of the Word of God (see Micah 5:2). Praise God! This re-introduces us to the fourth horn, namely Rome.

4. THE FOURTH HORN-CUTTER: BARBARIAN TRIBES (THE CHIEFTAIN ODOACER)

The Roman Empire became divided into East and West in AD 395. Then the unthinkable happened, and it collapsed (in the West) by AD 476. But whom did God use to cause it to collapse?[19] It is remarkable story, that took place over a period of time. Various 'Barbarian' (non-Roman, uncivilized)

---

[18] A monumental day was when, in 168 BC, the Seleucid king Antiochus Epiphanes was forced to withdraw from Alexandria according to the order delivered by Popillius Laenas (see the end of Chapter 1). The Romans had conquered Macedonia just days before. Now Ptolemaic Egypt effectively came under Rome's protection and the Seleucid king had been forced to submit and retreat. The three kingdoms, Macedonia, Egypt and Syria, which were the successors of Alexander the Great's Greek world empire, had all simultaneously bowed to Rome's superior power. Rome could be viewed as having defeated Greece at that point, although there were further struggles ahead.

[19] The fourth series of Basic Bible Studies, on Future Prophecy, deals with the Roman Empire in more detail, and addresses questions such as: "What is the Roman Empire?" and "Will it ever come back again?" An alternative interpretation is that the fourth horn in Zechariah's vision refers not just to the historical Roman Empire but also to the future, revived Roman Empire. In this case, the fourth horn-cutter would refer to Jesus Christ Himself, who will return and set up His Millennial Kingdom on the earth and reign as king in Jerusalem (see Daniel 2:34-35 and 44-45; 7:23-27).

tribes began to come against the Romans from the north and east of Europe: first Germanic tribes, followed by the fierce Huns of Central Asia.

Germanic hordes began by migrating across the frontiers of the empire and, by around AD 400, were successfully invading large areas. These groups included the Goths (the Ostragoths and Visigoths), Vandals, Alans, Sueves and other wild hordes. They poured into Gaul and Spain, and even invaded Italy. Rome was sacked by Alaric and his Visigoths in AD 410, estabilizing and effectively ending the empire in the West. The Roman army withdrew from Britain in AD 409, as Angles, Saxons and Jutes went in.

The Vandals overran North Africa around AD 430; then, in AD 455, they sacked Rome. Meanwhile, the Roman provinces in the East were soon occupied and decimated by warring tribes, as the brutal Huns drove westwards from Asia and crossed the Rhine under Attila. Only a ceremonial emperor remained on the throne—a show for various Germanic rulers, who by now dominated the Roman army.

Who can we say was the horn-cutter? The last emperor was a young boy (since no one else would take the throne), to whom they gave the imposing name Romulus Augustulus, called after the founder of Rome and the first emperor. It was a German chieftain named Odoacer (sometimes spelt Odovacer) who came in and deposed Augustulus in AD 476, marking the official end of the Western Roman Empire. Germanic kings now governed every portion of the former empire.

Therefore, if I am looking for one individual to identify as the fourth horn-cutter, I would choose Odoacer, although you could choose another leader of the Vandals, Visigoths, Ostragoths, Huns or other group.

We have seen the four horns, and now we have also seen the four craftsmen, or horn-cutters. God used: the Babylonians (under Nabopolassar) to cut down Assyria; the Medo-Persians (under Cyrus the Great) to cut down the Babylonians; the Romans to cut down Greece; and hordes of wild tribesmen to cut down the great Roman Empire.

LESSONS WE SHOULD LEARN

The lesson for every nation of the world is this: He who touches the Jews touches the apple of God's eye (see Zechariah 2:8b). Woe betide the nation that starts mistreating the Jews, because soon it will be cut down by God!

This is the glorious message of Zechariah 1:18-21, but the obverse is also true: those who bless the Jews will be blessed by God. How marvellous! If our country would support the Jews, we would quickly find that our economy would start to come right. We would find that violence would diminish. We would be secure in our land and have peace, with no fear of other nations. If only we would start loving the Jews instead of mistreating them! History should teach us that any nation that comes against the Jews is effectively coming against itself.

These four verses in Zechariah are so important, yet they are so neglected. Their message should be preached from every pulpit in this land: We can be blessed by blessing the Jews!

We who are Christians should pray for Israel every day. We should pray that there might be a revival in the land of Israel. We must ask God that the Jews would turn back to Him. We need to pray that they will recognize that Jesus—the One they rejected—*is* their Messiah, and will understand that the fifth cycle of discipline came upon them because they rejected Jesus and then continued to disobey God. When the Jews turn back to God, they will begin to dwell in safety, and will prosper as a nation (without high inflation or other such difficulties).[20] We should ask God that they might know peace and security on every side, and that every nation would be confounded by the Jewish nation, because the LORD God of Israel will be seen to reign there—the Lord Jesus Christ who *is* the King of Israel!

What blessing there is in store for Israel. There are terrible times ahead for Israel too, but in the end those who believe are going to come through into a glorious place. May we pray for Israel and may we love every Jew whom we meet, giving them the gospel faithfully, even as Jesus would have done. Amen.

---

[20] There are now more believing Jews (Messianic believers) in the land of Israel than at any time since the 1st Century AD; and the number is steadily increasing. There is possibly a greater number worldwide today than ever before. Interestingly, inflation in the new state of Israel has come down from several hundred per cent to reach single figures during the 1990s.

13. THE BAPTISM WITH FIRE
The Judgment of Israel at the Second Coming of Christ (Background)

We are now going to consider Israel's "Baptism with Fire" or "Baptism of Fire". First, we will look at the background, and I will define what I mean by the Baptism with Fire. Then, in the next chapter, we will look at one of the parables which deals with the Baptism with Fire, namely the Parable of the Ten Virgins, or the Wise and Foolish Virgins. Before we get into the subject in detail, however, I want to dip quickly into another subject that will help provide the right context.

THE MYSTERY OF THE CHURCH

If you do not understand why the Church is called a "mystery" in the New Testament, you will find many passages in Scripture difficult to understand. Paul conveyed fundamental truths that he had learnt about the Church in his letter to the Ephesians, and he called the Church a "mystery" (Ephesians 3:3, 9)—simply because it was *mentioned nowhere in the Old Testament (the Hebrew Bible)*. The Jews, despite having all the Old Testament scriptures, did not have the slightest idea about the Church that God was going to establish. It was a mystery that God Himself had concealed.

Of course, now that we know about the Church, we can look back and recognize that many pictures or 'types' of the Church were given in the Old Testament, and can see how glorious these are. However, nowhere was the Church specifically mentioned. It was God's pearl that He kept secret until after Jesus died on the Cross. Satan did not know about the Church; the angels did not know about it; and the Jews, who thought that they knew all about God's plans, did not know about it either. The man whom God primarily used to reveal the mystery was the apostle Paul. He was a Jew; but he was called to be an apostle and teacher of the Gentiles (Romans 11:13; Galatians 2:8; 2 Timothy 1:11). To him, in particular, the revelation of the Church was given.

To understand the distinctive characteristics of the Church, let us first be clear about one other thing: in Old Testament times, many Gentiles *were* truly saved, as well as Jews. In fact, it was the Jews' task to preach the gospel to the Gentiles—to teach them about the one true God, the God of Israel.

For example, Abraham had three Amorites who were allies with him: Mamre, Eschol and Aner (Genesis 14:13). Rahab was a Canaanite woman, a dweller in Jericho, and she believed on the Lord because of the testimony of Israel! She heard how God had delivered Israel from the land of Egypt and it was enough for her to be saved (Joshua 2:9-11; Hebrews 11:31). What about Ruth? She was a Moabitess, but she became a wonderful believer. Or what about Melchizedek? We do not know for certain what nationality he was (he was probably a Jebusite—a tribe of really tough, wild people), but he was certainly a believer. And he was not only a believer—he was a king and a priest of God Most High. Just when Abraham needed to be ministered to, Melchizedek came on the scene (Genesis 14:18-20). There are many more examples.

It certainly was not a mystery, therefore, that the Gentiles could come to know God. The mystery was the Church, and how Gentiles would be included as part of the covenant people of God. After Jesus died and rose again, God was going to do something new and marvellous. Instead of there being Jews and Gentiles, with believers amongst both groups, God was going to combine the believers and make one 'body' out of them—*in Christ*. That is what the Bible teaches and that is what God revealed to Paul.

In the Body of Christ, the Church, there is neither Jew nor Gentile (Galatians 3:28). If that had been written in the Old Testament, the Jews would not readily have believed it, because they were proud of their unique position as God's chosen people. But Paul, a Jew, made known the mystery of the Church: that the two (believing Jews and Gentiles) were now one, reconciled to God in one body through the Cross (Ephesians 2:13-16).

Today, if you have believed on the Lord Jesus Christ, you belong to a new creation, called the Church. There is no longer any division between Jew and Gentile in the Church. We are one in Christ. All believers are Christ-ones (or "Christians"). The whole human race today can thus be viewed as three groups: unbelieving Jews, unbelieving Gentiles and Christ-ones.

Look at what Paul said about the Church and his own ministry in Ephesians chapter 3: "**How that by revelation He made known to me the** mystery (as I wrote before in a few words,[1] by which, when you read, you may understand my knowledge in the mystery of Christ)..." (Ephesians 3:3-4). The word translated "revelation" here is the same word found in Revelation 1:1, from which we get the title of the Book of the Revelation of Jesus Christ at the end of the New Testament. It is the Greek word *apokalypsis*, and it means 'disclosure' or 'uncovering'. It refers to a secret matter that was hidden, but is now clearly revealed.

God Himself revealed to Paul the glorious mystery that had remained hidden throughout the Old Testament period, probably while Paul was in Arabia or Damascus (Galatians 1:17): "**which in other ages was not made known to the sons of men, as it has now been revealed by the Spirit to His holy apostles and prophets**" (verse 5). Abraham did not know about the Church; Moses did not know about it; Zechariah did not know about it; Jeremiah did not know about it; ....even John the Baptist did not know about it. Jesus *did* know about the Church, of course, although His disciples did not understand it until much later. But then the mystery was revealed to the apostle Paul.

Paul defined the mystery: "**That the Gentiles should be fellow heirs, of the same body, and partakers of His promise in Christ through the gospel, of which I became a minister according to the gift of the grace of God given to me by the effective working of His power**" (verses 6-7). This is the amazing truth about the wonderful Church that we belong to: We who are Gentiles are fellow heirs with the Jews, in the one Body of Christ! In Christ, we share the same inheritance and promises as Jews.[2]

"**To me, who am less than the least of all the saints, this grace was given, that I should preach among the Gentiles the unsearchable riches of Christ, and to make all people see what is the fellowship of the mystery, which from the beginning of the ages has been hidden in God who created all things through Jesus Christ; to the intent that now the manifold wisdom of God might be made known by the church to the principalities and powers in heavenly places, according to the eternal purpose which He accomplished in Christ Jesus our Lord**" (verses 8-11). After Jesus Christ died, the Church came forth; and I think the

---

[1] Paul might have been referring to a letter he had written previously to the Ephesians, although we have no record of it.

[2] In the Old Testament Scriptures, God revealed a number of times that Gentiles would be blessed, but it was a mystery how exactly they could be blessed since they were not included in the covenants and promises God had made with His people, Israel. The Jews certainly never expected that Gentiles would become co-heirs with themselves of God's promises.

angels and demons were stunned. God's intention was that the Church should make His wisdom known to them.

I believe that Satan was completely shocked when the Church came forth. When Jesus rose from the dead, Satan did not realize immediately how this would quickly change everything and begin to affect thousands, and even millions, of people on the earth. But a new creation had begun. After Jesus ascended and the Holy Spirit was poured out upon the believers at Pentecost, Satan suddenly realized that only the Head had risen and ascended; Christ's Body was still down here on the earth. And every day that the Body of Christ stays here, it is growing, getting bigger and bigger. The moment anyone believes on the Lord Jesus Christ, he or she is joined to the Lord (1 Corinthians 6:17) and baptized into the one Body by the Holy Spirit (1 Corinthians 12:13). No member of the Body of Christ is Satan's property any longer: we are God's property. What a shock for the enemy!

One day soon, God is going to decide that it is time to resurrect Christ's Body on earth, and all believers will be taken up to be with Him in heaven. All of this *was* a mystery, but now it has been revealed. Praise God! It was kept secret from all the angels, including Satan, kept secret from the Jews, including all the prophets, and it was kept secret from all the nations. How privileged we now are, therefore, that the mystery has been revealed!

Hear what Paul wrote in chapter 2 of his letter to the Ephesians, a Gentile church: "**For He Himself is our peace, who has made both one, and has broken down the middle wall of division between us, having abolished in His flesh the enmity, that is, the law of commandments contained in ordinances, so as to create in Himself one new man from the two, thus making peace**" (verses 14-15).

Both Jews and Gentiles have been made one. If you are a Jew, and I am a Gentile, so what? We are one in Christ. Hallelujah! "**And that He might reconcile them both to God in one body through the cross, thereby putting to death the enmity. And He came and preached peace to you who were afar off** [Gentiles] **and to those who were near** [Jews]**. For through Him we both have access by one Spirit to the Father**" (verses 16-18).

It was because the Church was a mystery, yet to be revealed, that the Jews had so much trouble understanding it. They thought that the plan of God was simple. They assumed that all it consisted of was Jewish history. They expected their Messiah to come to them, that He would be pleased with them, that He'd quickly conquer all of their enemies, and that He'd immediately establish His Kingdom on the earth. That was all they could see. Thus, when Jesus came, the Jews were expecting a Messiah who would quickly overthrow the Romans and establish His Kingdom.

The disciples of Jesus, being Jews, shared this view of history. Therefore, as they followed Him, they began to have difficulty understanding some of the things He said. Jesus was convincing them that He was indeed their Messiah; nevertheless, He did not seem to want to become a conventional king or to overthrow the Romans. He kept speaking about His own suffering and death; and He said that He must soon go away (John 13:33; 14:2-4; 16:16-20).

The disciples could not reconcile Jesus' words with their aspirations; and they still could not grasp their meaning even after Jesus had died and been resurrected. In Acts chapter 1 we find the final question they asked Jesus before He was taken up into heaven. This was after the resurrection, and after Jesus had appeared to them during a period of 40 days, telling them about the Kingdom of God (Acts 1:2-3). Some of them had watched Him die; and they had seen Him as a resurrected man. Now Jesus commanded them to stay in Jerusalem and told them that they would be baptized with the Holy Spirit in a few days' time (Acts 1:4-5). They still assumed He was going to establish His Kingdom on earth any day.

"Therefore, when they had come together, they asked Him, saying, "Lord, will You at this time restore the kingdom to Israel?"" (Acts 1:6). "Is it now, Lord?" they were asking, "You've been resurrected for 40 days, but still You haven't done anything to overthrow the Romans. Is it now? Is that why we've all come together?" They still knew nothing about the Church.

"And He said to them, "It is not for you to know times or seasons which the Father has put in His own authority. But you shall receive power when the Holy Spirit has come upon you; and you shall be witnesses to Me in Jerusalem, and in all Judea and Samaria, and to the end of the earth"" (verses 7-8). Jesus was effectively telling His disciples, "Don't be preoccupied with the Kingdom for now. Rather, get on with being witnesses to Me! You are going to be involved in something new; and you need the power of the Holy Spirit upon you!" They were going to establish the Church; and they needed the power of the Holy Spirit, just as we do.

The Jewish teachers understood from the Scriptures that their Messiah was going to be king of Israel, that He would establish His Kingdom over the whole world, and that the Jews would be the world's teachers in this time of great prosperity and peace. Therefore, they had taught the Jewish people that, as soon as Messiah came, He would establish His Kingdom forever. The Jews therefore had trouble understanding Jesus, because they believed this incomplete view of history.[3]

There *were*, however, some passages which portrayed the Messiah differently. In Isaiah chapter 53, for example, the Jews could identify a suffering servant, who was going to come and be rejected. He was going to be beaten up, crushed and led like a lamb to the slaughter. Other prophets revealed how the Messiah would be pierced, hinting that He would be crucified (Psalm 22:16; Zechariah 12:10).

The teachers could not reconcile these two groups of scriptures; so they chose to ignore or explain away those that described a suffering Messiah. They decided that it was not going to be like that. No! Their Messiah was only going to come as a conquering king, in power and great glory, to rid them of their enemies and establish Israel as the top nation!

We happen to be in the Church, with the benefit of further history and the whole Bible to teach us, so we can now see the fuller picture. The Lord Jesus, the Messiah, came for a first time to Israel—but not as a conquering king and not to establish His Kingdom as a worldwide, political and physical entity immediately. Rather, He came to die on a cross for the sins of the whole world, as a suffering servant—the Lamb of God.

Jesus came Principally to Israel

Jesus was sent specifically to Israel first time, so that the Jews might believe on Him as their Messiah. His mission was only to minister to Israel, as He made clear on several occasions. But Israel, as a nation, rejected Him.

In Matthew chapter 15 we read about a remarkable woman who came to see Jesus. We know she was a believer because she addressed Jesus as "Lord" and she worshipped Him: **"Then Jesus went out from there and departed to the region of Tyre and Sidon. And behold, a woman of Canaan came from that region and cried out to Him, saying, "Have mercy on me, O Lord, Son of David! My daughter is severely demon-possessed." But He answered her not a word"** (Matthew 15:21-23a). It

---

[3] See for example John 12:30-35. The Jews understood that their Messiah would remain forever, so they could not understand Jesus' teaching that He, the Son of Man, would soon be lifted up to die.

seems that Jesus just stood there and, at first, would not answer this woman.

"**And His disciples came and urged Him, saying, "Send her away, for she cries out after us""** (verse 23b). The disciples were Jews, but here was just a Canaanite woman. Therefore, they said to Jesus, "She's bothering us, Lord. Send her away!"

"**But He answered and said, "I was not sent except to the lost sheep of the house of Israel""** (verse 24). Jesus was Israel's king. "I've come to minister only to Israel," He said to her. I wonder whether that would have put you off. Jesus wanted to see what her faith was like. Sometimes God does seem to turn His back on us; and it's then that He really sees our true character—and so do we.

Now comes one of the most beautiful passages in Scripture. I am very fond of this woman indeed. She was not put off by Jesus' answer; and she was not going to be put off. "**Then she came and worshipped Him, saying, "Lord, help me!""** (verse 25). Jesus seemed to be ignoring her. He seemed to have put her off. But she was still thrilled with Him! She knew whom she wanted to worship. Therefore, she worshipped Him and asked for help.

"**But He answered and said, "It is not good to take the children's bread and throw it to the little dogs""** (verse 26). Now Jesus was being 'derogatory', calling her a dog! "It is not right that I take the children's food—the Jews' food—and cast it to Gentile dogs like you!" Jesus answered.

Incredibly, this Canaanite woman was still not put off a bit. She understood. "**And she said, "True, Lord, yet even the little dogs eat the crumbs which fall from their masters' table""** (verse 27). The word translated "little dogs" meant a 'puppy' or a 'gentle dog'—the type of small, frightened, weak little dog that you might keep as a pet. "That's true," she said, but her attitude was, "Lord, I just want crumbs from You. That will be good enough for me. It would only take a crumb from You and my daughter will be healed."

"**Then Jesus answered and said to her, "O woman, great is your faith!""** (verse 28a). There is no verb in the last phrase, which emphasizes it: "Great your faith!" Jesus recognized her tremendous faith. "**"...Let it be to you as you desire." And her daughter was healed from that very hour**" (verse 28b).

The Jews could never claim that Jesus was so busy ministering to Gentiles that He neglected them. He came specifically to the Jews and ministered to them first, always. But when Gentile believers came, they received from Him exactly what they asked for, according to their faith. Many of the Jews were proud and despised Jesus. But this Canaanite woman probably travelled some distance to come and ask Jesus for mercy.

Let us have a quick look at another passage on this subject, in Matthew chapter 10. Jesus had called His twelve disciples to Him, and was sending them out. Notice what He commanded them to do: **"Do not go into the way of the Gentiles, and do not enter a city of the Samaritans. But go rather to the lost sheep of the house of Israel. And as you go, preach, saying, 'The kingdom of heaven is at hand.' Heal the sick, cleanse the lepers, raise the dead, cast out demons. Freely you have received, freely give"** (verses 5b-8). Jesus wanted them to minister specifically to Israel. That was what He had come to do, so that was what they should do also.

God's Timetable of History

Jesus Christ came to Israel, but His own people rejected Him. Then the Church came in; and it is still on the earth today, after nearly 2000 years. We understand this now, but they did not know it then. We do not know the number of years that the Church will remain on earth, but one day God will suddenly remove the Church. Both Jew and Gentile in the Body of Christ will be caught away, in this Rapture of the Church.

Seven more years of Jewish history will follow. This period, often called The Tribulation, will be the most terrible time of Jewish history. Afterwards, Jesus the Messiah will come again to Israel. This time, He *will* come in power and great glory, as the Kings of kings. This is the Second Coming, or Second Advent, of Christ. And this time He *will* establish His Kingdom—the Kingdom of God, or the Millennium—on this earth.

The Jews did not understand all this. They could not understand it. They looked and they looked, but, because they could not see the Church, they did not grasp God's timetable. Many passages in the Old Testament talk about Jewish history up to the time when Christ came first time, but then the description suddenly jumps over to the Kingdom period. The writers jumped right across 2000 years of Church history.[4] The mystery of the

---

[4] See for example Isaiah 61:1-2. Notice how, in Luke 4:18-19, when Jesus quoted this prophecy, He abruptly stopped halfway through Isaiah 61:2. He had come to proclaim the acceptable year of the LORD, but the day of vengeance would only follow after the Church age, more than 2000 years later. More examples are given in BBS 47, entitled "The Mystery of the Church".

Church was like the comma or space between the phrases or verses; but God had not yet revealed what would come in between. It is only explained in the New Testament.

If we bear this in mind, it is very helpful, because I find that many Christians are so preoccupied with the Church that they think everything in the Bible applies to the Church first. We can certainly learn much about the Church from the principles, historical accounts and prophecies contained in the Old Testament, of course, but to apply them *all* solely to the Church is a mistake. In fact, some passages become incomprehensible if we try to apply them to the Church!

Rightly Dividing the Word of God: What the Baptism of Fire is not

I am making this point now because, as soon as we talk about baptism with fire, most Christians immediately think, "I wonder if I've been baptized with fire?" and they start thinking about a baptism with power. They immediately relate it to themselves.

I bought a booklet a few years ago entitled "*Baptism with Fire*", but when I read it, it was all about baptism with the power of the Holy Spirit. Its author obviously assumed that the two things were the same, so he tried to relate everything to do with baptism with fire to the Church. I do not know what the *Trade Descriptions Act* would say about that: having one name on the outside and talking about something else inside! It is quite wrong.

If you have studied principles in the Bible, you should know that this approach was wrong because fire almost always represents judgment in the Bible. It is not used to illustrate power, but rather holy judgment. Fire is sometimes used in the context of purifying, but even that is a form of judgment: the judgment, or separation, of dross to leave pure material. Therefore, when we talk about baptism with fire, we must be talking about a judgment. It is not the same as baptism with the Holy Spirit. Muddling up these two baptisms involves taking verses out of their context and misapplying them.

For example, people often quote John the Baptist saying that Jesus would come and baptize with fire (see Matthew 3:11), but ignore the fact that the context was judgment. They use it as a pretext to talk about baptism with the Holy Spirit. We will look at John's words in more detail later.

In many instances such a misapplication does not matter too much. God is such a genius that many things in the Bible do have wonderful parallels in the Church, and it is glorious to recognize those parallels. But we should stay true to the plain meaning of the Word of God first.

Some Christians think that baptism with fire must be the refining that goes on in believers—the testing of our faith mentioned in 1 Peter 1:7. Making such an application to the Church is fine, so long as we don't lost sight of what it really refers to. We need to understand what passages mean in their original context for Israel. There often is a dual application in the things we learn. The moment we are saved, God *does* want to purify our lives by the Holy Spirit; that is true. But if we restrict our understanding of baptism with fire to that, then we have missed most of the glory of the whole subject. Once we recognize that there are substantial passages in the Old Testament that describe a future event involving baptism with fire, we realize that there is more to this subject. Let me therefore define what I understand the Baptism with Fire to be.

THE BAPTISM WITH FIRE

The Baptism with Fire refers to *the judgment of Israel at the end of the Tribulation, at the Second Coming of Jesus Christ.*

In Matthew chapter 24, the Lord gave a beautiful analogy of what is going to happen; and we shall see in this passage how many Christians have been guilty of assuming that everything applies firstly to the Church. The whole context of Jesus' teaching in Matthew 24 is about the Temple, the Tribulation, armies coming against Jerusalem and Jesus coming again as king in mighty power. It is not about the Church.

Jesus said, **"But of that day and hour no one knows, no, not even the angels of heaven, but My Father only"** (Matthew 24:36). No one at all knows the day or hour when Jesus will come again to establish His Kingdom, except the Father. This is the point Jesus repeated later in Acts 1:7, when His disciples asked Him if He was at that time going to restore the kingdom to Israel.

The analogy is in verse 37: **"But as the days of Noah were, so also will the coming of the Son of Man be."** Do you see the picture? Jesus was describing what things will be like when He comes again. **"For as in the days before the flood, they were eating and drinking, marrying and giving in marriage, until the day that Noah entered the ark, and did not know until the flood came and took them all away, so also will the coming of the Son of Man be"** (verses 38-39). This simply means that people will be so occupied with the cares of this life that they won't have time for God. That is what it is going to be like then; and it is true now, too.

This is *not* describing the Rapture of the Church because, at the Rapture, we will meet the Lord in the air. Here, the Son of Man is coming *to the earth*. This is at the end of the Tribulation, seven years *after* the Rapture of the Church.

Let us consider the analogy further, to help us understand what is going to happen at the end of the Tribulation. Before Noah's Flood, believers and unbelievers were living on the earth together. Then God sent judgment, and floodwaters came upon the earth. Every unbeliever died and did not remain on the earth after the Flood. The believers in the Ark were saved. The unbelievers were thus removed, while all the believers remained on the earth. I'm going to say that again: in the days of Noah all the *unbelievers were taken away*, but the *believers stayed* on the earth. When the floodwaters receded, Noah and his family came out from the Ark and began multiplying; and soon a huge civilization developed again.

What then is going to happen at the end of the Tribulation? As in the days of Noah, all the *unbelievers* are going to be taken away, and all the believers will remain to re populate the earth! The Kingdom cannot be established until the unbelievers have been removed. Then, I believe, there is going to be a 'population explosion' on the earth.

"Then two men will be in the field: one will be taken and the other left. Two women will be grinding at the mill: one will be taken and the other left" (verses 40-41). The unbeliever is taken; the believer is left behind. Do you see? It does not matter too much if you talk about the Rapture of the Church using this passage, but, it is important to be true to the Word of God and understand the plain meaning first. To be strictly true to the context, it is clearly the *unbeliever* who will be taken away, just as in the days of Noah. I am sorry if this is a shock to you! But I hope this might cause you to re-think this and some other passages also.

Jesus will come again, and He will separate all unbelievers from the believers on the earth. It will be a separation, or judgment. That is the Baptism with Fire—particularly as it applies to Israel. Let us see this described in the Old Testament before we go any further.

EXAMPLES OF THE BAPTISM WITH FIRE IN THE OLD TESTAMENT

Ezekiel 20:33-38

"As I live," says the Lord GOD, "surely with a mighty hand, with an outstretched arm, and with fury poured out, I will rule over you. I will

bring you out from the peoples and gather you out of the countries where you are scattered, with a mighty hand, with an outstretched arm, and with fury poured out. And I will bring you into the wilderness of the peoples, and there I will plead My case with you face to face"** (Ezekiel 20:33-35). The word translated "**plead My case**" is the Hebrew verb *shaphat*, which means 'to judge'. (The NASB translates it correctly as "enter into judgment".) At the end of the Tribulation, all the Jews are going to be regathered from every nation of the world. They are going to be taken into a wilderness area and God is going to judge them face to face.

"**"As I entered into judgment with your fathers in the wilderness of the land of Egypt, so I will enter into judgment with you," declares the Lord GOD**" (verse 36, NASB). Do you recall what happened to their fathers in the wilderness? The people of Israel were judged by God. Only two believers entered the Promised Land; the rest of the people died in the wilderness. Similarly, not one unbeliever is going to enter into the Kingdom that Jesus will establish after He returns.

"**And I will make you pass under the rod** [or, shepherd's crook], **and I will bring you into the bond of the covenant**" (verse 37). To "pass under the rod" refers to separation, or judgment. A shepherd used to take his sheep and, as they passed under his rod, or crook, he would separate them into groups. He might separate his own sheep from those not belonging to him, or from other animals, such as goats. God will restore Israel and bring her into all of her inheritance. The covenants are all going to be restored and fulfilled in the Kingdom. (This is too big a subject to deal with here.)

"**I will purge the rebels from among you, and those who transgress against Me; I will bring them out of the country where they sojourn, but they shall not enter the land of Israel. Then you will know that I am the LORD**" (verse 38). This is the Baptism with Fire. All the rebels among the Jews will be purged out before Israel enters in and possesses all of her land in the Kingdom.

Zechariah 13:8-9

"**And it shall come to pass in all the land,**" says the LORD, "**That two-thirds in it shall be cut off and die...**" (Zechariah 13:8a). During the Tribulation, two-thirds of the people in the land will perish. It will be a terrible, terrible time—the worst time the Jews have ever known. In Deuteronomy 4:30 it is called a time of "**distress**". Jeremiah called it "**the time of Jacob's trouble**" (Jeremiah 30:7); and that's exactly what it is going to be.

Two-thirds of the people in all the land will die, **"but one-third shall be left in it: I will bring the one-third through the fire, will refine them as silver is refined, and test them as gold is tested"** (verses 8b-9a). Here we have a mention of actual fire. When silver is refined, the dross is skimmed off from the surface and removed. All the unbelievers in Israel are going to be removed, leaving only believers. Then the believers will be refined through the fire. That is what I mean by the Baptism with Fire.

Then, **"They will call on My name, and I will answer them. I will say, 'This is My people'; and each one will say, 'The LORD is my God'"** (verse 9b). Praise the Lord!

Malachi 3:2-6

"But who can endure the day of His coming? And who can stand when He appears? For He is like a refiner's fire and like fuller's soap" (Malachi 3:2). That is how fearsome and terrible it is going to be when Jesus comes again.

A "fuller" was a laundry-man. (The Fullers' Pool in Jerusalem was where the people went to do their washing, for example.) Fuller's soap was really powerful stuff; it had to be in those days! The moment you put fuller's soap in the water with your washing, all the insects and lice died off, and all the rubbish floated to the surface. That is what this judgment is going to be like. All of the 'dirt', 'scum' and 'impurities' are going to be removed, leaving behind only clean linen. That's the Baptism with Fire; and it will take place at the end of the Tribulation when Jesus Christ the Messiah returns.

"He will sit as a refiner and a purifier of silver; He will purify the sons of Levi, and purge them as gold and silver, that they may offer to the LORD an offering in righteousness. Then the offering of Judah and Jerusalem will be pleasant to the LORD, as in the days of old, as in former years" (verses 3-4). God is going to refine all the remaining people. Even the sons of Levi, including the priests, are going to be purified.

"And I will come near you for judgment; I will be a swift witness against sorcerers, against adulterers, against perjurers, against those who exploit wage earners and widows and the fatherless, and against those who turn away an alien—because they do not fear Me," says the LORD of hosts. "For I am the LORD, I do not change; therefore you are not consumed, O sons of Jacob" (verses 5-6). This clearly is a judgment—the Baptism with Fire.

AFTER THE BAPTISM WITH FIRE

What is going to happen to the believers when they go through into the Kingdom? Here is the glory of it, because they are *all* going to be baptized with the Holy Spirit! The whole earth is not only going to be populated by believers, but the believers are all going to have the Holy Spirit poured out upon them. How do we know this? Because another well known prophecy tells us this: the prophecy of Joel, chapter 2. It will be a wonderful time!

The prophecy begins, "**And it shall come to pass afterwards** [after the Second Coming] **that I will pour out My Spirit on all flesh; your sons and your daughters shall prophesy, your old men shall dream dreams, your young men shall see visions; and also on My menservants and on My maidservants I will pour out My Spirit in those days. And I will show wonders in the heavens and in the earth: blood and fire and pillars of smoke. The sun shall be turned into darkness, and the moon into blood, before the coming of the great and terrible day of the LORD. And it shall come to pass that whoever calls on the name of the LORD shall be saved. For in Mount Zion and in Jerusalem there shall be deliverance, as the LORD has said, among the remnant whom the LORD calls**" (verses 28-32).

Notice that God is going to pour out His Spirit on "**all flesh**"—and that means *all*. Every single person on the earth after the Second Coming is going to have the Holy Spirit poured out upon them, at the beginning of God's Kingdom. And Joel goes on to define it: Both men and women are going to receive of God; age won't matter; and class won't matter either. The rest of the passage tells us what is going to happen at the Second Advent. There are going to be wonders in the heavens. Jesus reiterated this in Matthew 24:29-30.

What a fantastic beginning it will be to the Kingdom! There was a parallel when the Church began, as we all know. However, once again, we must not be so preoccupied with the parallel that we forget that Joel was describing what will happen at the start of the Kingdom—which will be even more remarkable and glorious. Now let us go to Acts chapter 2 and see what actually happened at Pentecost.

THE PARALLEL OF PENTECOST

Peter quoted the passage from Joel that we have just read (with some very minor changes) on the Day of Pentecost. The Holy Spirit had come upon the disciples in such power, and they were making such a noise, that a multitude of the Jews in Jerusalem gathered together. They were confused because of all the languages that they heard being spoken and supposed that the disciples must be drunk, even though it was only the third hour of the day (see Acts 2:1-13). The devout Jews from every nation knew the Book of Joel 'backwards' of course; they could probably recite it all.

Peter, having been filled with the Holy Spirit, stood up and preached to the Jews. His message was essentially this: "Why are you so surprised? Haven't you read the prophet Joel? Didn't he say that this would happen in the Kingdom? I thought you knew all about this!"

The Holy Spirit had been poured out, but not on all flesh—only on the gathered believers. The signs of prophecy, visions and dreams had *not* been given. Rather, the followers of Jesus Christ had spoken in other tongues—which the prophet Joel had *not* talked about. Peter was clearly saying, "This *is like* the event which the prophet Joel spoke of."[5] He was in no way saying that what had occurred was the complete and final fulfilment of the prophecy in Joel. This is clear, because he went on to quote more of Joel's words: **"I will show wonders in heaven above and signs in the earth beneath: blood and fire and vapour of smoke. The sun shall be turned into darkness, and the moon into blood, before the coming of the great and notable day of the LORD"** (Acts 2:19-20). None of these signs came to pass on the Day of Pentecost, in AD 33, even though the Holy Spirit truly had been poured out upon the believers.

Peter was quoting about the great Day of the LORD, when Jesus will come again. He was saying, "Don't be so amazed, you Jews! This is a *parallel situation* to that great and terrible Day of the LORD. What you see today *is* a work of God! The Holy Spirit has been poured out upon us, just as He will be poured out on all flesh in the Kingdom!" Pentecost was a foretaste of that glorious time at the start of the Millennium, when all people on the earth shall be baptized with the Holy Spirit.

JOHN THE BAPTIST'S MESSAGE

We are now ready to look at Matthew chapter 3. Remember that John the Baptist came and ministered to the Jews, to prepare them for the coming of their king and Messiah.

---

[5] Some scholars say that the phrase Peter used in Acts 2:16, "But this is what was spoken by the prophet Joel", was a Greek idiom meaning 'But this is like that...'. Peter was saying, "This is a similar thing to what Joel talked about." The Jews would have been very interested and attentive to what Peter had to say. No prophecy actually described the Holy Spirit being poured out on the Day of Pentecost in AD 33, because the Church was a mystery in the Old Testament.

John preached a message of repentance to Israel and baptized those who came to him. **"But when he saw many of the Pharisees and Sadducees coming to his baptism, he said to them, "Brood of vipers! Who has warned you to flee from the wrath to come?""** (verse 7). John was talking about judgment. "There is wrath coming upon this world," he was saying, "but who's told *you* to escape from it?" John was thus saying quite offensive things to the Pharisees and Sadducees—because he knew what was in their hearts. They were religious people; but they did not want to hear the truth.

The situation was this: More and more people were coming to John, so the Pharisees and Sadducees were jealous and afraid that they would lose their control over the people. Many of them therefore decided to go and be baptized by John, so that the people would think they were involved in this new 'movement'. They had no intention of humbling themselves and turning away from their sins. The moment John saw them coming, in their pride, dressed in their long robes, he said to them openly, in front of all the crowds, **"Brood of vipers!"**—and this meant 'children of vipers'. That surely upset them!

As soon as you light a fire, vipers scuttle away to their holes. John had seen it happen often in the desert. In effect, John was saying to them, "You're scuttling away from the fire, are you? Judgment is coming, and you're trying to avoid it, are you?" But they could not escape, because they had not truly repented. That was John's point. They were religious men, outwardly devout, but they had not repented.

John defined what was required in verse 8: **"Therefore bear fruits worthy of repentance"**. They needed to give up their hypocrisy, pride and self-righteousness, repent, and then prove that they had done so by a changed life. John was also telling all the people to believe on the One coming after him—the Lord Jesus, the Lamb of God. But the Pharisees and Sadducees were so proud. They thought, "We're Jewish, and we keep the Law, so God must be pleased with us. We are better than everyone else, so we must be saved!" In the same way, some people today think, "I go to church every Sunday and I live a good life, so I must be saved." But it is not true.

"And do not think to say to yourselves, 'We have Abraham as our father.' For I say to you that God is able to raise up children to Abraham from these stones" (verse 9). John probably pointed to the pebbles in the Jordan, and said, "Out of these stones in the Jordan, God could raise up Jewish people. Don't think that being Jewish automatically saves you. It certainly does not."

"And even now the axe is laid to the root of the trees. Therefore every tree which does not bear good fruit is cut down and thrown into the fire" (verse 10). The implication was that trees bearing good fruit will remain standing. Trees which do not will be cut down and burnt up. "There's going to be a judgment," John was saying, "so watch out, you Pharisees and Sadducees! The axe is coming and it's going to cut *you* down—unless you truly repent!" The whole passage is about judgment.

Who was going to carry out this judgment? John made it clear that it was not him. One coming after him would do it, who was much greater. **"I indeed baptize you with water unto repentance, but He who is coming after me is mightier than I, whose sandals I am not worthy to carry. He will baptize you with the Holy Spirit and fire"** (verse 11). John was referring to the time when Jesus will come as a mighty king. The judgment then will involve a baptism with the Holy Spirit *and* a baptism with fire, because, when the Lord judges the Jews at the end of the Tribulation, those who pass through the fire will all be baptized with the Holy Spirit. The unbelievers, however, will be removed.

In case you think I am twisting the passage to make these baptisms refer to judgment, notice the next verse: **"His winnowing fan is in His hand, and He will thoroughly purge His threshing-floor, and gather His wheat into the barn; but He will burn up the chaff with unquenchable fire"** (verse 12). John talked logically, point by point. In verses 7 to 10 he had talked about judgment; in verse 12 he is talking about judgment. He surely would not have suddenly changed topic to talk about the Holy Spirit coming in power upon the Church in verse 11.

A "winnowing fan" was a grain shovel. Reapers used to pour all of their harvested grain on to the floor of a particular 'room' or enclosure, where animals would tread it down until the chaff and wheat fell apart. Then they would take a grain shovel, throw the mixture of wheat and chaff up into the air, and the wind would blow the chaff away, leaving only the wheat. This is another good illustration of the Baptism with Fire: the chaff will be separated from the wheat, so that only wheat will remain. Jesus is going to thoroughly clean His threshing-floor: He will clean the whole floor out— by removing all the chaff (all the unbelievers). He will gather His wheat into the barn, but the chaff will be burned up with unquenchable fire. This is going to happen at the end of the Tribulation, at the Second Coming of Christ, and the wheat (believers) will go through into the Kingdom.

The whole passage is clearly about judgment. John was not talking about power in the Church. Nor was John talking about the purity of the Church, since neither John nor any of the people yet knew about the Church.

Jesus referred to the Parallel Event in the Church

If we turn to Acts chapter 1, however, we see that Jesus did later allude to John's message and 'redefine' it, because part of it *did* apply to the Church. He did not quote John exactly, however, which is very interesting: He missed out John's reference to the fire. Why? Because Jesus was talking to those who were going to make up the Church. He said, **"For John truly baptized with water, but you shall be baptized with the Holy Spirit not many days from now"** (Acts 1:5). He did not say, "You shall be baptized with the Holy Spirit *and fire* not many days from now." No! He missed out the reference to fire; and this was quite deliberate. Jesus always spoke precisely, as do the Scriptures that God inspired.

Jesus was referring to the Day of Pentecost. He made no mention of fire because the Baptism with Fire was an event far in the future—after the Church has been taken away. Again, the baptism with the Holy Spirit at Pentecost was a parallel, at the start of the Church age, with what is going to happen at the start of the Millennium. As we have noted, it is wonderful to recognize these parallels, so long as we understand the plain meaning of Scripture also.

There are many parables that deal with the Baptism with Fire: the Wheat and the Tares (Matthew 13:24-30; 36-43), the Good and the Bad Fish (Matthew 13:47-50), the Faithful and the Evil Servant (Matthew 24:45-51), the Wise and Foolish Virgins (Matthew 25:1-13), and so on. These all concern the time when God will judge Israel and separate unbelievers from the believers. The believers will go through into the Kingdom, but unbelievers will be taken away and kept for eternal judgment.

Having covered all of this background, we are now almost ready to consider the Parable of the Wise and Foolish Virgins. May God bless His Word to our hearts. And may we be faithful in every part to Him, rightly dividing the Word of God.

14. THE WISE AND FOOLISH VIRGINS
The Judgment of Israel at the Second Coming of Christ

When Jesus Christ returns, the Bible says that God will "**whistle**" (or "hiss") for the Jews all around the world (see Zechariah 10:8), and gather them to the land of Israel, where He will judge them face to face. Unbelievers will be removed, but the believers will be refined through fire and brought through into the Kingdom. This is the Baptism with Fire.

The Parable of the Ten Virgins, or the Wise and Foolish Virgins, describes this. However, before we can go through the details of the parable, we still have a bit more background to cover.

How to Interpret a Parable

The word 'parable' comes from two Greek words: *para*, which means 'by the side of' or 'alongside', and *ballo*, which means 'to throw' or 'to throw down'. A parable is thus something thrown down alongside something else. There is a point of truth; and a parable is a story thrown down alongside it to illustrate that truth. Every public speaker or writer uses such stories at times to demonstrate what he or she is saying. I have used quite a number in this series of studies already.

When talking about the security of our kindred relationship with God, I said that, once we are born again, we become children of our Father in heaven. The parable I gave was this: In our natural families, it doesn't matter if we change our name, change our looks, change our nationality or anything else; we can never alter the basic relationship underneath. We are still our father's child. Similarly, once we are born again as our heavenly Father's child, that kindred relationship can never be altered.

Watchman Nee used a parable when he talked about the phrase "**in Adam all die**" (1 Corinthians 15:22).[1] He argued that if your great-grandfather

---
[1] Refer to Chapter 2 in "The Normal Christian Life" by Watchman Nee (various publishers).

had died when a small boy, you would not be here now; you effectively would have died 'in him'! And not only would you have died, but all his descendants would have died in him. The point he was demonstrating was that, when Adam sinned and died *spiritually*, we all also died spiritually in Adam.

When you consider a parable, clearly you have got to make sure that you apply the story to the corresponding point of truth. Otherwise, you will be in trouble! If you take the parable and don't understand the truth it applies to, you might end up having to force or twist the parable to fit it with the point you are trying to demonstrate. An opposite, more serious problem is that you might have to change the truth to fit in with the parable!

Jesus was the best teacher this world has ever seen. He used parables a great deal; and His parables were always given to demonstrate a particular teaching. Unfortunately, people often forget what Jesus was talking about at the time He delivered the parable. Without understanding the context of the parable, they take a point that they wish to demonstrate from somewhere else and then try to lay the parable alongside it. Inevitably, this leads to problems. Sometimes, it doesn't matter too much. For example, we saw in the last chapter how Jesus spoke about two men in a field, one of whom would be taken and the other left (Matthew 24:40-41). We saw how this parable, in context, applies to the Second Advent of Christ and the Baptism with Fire. Some people apply it inaccurately to the Rapture of the Church, but this isn't too serious—not much damage is done.

The Parable of the Ten Virgins must surely be the most frequently 'mutilated' of all Jesus' parables! It has probably caused more people difficulties than any other parable. Many preachers have wanted to explain the parable, but have backed out. Some make a good point from it and then say, "But I don't understand the rest". At least that is being honest.

It is tempting to say that, with this particular parable, the details do not matter, and the only point Christ was trying to emphasize was that we have got to be alert. However, Jesus went right through some of His other wonderful parables in meticulous detail, to explain the truths He was teaching. It therefore seems to me that every part of every parable Jesus gave must have some meaning.

In the Parable of the Ten Virgins there are five foolish virgins, who have no oil, and there are five wise virgins. The story has been used to support a number of unbiblical theories about salvation, the Second Coming, the Holy Spirit, and all sorts of other things! Some people have claimed it proves that, unless you are filled with the Holy Spirit, you are not saved.

They say a virgin represents a believer: the foolish ones have not been filled with the Holy Spirit, whereas the wise ones have been, so only the wise ones are saved. That is simply non-biblical. As soon as you compare that interpretation with other passages in the Word of God, it just does not match up. Using this parable as a basis for their doctrine, these people have gone into serious error—and can do a great deal of damage. They have not simply adjusted the parable to fit a point of truth, but have derived erroneous teaching from their own understanding of the parable. They have actually altered biblical teaching on salvation and the Holy Spirit, based on a parable taken out of context!

The one thing we must always do when we are studying a parable is to make sure that we get the context right. Jesus did not suddenly interrupt the chain of thought in His teaching and recount a story with no relevance to what He was saying. A parable was always a demonstration of His teaching. He would state His case, He would develop His case, and then He would give a parable to demonstrate the case.

The story of the ten virgins therefore has to be thrown alongside the point that Jesus was making and was seeking to demonstrate. We will see what point that was a little later on. However, first we need some historical background, because the parable relates to a wedding.

THE PICTURE OF CHRIST AND THE CHURCH AS A BRIDEGROOM AND BRIDE

Many wonderful descriptions are given of Christ and His Church in the New Testament. These are really parables—little pictures for us to lay down alongside the truth of Christ's relationship with the Church. They each demonstrate particular facets of the marvellous relationship we have with the Lord. I shall remind you of six such parables.

1. Christ is the Vine, and we are branches of the vine (John 15:1-8). This is a wonderful picture of Christ and those who are His disciples—the members of His Church. It demonstrates various principles about abiding in Christ and fruitfulness.

2. Jesus is the Shepherd, and we are His sheep (John 10:11-16; 1 Peter 5:4; Hebrews 13:20). This of course emphasizes that the Church really needs a shepherd to protect it, guide it, care for it and comfort it. Jesus is the perfect Shepherd for us.

3. Jesus is the great High Priest, and we are priests unto God (Hebrews 4:14; Revelation 1:6).

4. Jesus is the last Adam, and we are part of God's new creation in Christ (1 Corinthians 15:45; 2 Corinthians 5:17).

5. Jesus is the Head of the Body, and we are members of His Body (1 Corinthians 12:12-27; Ephesians 4:15-16; Colossians 2:19).

Note that all of these pictures apply *now*. It is true now that Jesus is the Vine and we are the branches. It is true now that He is our Shepherd and we are His sheep. It is true now that He is our great High Priest, the last Adam, the Head of the Body, and so on. But there is another marvellous picture that will be true *in the future*; and that is the picture of Christ as the Bridegroom and the Church as His bride. At the present time, we are still down here on this earth, not yet married to Christ. However, Christ has chosen us as His bride and He is 'wooing us'.

In 2 Corinthians chapter 11, for example, Paul talked to the Corinthian church and said, "**For I am jealous for you with godly jealousy. For I have betrothed you to one husband, that I may present you as a chaste virgin to Christ**" (verse 2). In other words, "Because Christ is so marvellous, and you are betrothed to Him, this is what I want you to be like in your love relationship with Him..."; and Paul went on to teach them how they should be pure, devoted to Christ and not led astray.

There is a beautiful passage in Ephesians chapter 5 that is read at many marriage services (verses 22-33). It contains two pictures. We find the picture of Christ as Head of the Body, but we also get the picture of Him as the husband and lover of the Church. Christ is coming, and He is deeply 'in love with' the Church. He has given Himself for her; and there is going to be a wonderful husband and wife relationship between them.

THE FUTURE WEDDING AND WEDDING FEAST OF CHRIST AND THE CHURCH

The point we must understand is that Christ soon will be the Bridegroom, while the Church is His bride-in-waiting. At the present time we are engaged, or betrothed, to Christ. We are not yet married, but we have the 'engagement ring' of the Holy Spirit as our guarantee.[2]

---

[2] In Ephesians 1:13-14, Paul said that we have been "**sealed with the Holy Spirit of promise, who is the guarantee of our inheritance until the redemption of the purchased possession**". The Greek word used for an 'engagement ring' is derived from the word here translated "**guarantee**" ("earnest" in the AV), which means a 'deposit' or 'downpayment', given as a guarantee that the full amount will be paid soon.

THE WISE AND FOOLISH VIRGINS

When will the relationship of husband and wife come about? On the wedding day, of course! Indeed, every person who is a believer in the Lord Jesus Christ has a wedding coming up, whether they are married in this world or not! And it is going to be the wedding of the universe! There won't have been another wedding like it.

When will the wedding take place? It will take place just before the Second Coming of Christ. Remember that, at the Rapture, all the believers (both alive and dead) who constitute the Body of Christ will be taken up from the earth and caught away into heaven. After the Church arrives in heaven, rewards will be given out, and the bride-to-be will be decked in beautiful attire—in fine righteousness and wonderful crowns. These rewards will be given because of our good works on this earth—those inspired and led by the Holy Spirit and carried out in obedience to God. There will be tribulation on the earth; but there will be a wedding day up in heaven.

In Revelation chapter 19 we find that, when the Lord Jesus returns to the earth, He is a married Man. He comes back with His bride! He comes back together with His Church in glory, as if to show her off down below on the earth.

"And I heard, as it were, the voice of a great multitude, as the sound of many waters and as the sound of mighty thunderings, saying, "Alleluia! For the Lord God Omnipotent reigns!"" (Revelation 19:6). Revelation chapter 18 ends a long description of the terrible Tribulation period on the earth. Chapter 19 then deals with the Second Coming of Christ, so we see God Omnipotent reigning. Jesus is about to come back to the earth, to reign there.

"Let us be glad and rejoice and give Him glory, for the marriage of the Lamb has come, and His wife has made herself ready" (verse 7). Oh, how glorious this is! There is so much talk about how Christ is going to prepare His Church, and indeed Christ *is* preparing His Church. But another aspect of the glory is that the Church makes herself ready. **"And to her it was granted to be arrayed in fine linen, clean and bright, for the fine linen represents the righteous acts of the saints"** (verse 8).

We have the marvellous privilege of helping to determine what type of wedding dress the Church is going to have. If we live in obedience to the Spirit now, we will be arrayed with beautiful clothes and jewels. If we do not, our works shall be burnt up and we shall suffer loss of reward. I am sure that the Lord Jesus does not want His bride dressed plainly. Our best quality works will come through the fire when they are judged—those done in obedience to God: the gold, silver and precious stones—and we shall receive a reward for them and be adorned on that day! Oh, it is a wonderful truth. The bride is making herself ready.

That is why it is right to be fervent for the Lord now, on this earth. Even after the earth passes away you are going to be arrayed in the wonderful clothes you have made for yourself by His grace. By co-operating with the Holy Spirit now you will get rewards for the works you are doing. And who is it for? It is all for Him! A bride spends hours preparing herself: not to show off, but for her bridegroom—because she loves him so much. That is part of the picture. That is why we should spend time asking God to deal with our lives and should ask the Holy Spirit to lead us in our lives: so that we might be the best dressed bride for our wonderful Saviour. He deserves it!

"Then he said to me, "Write:…"" (verse 9a). An important point of truth was coming up, so John was told to write it down. **"…Write: 'Blessed are those who are called to the marriage supper of the Lamb!'"** (verse 9b). The marriage supper means the wedding reception, or feast. In other words, "Blessed are the guests who are called to the great wedding feast of Jesus and His bride!" Oh, the bride is going to be blessed; but the guests are going to be blessed also. We are going to see who the guests are later on.

The Context of the Parable

It is essential to see the context of the parable; so let us see what Jesus was talking about in Matthew chapter 25. For the context, we have to turn back to the beginning of Matthew chapter 24.

"Then Jesus went out and departed from the temple…" (Matthew 24:1a). Jesus had been speaking for quite some time *in* the Temple (as recorded in the previous three chapters of Matthew's Gospel). He had slammed the religious leaders in His "Temple Discourse". He wanted them to realize that their religion would not get them anywhere; only salvation would get them somewhere with God. They needed to repent and believe on Him. Jesus finally left the Temple, making towards the Mount of Olives. As they were leaving, He told His disciples not to be unduly impressed by the Temple, for it would soon be utterly destroyed (verses 1b-2). What follows in chapters 24 and 25 is often called the "Olivet Discourse": it is what Jesus said to His disciples on the Mount of Olives.

"Now as He sat on the Mount of Olives, the disciples came to Him privately, saying, "Tell us, when will these things be? [when is the Temple going to be thrown down?] **And what will be the sign of Your**

coming, and of the end of the age?'" (Matthew 24:3). These questions began the Olivet Discourse. The context of the parable is therefore a description of what is going to occur before the Second Advent and the end of the age. Jesus described various signs: **"For many will come in My name, saying, 'I am the Christ.' and will deceive many. And you will hear of wars and rumours of wars. See that you are not troubled; for all these things must come to pass, but the end is not yet. For nation will rise against nation, and kingdom against kingdom. And there will be famines, pestilences, and earthquakes in various places"** (Matthew 24:5-7). These are the signs. Then Jesus said, **"All these are the beginning of sorrows"** (verse 8).

Further on, Jesus spoke about the Temple: **"Therefore when you see the 'abomination of desolation,' spoken of by Daniel the prophet, standing in the holy place"** (whoever reads, let him understand), **"then let those who are in Judea flee to the mountains"** (verses 15-16). Daniel spoke about this "abomination of desolation" (Daniel 11:31; 12:11; see also 9:27)—meaning an 'abomination that makes desolate' or 'abomination that causes horror'. This probably refers to a statue or image that will be set up in the Temple halfway through the Tribulation period. Jesus was describing events that shall occur during the seven-year period up to His Second Advent.[3]

If you read through Matthew chapter 24, you will see clearly that it is about the Tribulation. Then, in verse 29, we come to the Second Coming of Christ: **"Immediately after the tribulation of those days the sun will be darkened, and the moon will not give its light; the stars will fall from heaven, and the powers of the heavens will be shaken. Then the sign of the Son of Man will appear in heaven, and then all the tribes of the earth** [or, the land] **will mourn, and they will see the Son of Man coming on the clouds of heaven with power and great glory"** (verses 29-30). This is the Second Advent. Jesus was not talking about the Rapture of the Church.

Jesus then went on to describe how His angels, with a great trumpet blast, will gather together all His elect (all the believers and all the Jews) from one end of heaven to the other. He then gave parables to demonstrate what He had been talking about, including the Parable of the Ten Virgins in Matthew 25:1-13. (Remember that there are no chapter divisions in the original Scriptures. It is all the Olivet Discourse.)

---

[3] The Tribulation period is described in more detail in Basic Bible Studies 49 to 58.

After Jesus talked about the ten virgins, He told the Parable of the Talents (Matthew 25:14-30). He then made clear that He was still talking about His Second Coming: **"When the Son of Man comes in His glory, and all the holy angels with Him, then He will sit on the throne of His glory. All the nations will be gathered before Him, and He will separate them one from another, as a shepherd divides His sheep from the goats"** (Matthew 25:31-32). This is the Baptism with Fire, which follows the Second Advent. The whole context of Matthew chapters 24 and 25 is clearly the Tribulation, followed by the Second Coming of Christ and judgment.

What is the Parable of the Ten Virgins about then? It clearly is *not* about the Church. If you start trying to apply it to the Church, it will lead to trouble. That is why many people have had such difficulty interpreting it: they have thrown it alongside the wrong point of truth, because they have taken it right out of its context.

The bridegroom in the parable is not coming *to* his wedding, but is coming *from* his wedding to the wedding feast: **"And while they were going away to make the purchase, the bridegroom came, and those who were ready went in with him to the wedding feast; and the door was shut"** (Matthew 25:10, NASB).[4] It is the marriage *feast* that is in view here. The marriage has already taken place. The marriage of Jesus takes place in heaven. The banquet will take place back on the earth.

The same thing is made clear in Jesus' similar parable in Luke chapter 12: **"Let your waist be girded and your lamps burning; and you yourselves be like men who wait for their master, when he will return from the wedding, that when he comes and knocks they may open to him immediately"** (verses 35-36). There it is: the bridegroom will return *from* the wedding. Therefore, he will come to the wedding feast with his bride. They used to wear very long robes in those days, so Jesus was saying to His disciples, "Make sure that you've got a belt, or girdle, around your waist so that, when you need to run or do your job quickly, you can tuck your outer garment into your belt and it won't hinder you!" They were also told to have their lamps burning, meaning, "Make sure your testimony is clear and bright!" The point was, "Be ready for the coming of the Son of Man!" (see verse 40).

Next we need to understand who the virgins represent in Matthew 25. In the ancient world, kings used to have harems in their palaces. There is a lot

---

[4]The AV and NKJV say "wedding" rather than "wedding feast" in this verse.

written about these harems. There was not just one group of women in the royal court. There were actually three: the queens, who were married to the king; the concubines; and the virgins. Virgins had one task only: to wait on a queen. They used to dress the queen; they used to bathe her; they used to make sure her hair was combed beautifully; they used to make sure all her dresses were ready for her to wear. A virgin was usually a friend of the queen, for the queen would choose whom she wanted to serve her.[5] The word 'virgin' thus came to mean the friend of a bride. In the parable, the virgins were there to wait on the bride. We shall soon see whom they represent.

The Format of a Wedding

As soon as we think of a wedding, we immediately tend to think of one of our weddings, or perhaps of a modern Jewish wedding. In our day, in Britain, the father of the bride gives away his daughter. He effectively presents his daughter to the bridegroom. However, it was entirely different in the ancient world. To apply what goes on today to the parable leads to confusion. Let me therefore describe what a wedding was like in Jesus' day.

First of all, a wedding was usually arranged by the parents. They decided who was going to marry whom, and the bride and groom were not usually allowed to be alone together beforehand. They could see one another, but they needed someone else with them until the marriage day actually came. If the couple liked the choice, that was fine. Then the parents would set a particular day for the marriage.

The bride-to-be used to live with her parents. On the evening of the wedding, the bridegroom would hire a carriage or chariot (it would be quite an elaborate one), and he would leave his home and travel through the streets until he arrived at the home of his bride. Inside, she was all ready. She had been preparing herself for him. He would knock on the door and wait. Then his bride would come out, and they would say their goodbyes. The bride would then get into the carriage with the bridegroom and they would set off together. From that time forth, they were man and wife. That was the marriage ceremony. It was simple; that was all there was to it!

This of course derives from Adam and Eve. In Genesis, God said, **"Therefore a man shall leave his father and mother and be joined to**

---

[5] In the Song of Songs, the "daughters of Jerusalem" were probably virgins who were there to wait on Solomon's queens.

his wife..." (Genesis 2:24), so the wedding ceremony at the time of Jesus was a simple matter of leaving your parents. The bride was taken away from her parents by the bridegroom. This had never happened to her before; she had always lived under their protection until that time.

That was not the end of it, however. The couple then travelled to the bridegroom's house, where a reception was held—and they had a tradition for this wedding feast also. All the friends of the bridegroom would be inside the house with the door closed. They had prepared the inside of the house. The friends of the bride would have to stay outside the house until the bride came with her husband. Then they could go in together and celebrate. This procedure was quite beautiful and meaningful.

Sometimes the bride and groom had to travel many miles to get back to the bridegroom's house; so the friends inside the house used to put a lookout to watch for them coming along the road. It was usually around midnight when they came, since this all used to take place after the first stars had appeared, so it would be late into the evening. When the lookout saw a light in the distance, perhaps a torch burning on the chariot, he would immediately call back to the friends of the bride who were outside the house, "He's coming. Quick, get ready for them!" And they used to form two lines from the door out towards the chariot, so that the bride and groom could walk down between them into the wedding feast.

You have probably guessed the rest by now! Since it was dark, they used to have lamps and, as the couple approached, the young women would light their lamps. There would thus be two lines of lights, and the bridegroom and his new wife would proceed down this avenue of lights into the bridegroom's house, where the feast was prepared. After the friends of the bride had come in after them, the door was shut. A big party was then held to celebrate the marriage.

That was a wedding. The actual marriage ceremony was simply the taking away of the bride from her home by the bridegroom. The reception, however, was this more elaborate ceremony involving the friends of the bridegroom inside the house and the friends of the bride outside. All the disciples to whom Jesus told the parable would have understood the scene Jesus was describing. Most of them were probably married themselves.

THE CHARACTERS INVOLVED IN THE PARABLE

There were thus four people or groups involved at a wedding feast: the bridegroom, the bride and the two groups of friends. In the parable, only two of them are mentioned directly. However, all four are certainly involved.

THE WISE AND FOOLISH VIRGINS

The first person is the bridegroom. He is the Lord Jesus. The second person, who isn't mentioned except by implication, is the bride. She is the Church. The Church is coming back from the wedding with the bridegroom, to the wedding feast.

The third group is the virgins, the friends of the bride. Who are they? In Revelation 14:1-4, we have an interesting description of some of the Jews who will be alive during the Tribulation: they are described as "virgins". The friends of the bride are those Jews, during the Tribulation, who are expecting the Lord, their Messiah, to come.

The friends of the bridegroom are also not mentioned directly. They are already inside the house. They represent all those believers who are not in the Church: all those who became believers during the Old Testament period, before the Church, as well as all the believers who will die during the Tribulation. They will be 'inside the house' already when the Lord returns—where the wedding feast is prepared. Of course they will be!

Can you see the beautiful picture? It all fits perfectly. We have not had to fiddle anything. We are now finally ready to go through the parable itself; and we shall see a few more details as we go through. It *is* a complex parable. That is why we have had to cover so much background.[6]

THE PARABLE OF THE TEN VIRGINS (MATTHEW 25:1-13)

As we have noted, Matthew chapter 25 is not separate from chapter 24; it was all one conversation. Jesus talked about the coming of the Son of Man in chapter 24, then He immediately continued: **"Then the kingdom of heaven shall be likened to ten virgins who took their lamps and went out to meet the bridegroom"** (Matthew 25:1). "Then" means 'at that time'. Thus, at the time of the Second Advent, the kingdom of heaven is going to be like this: like ten virgins waiting to meet a bridegroom. The bridegroom will be about to return to his house with his bride, and the virgins will be waiting, holding their lamps, to go forth and meet them.

"Now five of them were wise, and five were foolish. Those who were foolish took their lamps and took no oil with them, but the wise took oil in their vessels with their lamps" (verses 2-4). I believe that this is specifically talking about the *Jews* who will be expecting their Messiah to

---

[6] If we had not laboured over the background, we would not be able to understood the parable. To see the glory in the Word of God, we often need to be prepared to study and discover the background. But the investment is well worth it!

come; but not all of them will be saved. The Holy Spirit is represented by the oil. Five of the virgins are born again. They are looking for Jesus to come back. They have believed on Him as their Messiah. They understand how He bore their sins and died for them. They have oil for their lamps. The other virgins, the five foolish ones, are also expecting the Messiah, but they have never actually stopped to ask the Lord to save them. They are probably very religious, possibly orthodox, Jews who have been working busily for God, to show Him just how righteous they are. However, they have never actually been born again. They think that, by their own works, because of their religious zeal, they are going to be able to face their Messiah when He comes. But they will be in for a shock, as we shall see.[7]

Just before a bridegroom came, the waiting virgins used to pour oil from their vessels into their lamps and light them up. A lamp represents a testimony (cf. John 5:35). The virgins in the parable *all* have a testimony. The foolish ones have just got their lamps. "We've been living perfectly good lives. Why do we need the Holy Spirit?" is what the foolish virgins are effectively saying.

"But while the bridegroom was delayed, they all slumbered and slept" (verse 5). Sometimes a bridegroom and bride were delayed. Here there has been a delay—seven years of tribulation in fact. The Jews were expecting their Messiah to come earlier. In view of the delay, they have *all* begun to fall asleep. (The word "slept" is in a continuous tense, suggesting that the virgins kept dozing off.)[8]

---

[7] We have such religious people today, who spend all their days talking about the Bible, talking about theology, and even talking about Jesus, but they are not born again. Yet we have other people who are born again, who also spend their days talking about the same things. It is no wonder the world is confused! Jesus described it like this: He said the kingdom of heaven is like a mustard seed (see Matthew 13:31-32). If you plant a mustard seed and it grows into a big tree, the birds of the air come and settle in the branches, so that soon you cannot tell which is the mustard tree and which are the birds of the air. The organized church today is rather like this. The "birds of the air" (false believers) are perching in the branches, saying, "I'm part of this tree"; but they are not.

[8] This of course could be applied to the Church too. 'Sleeping' is a major problem in the Body of Christ today, just as it will apply to Tribulational saints and religious unbelievers. Do you remember the thrill of first being saved? The message of the gospel burned in your heart; you just had to get it out to everyone. But now we tend to go to sleep. Satan is the best anaesthetic out! He tries to put us to sleep. He tries to curb our enthusiasm and our zeal. Do you remember the thrill of first having fellowship with other believers? Oh, how Satan comes and messes that up, doesn't he? It's not long before we start seeing only faults in others. What has happened? Satan has put us to sleep as far as the glory of the Body of Christ is concerned—he never puts us to sleep as far as the problems are concerned! Do you remember when the Word of God came alive to you, when you understood it for the first time? Oh, the thrill of it! But what now? Are you too tired to go to a Bible study? May God awaken us by His Holy Spirit!

THE WISE AND FOOLISH VIRGINS

After the Rapture of the Church, the Jews will realize that their Messiah is coming very soon. They will read Matthew 24 and 25, Daniel and the other prophets, and, at first, they will marvel at what they find. They will be really expectant—for a while! But then, gradually, they will start falling asleep.[9] Most Jews will be expecting their Messiah to come, but the reality will have gone from them. The unbelievers won't realize that Jesus is the Messiah and that He has had a wedding to go to first. This parable will be a warning to the Jews, "Don't let this happen to you!"

"And at midnight a cry was heard: 'Behold, the bridegroom is coming; go out to meet him!'" (verse 6). The lookout has seen something. Perhaps he has heard the sound of the chariot approaching. This is it, the midnight cry: "Quick, you virgins, get ready! Light your lamps. Come on, He's here!"

"Then all those virgins arose and trimmed their lamps" (verse 7). They *all* get up. The born-again ones get up; they know Jesus is coming. The religious ones get up too, thinking, "Now our Messiah will see how good and zealous we are!" But they are trusting in their own 'good' works. To 'trim a lamp' means to prepare it for lighting. They all cut the top off their wicks and light their lamps. By now the bridegroom is very near; the chariot is in sight.

The moment Jesus starts appearing will mark the end of the time of grace. There is no second chance after Jesus comes back. Just as the bridegroom appears, the foolish virgins realize that their religious activities are worthless. Their own good deeds, compared with the glory of Christ, amount to absolutely nothing. They have not got what is required; they are not born again. Their good works, they suddenly realize, are filthy rags in the sight of God—and they start panicking.

"And the foolish said to the wise, 'Give us some of your oil, for our lamps are going out'" (verse 8). Consider the two sets of lamps. Those containing oil are burning with a clear flame, giving a wonderful light. The others, however, are flickering and smouldering, causing a lot of smell and a lot of smoke. The foolish virgins lit their wicks, but the flames are diminishing because of a lack of oil. That is the difference between born-again people and religious people. Religious people have a faint glow at times; but they actually confuse the issue of the gospel. They are like a smoking wick, not producing a clear flame. The religious Jews suddenly

---

[9] In fact, probably the only ones who will remain fervent will be the 144,000 Jews who are "sealed" (see Revelation chapter 7). It seems that they will be evangelists, who will preach during the Tribulation.

realize that their flame is no good for the Bridegroom who is coming. Instead of turning to God, they turn to the believers, "Quick, give us some of your oil!" they implore. However, it is too late! The Bridegroom has come; and they cannot be born again now. They'd had opportunity to be saved, but they had ignored or rejected it because they loved religious observance.

"But the wise answered, saying, 'No, lest there should not be enough for us and you; but go rather to those who sell, and buy for yourselves'" (verse 9). What does this mean? There is only one way to receive the Holy Spirit, and that is by believing on the Lord Jesus Christ. You cannot buy the glorious person of the Holy Spirit. What are the wise virgins saying, then? "You've trusted in your own works all this time. You think your religion has worked. Go on, then, try and buy some of this oil that you need so badly!" It was a pointed remark to the foolish ones about their religion. They had their religion—their 'money'. "You try purchasing oil with what you've got!"

A panic begins; and it is described in several other passages of the Bible. The unbelievers will begin to hide their faces; they will begin to run; they will plead for the mountains to fall on them (cf. Luke 23:29-30; Revelation 6:12-17). They will realize that they are not good enough; and they will realize that it's too late.

"And while they went to buy, the bridegroom came, and those who were ready went in with him to the wedding [feast]; and the door was shut" (verse 10). The five wise virgins—the believers who are alive at the Second Advent—go in with Christ to the wedding feast. They join the Old Testament believers, and they have a glorious celebration. Jesus has returned, with His bride, and they are overjoyed to see Him.

The shutting of the door represents the Baptism with Fire—the actual judgment, or separation, of unbelievers from believers. The believers are now inside the house with Jesus, where they join in the feast. The unbelievers, however, are excluded. As Revelation 19:9 tells us, **"'Blessed are those who are called to the marriage supper of the Lamb!'"** Oh, how blessed they are! Yes, indeed. They are believers in the Messiah. The Holy Spirit has set them apart; and they are welcomed inside.

"Afterwards the other virgins came also, saying, 'Lord, Lord, open to us!'" (verse 11). This immediately reminds us of that scripture, **"Many will say to Me in that day, 'Lord, Lord, have we not prophesied in Your name, cast out demons in your name, and done many wonders in your name?' And then I will declare to them, 'I never knew you; depart from Me, you who practise lawlessness!'"** (Matthew 7:22-23).

At the present time, no one can confess that Jesus is Lord except by the Holy Spirit (see 1 Corinthians 12:3). If today someone truly says, "Jesus is Lord", he or she is a born-again believer. But the Scriptures make clear that, when Jesus comes again as judge, *every* knee shall bow and *every* tongue confess that He is Lord (Philippians 2:10-11; Romans 14:11)—not just those of believers, but *every* knee and tongue. Therefore, at the time of judgment described here, everyone will recognize that Jesus is Lord; but not everyone will be saved.

I believe that, during the Tribulation period, the 'religious church' will have the greatest revival ever. If you think that the religious church, or 'counterfeit church' is going to die out, you are seriously mistaken. Rather, it is coming in for its heyday. Also, during the Tribulation, Satan will work many miracles. Fantastic things will take place—some of which are described in 2 Thessalonians chapter 2. Great miracles will be performed; and many of the religious, unregenerate people, who have worshipped the Beast and joined with the False Prophet, will perform miracles themselves. They will think that, on the basis of their works, they will get into heaven. However, they will be deceived.

Returning to the parable, we see the bridegroom's response: **"But He answered and said, 'Assuredly, I say to you, I do not know you'"** (Matthew 25:12). The foolish virgins do not know the Lord. Jesus therefore says to them, "Depart from Me. I don't know you, and I never will know you. It's too late." That is the Baptism with Fire. These people do not have God's Spirit indwelling them.

The parable ends with this warning: **"Watch therefore, for you know neither the day nor the hour in which the Son of Man is coming"** (Matthew 25:13). Jesus was repeating what He said in Matthew 24:36, that no one knows the day or hour of the Second Coming, except the Father.

Conclusion

The purpose of this parable is to tell believers during the Tribulation, "Stay alert! Be ready! The Son of Man is coming any time. Don't slumber and sleep. Wake up!" It is also a warning to those Jews who have not been born again that they need to be saved. I would summarize the message as this: *a lack of foresight is inexcusable*. A lack of reality concerning what is about to happen has no excuse whatsoever.

"Neglect," Jesus was warning the unbelievers, "is going to cost you very dear. Don't neglect the fact that I am coming soon. Don't neglect your need of repentance and faith in Me." The Jews will read this parable during the Tribulation and I believe that they will understand it. It is going to be a major help, as well as a warning. Ignorance of the exact time of Christ's coming will be no excuse.

Indeed, may *our* ignorance of the exact time when Jesus will come again for His Church similarly be something that spurs us on to remain ever fervent for the Lord. We do not know when the Rapture is going to occur, just as the Jews won't know exactly when the Second Advent is going occur. The principle is the same. Just because we do not know the exact time, we must not use that as an excuse to become worldly or to fall asleep. Rather, keep yourself for Christ! Serve Him; love Him; remain on fire for Him!

To use a well known exhortation: We should live today as if Christ died yesterday, rose today, and is coming again tomorrow! That is the key for us all. The Rapture might take place today or tomorrow. It might be in one year's time; it might be in five years; we don't know. Whenever it will be, we should live for the Lord today.

This parable applies particularly to those who will be alive just before the Second Coming of Christ; but it has a message for us now. The world needs us to be on fire for the Lord—to have a clear, bright testimony—to be burning and shining for the Lord. Let us make sure that we learn from this parable. If you are born again, but are slumbering, then wake up! He is coming for us very soon, and the world needs Him.

15. THE GREAT WHITE THRONE
The Judgment of Unbelievers

We come now to the final and most devastating of all judgments. It is the Last Judgment, before the great white throne of God, described in Revelation 20:11-15. It is the final judgment that will affect this present earth and this present universe. It is the time when God will judge all unbelievers.

When we read the word "white" in Scripture, it is a reference to purity and to absolute righteousness. Therefore the great white throne—which is great because it has a great Judge sitting on it in power and glory—represents the holiness and righteousness of God.

I pray that as I speak about this judgment, its reality will grip every person. It is so important for all of us to understand. We all have neighbours and friends who do not believe in God's great white throne; but, whether they believe in it or not, the day is coming when they are going to stand before the Lord Jesus enthroned there. It is going to be the most terrible and dreadful day. In fact, the fear that will be attached to that day is something we can wish on no one. It is something that the Lord Jesus Himself wishes on no one. Nevertheless, as surely as the Bible is the Word of God, this judgment day is coming.

Every person will see God's throne; but every unbeliever will stand in dread before it for judgment. For the unbeliever, after the great white throne will come the eternal, burning lake of fire. An end so awful, so horrific, is almost beyond human comprehension.

I want to remind you first of all that judgment has been restrained for thousands of years because God loves every single person in this world so much. The final judgment should have come thousands of years ago, because the human race has deserved it. However, God wanted to supply the remedy for us all first. In His grace, He has waited for as many people as possible to receive His remedy—the great salvation He has provided—so that they won't have to appear before Him for judgment. He wants to bring many sons to glory. There is only one remedy: to believe on the Lord Jesus Christ and be saved. The sufferings Christ went through on the Cross, and leading up to the Cross, were so awful because the doom faced by every single person on this earth was so awful. When God considered the lake of fire, He wanted to provide a way out for us. There was no other hope for us. Therefore, salvation was an essential part of His plan.

Today, if you are reading this book and you are without Christ and without hope, then it is essential that you understand this: the great white throne is coming to *you*, as well as to the rest of this world. Your reaction to it will depend on whether or not you have believed on Christ. If you have believed on Him for salvation, it holds no fear. However, if you do not believe, this day of judgment *is* coming; and it's going to be frightening.

Some people, of course, believe that death is going to provide a rest for them. Many people, and I used to be one of them, think that death marks the end of consciousness and that there is nothing afterwards. That is a lie of Satan. If you are trusting in death as the final escape, you will be in for a very bad shock indeed, for death is not the final thing. The day is coming when every unbeliever will stand in the majestic presence of God, and will feel as if they want to shrink away or shrivel up. They are going to long for everything to end. They will beg for annihilation, but will not receive it.

Jesus suffered in such agony because of the awesome reality of what is coming on that day. We should never underestimate what Jesus went suffered, nor fail to realize that He would not have had to endure what He did if the prospect awaiting us had not been so extremely serious. What we are talking about here is so dreadful because it is real. It is true and unchangeable. The lake of fire *is* coming; and it is coming soon. There is going to be a judgment day. Therefore, even today, believe on the Lord Jesus Christ and be saved!

For some reading this, it may be your last opportunity to believe on the Lord. You do not know what is going to happen. You could collapse and die today. This could be the most important moment of your life if you do not yet have Christ. It is essential that you put your trust in the Lord Jesus Christ, who died for your sins. The promise of the Word of God is clear: **"Believe on the Lord Jesus Christ, and you will be saved"** (Acts 16:31b). If you believe on Him, you will be delivered from the judgment that is coming upon the world. Make sure that today is the day, if you have not yet believed on the Lord. God loves you. He does not want you to stand before His throne in the prospect of judgment. He does not want any member of the human race to be cast into the lake of fire. That is why He has provided such a wonderful salvation.

To those who are Christians already, I pray that the reality of what we are talking about is going to grip you so much that you will be occupied and constrained by it, because the very people whom you meet today are going to see God's great white throne. It is certain. And we have a job, as watchmen, to warn people of what is coming to them.

We live in days when people do not like talking about Hell. They do not like talking about judgment and they do not like talking about the lake of fire. This is all deception. It is a result of the enemy's lies. If Satan can convince people that they will not exist after death, then they will proceed ignorantly and fearlessly towards the lake of fire. We have got to make sure that we give them the message loud and clear. Peter foretold how "**scoffers will come in the last days, walking according to their own lusts, and saying, "Where is the promise of His coming? For since the fathers fell asleep, all things continue as they were from the beginning of creation**" (2 Peter 3:3b-4). The world might not think that Jesus will come again; but come He will.

It would be quite wrong of me, since I am talking about the final judgment, not to begin on a serious note like this. Let us now move on to consider the details of this judgment, to see what will take place and when it is going to occur.

ALL WILL BE RESURRECTED: BELIEVERS AND UNBELIEVERS

Let me first say something that is so obvious, or so often assumed, that very few people ever say it or even realize they believe it. It is this: *Every single person who has ever lived and died on the earth is going to be resurrected.* Believers *and* unbelievers alike are going to be resurrected. Have you ever thought of this before?

By 'resurrection' I do not mean resuscitation, reviving or revitalization, which refer to bringing someone back to life temporarily. In hospitals today, for example, it is not uncommon for people whose hearts have stopped beating, or who have stopped breathing, to be resuscitated or revived. However, that does not mean that they will not die again later. It simply means that they have been brought back to life for a while.

Lazarus was brought back to life by Jesus (see John chapter 11) after he had been dead for several days. Jesus truly raised him up from death. Nevertheless, Lazarus is definitely not alive today.

Resurrection means *bringing someone back to life for ever and ever, so that he or she will never die again*. Every person on the face of the earth who has died, believer and unbeliever, is going to be resurrected—not resuscitated, revived or raised up temporarily. Believers will then live forever with God; but unbelievers will go into the lake of fire forever. It is the fact of resurrection that makes our salvation so wonderful and the destiny of unbelievers so awful. Resurrection is certainly for ever and ever.

Knowledge of this truth has been around for thousands of years. It is not something new that came in with Christ or the apostle Paul! In the Old Testament Job spoke of resurrection (see Job 19:25-27), as did Daniel: **"And many of those who sleep in the dust of the earth shall awake, some to everlasting life, some to shame and everlasting contempt"** (Daniel 12:2). This clearly means future resurrection. Some, which refers to believers, shall awake to everlasting life, but some others (unbelievers) shall awake to shame and everlasting contempt. There are thus *two* resurrections, or types of resurrection; but resurrections they are, both of them.

Now let us see what Jesus said about these two resurrections in John chapter 5. This is the passage we went through right at the beginning of this book, when we discovered that Jesus is God's appointed Judge.

"Most assuredly, I say to you, he who hears My word and believes in Him who sent Me has everlasting life, and shall not come into judgment, but has passed from death into life" (verse 24). This is a promise for you if you are a believer. You will not come into judgment. The great white throne is not for you. You will see it, but you will not come before it for judgment.

"Most assuredly, I say to you, the hour is coming, and now is, when the dead will hear the voice of the Son of God; and those who hear will live. For as the Father has life in Himself, so he has granted the Son to have life in Himself, and has given Him authority to execute judgment also, because He is the Son of Man. Do not marvel at this; for the hour is coming in which all who are in the graves will hear His voice..." (verses 25-28). All who are in the graves—every single person who has ever died—will hear the voice of Jesus Christ.

"And come forth—those who have done good, to the resurrection of life, and those who have done evil, to the resurrection of condemnation" (verse 29). The dead are *all* going to come forth. This means resurrection. Just as Daniel said centuries before, there will be *two* resurrections: one to life and the other to condemnation.

Jesus described the difference between those who do good and those who do evil in John chapter 3: **"He who believes in Him is not condemned; but he who does not believe is condemned already, because he has not believed in the name of the only begotten Son of God. And this is the** condemnation, that the light has come into the world, and men loved darkness rather than light, because their deeds were evil. For everyone practising evil hates the light and does not come to the light, lest his deeds should be exposed. But he who does the truth comes to the light, that his deeds may be clearly seen, that they have been done in God"** (verses 18-21). Those who do good come to the light—they come to Jesus and are born again. They love light rather than darkness. However, those who do evil do not come to the light, for they love darkness and hate the light. They will not come to Christ, believe in Him and be born again.

The Timing of the Two Resurrections

The two resurrections will both last forever. One is to eternal life, whilst the other is to an eternity in the lake of fire. Another difference between them is that they will occur at different times. Believers will be resurrected at least 1000 years before all the unbelievers, prior to the start of the Millennium. By the time of the Second Advent of Christ, all believers will be raised up. All unbelievers will only be resurrected after the end of the Millennium.

1 Corinthians chapter 15 deals with the subject of resurrection in some detail. It is a glorious passage, and one of my favourites. It describes death being conquered—by resurrection. Perhaps you have never understood before what it means for death to be conquered?

"But now Christ has risen from the dead, and has become the first-fruits of those who have fallen asleep" (verse 20). Christ rose from the dead, with results that will last forever. Having risen, He is risen forever. There will never come a day when Christ will not be risen. Hallelujah! May that be a great source of comfort to us all. The phrase **"those who have fallen asleep"** means those who have died physically, right from Adam onwards. They are in the claws of death, asleep, waiting to be resurrected.

Christ too was once in the claws of death, but He is now risen from the dead. And He is the first-fruits. The first-fruits were always harvested first, as a sign that the rest of the harvest would soon be brought in. They were the part of the harvest lifted up to God at the beginning. Therefore, as surely as Christ, the first-fruits, is now risen from the dead, so the rest of mankind is going to be resurrected soon. That is the point Paul was making.

"For since by man came death, by Man also came the resurrection of the dead" (verse 21). By the first man, Adam, death came to all. Both physical and spiritual death came to all human beings because of Adam's sin, although Paul specifically had *physical* death in view here. We all are destined to die physically because of Adam's sin. However, by another Man, Jesus Christ, came the resurrection of the dead.

"For as in Adam all die, even so in Christ all shall be made alive" (verse 22). The "all" here means literally all! This does not mean that all shall be saved—that all shall be made *spiritually* alive. Rather, the previous verse shows what it means: Paul was talking about *physical* resurrection. Both unbelievers and believers will all be made alive physically because of Christ, who is the first-fruits of all those who have died physically.

"Each one in his own order"

Verse 23 begins: **"But each one in his own order"**. Those who are dead are not all going to be resurrected together. They are going to be resurrected in a particular order. The word translated "order" here was in fact a military term used for a company in an army. An army had battalions and each battalion had four companies. Paul was therefore saying that the 'battalion' of all human beings is going to be resurrected in companies—that is, in four specific groups. I am going to call them: "A Company", "B Company", "C Company" and "D Company". Let us therefore identify who is in each company, because this is important.

A Company

The first company is **"Christ the first-fruits"** (verse 23b). It therefore comprises just one Man, the Lord Jesus Christ. Three days after He died, Jesus rose from the dead, as the first-fruits. Therefore, the resurrection of A Company has already taken place. The resurrection of the other three companies is yet to come.

B Company

Next Paul said, **"afterwards those who are Christ's at His coming"** (verse 23c). Those who are Christ's are believers. We know from other scriptures that believers will be raised up in two groups, at the Rapture and at the Second Coming. These two groups are therefore B Company and C Company.

At the Rapture, B Company will be raised. It will comprise all the members of the Church who have died. The Lord Jesus will come for His bride, to take her to their magnificent wedding in heaven.

The dead in Christ will rise first (see 1 Thessalonians 4:13-18). Therefore, if members of your family who were believers have died, they are going to be resurrected before you—unless you also die before the Rapture! "**Then we who are alive and remain shall be caught up together with them in the clouds to meet the Lord in the air. And thus we shall always be with the Lord**" (1 Thessalonians 4:17). Those believers who are alive at the Rapture will not die physically, but shall be changed. "**Behold, I tell you a mystery: We shall not all sleep, but we shall all be changed**" (1 Corinthians 15:51). Thus those who have died in Christ will be resurrected; then those who are alive will be changed and caught up together with them. That is B Company, and it is a wonderful resurrection.

C Company

Which believers are in C Company then? They will be raised up at the end of the Tribulation, seven years after the Church has been taken up. These are all the remaining believers who have died: hence, all of the Old Testament saints and all those who die as believers during the Tribulation. C Company thus includes Rahab, Ezekiel, Jeremiah, Daniel, Abraham and all of the other Old Testament saints, including Adam; they are all going to be raised up!—And so will all the believers who are martyred or who die during the Tribulation. How wonderful!

At the end of the Tribulation, by the time of the Second Advent of Christ, all believers throughout history will thus have been raised up. That is why I said earlier that all believers will be resurrected before the start of the Millennium. The Bible defines this as the "first resurrection" (Revelation 20:4-6), as we will see later. It is what Daniel spoke about and what Jesus spoke about—the resurrection of believers to eternal life.

Those believers who survive the Tribulation and are still alive at the Second Advent will also go through into the Kingdom with the resurrected believers. They will not die. Rather, *at the end of the Millennium* they will be changed, just as those believers alive at the Rapture will be changed. Now we have only got D Company to go.

D Company

D Company comprises unbelievers: all the unbelievers who died during the Old Testament period up to the time of Christ, all unbelievers who have died or will die during the Church age up to the Rapture, all those unbelievers who will die during the Tribulation and all those who will die during the Millennium. They will all remain dead until after the end of the Millennium, when they all will be resurrected together. However, theirs is not a resurrection unto everlasting life; it will be a resurrection unto judgment—to condemnation, shame and everlasting contempt. D Company is thus raised up at least 1000 years after C Company. The resurrection of the whole of mankind will then be complete.

"Then comes the end, when He delivers the kingdom to God the Father, when He puts an end to all rule and all authority and power" (1 Corinthians 15:24). At the end of the Millennium there will be a final revolt against God, as we will see below (Revelation 20:7-10). The Lord Jesus will smite the rebels down, and He will present the Kingdom, which will then be fully His, to His Father. Satan will be gone, cast into the lake of fire; and all unbelievers will have been resurrected, judged and also cast into the lake of fire. **"For He must reign till He has put all enemies under His feet"** (verse 25).

Death is Finally Defeated

"The last enemy that will be destroyed is death" (1 Corinthians 15:26). Death will not be completely destroyed until the final company is resurrected. Many people interpret this verse to mean that death will have no further *influence*. But it means much more than that! It means that any influence or effect that death *has ever had*, since the earth was established, will be reversed, repealed and annulled! After the final resurrection of all unbelievers at the end of the Millennium, not one person will still be held captive in death!

Death at the present time has millions of victims, and the number is increasing every day. Death has been gathering them in, ever since Adam sinned. Just one Man, Jesus Christ, has so far been raised up out of death permanently—the first-fruits of all those who have died, or who will die. A Company is risen! But B Company, then C Company and, finally, D Company will also each be raised up in turn, until every single one of death's victims will have been removed from its grip.

Death seemed to have won, to have captured its victims forever. However, when Christ rose from the dead, it began to lose its grip. Very soon, when the dead in Christ rise and the Church is raptured, death will be clearly losing the battle. Then, at the Second Advent, the battle will be almost lost. And finally, after the end of the Millennium, every single person will have been resurrected. Death will no longer have conquered, or overcome any member of the human race. The Lord Jesus will then have all of His enemies under His feet. His complete victory over death will finally be realized! Death will own no one. The Lord will have provided resurrection for all. That is why the last enemy that shall be destroyed is death. That is what this means. Hallelujah!

However, death is not completely destroyed yet. We only have to look around us to see this! Yet it *will* be completely destroyed after the end of the Millennium. Death is going to be empty. That is why this point about the future resurrection of all *un*believers, as well as believers, is so important. If unbelievers shall always remain dead, then death would have won a partial victory: it would still hold some people in its grip forever. But no! In Christ, all shall be resurrected! "**In Christ all shall be made alive**" (verse 22b). Praise His wonderful name!

"**The last enemy that will be destroyed is death. For "He has put all things under His feet." But when He says, "all things are put under Him," it is evident that He who put all things under Him is excepted. Now when all things are made subject to Him, then the Son Himself will also be subject to Him who put all things under Him, that God may be all in all**" (verses 26-28). The Father will never be put under the Son. He will never become subject to His Son. The Son has accomplished the actual work of salvation, but still He will be subject to His Father. He wants to give all the glory to His Father. He desires to take no credit for Himself, no glory for Himself. He is occupied only with the glory He can give His Father. Oh, may we be like that—not wanting any glory for ourselves, but putting God's glory first!

Further on in 1 Corinthians chapter 15, Paul made this triumphant declaration: "**So when this corruptible has put on incorruption, and this mortal has put on immortality, then shall be brought to pass the saying that is written: "Death is swallowed up in victory." "O Death, where is your sting? O Hades, where is your victory?"**" (verses 54-55). Death will have no sting left. It will be swallowed up by Christ's victory! Death is already losing its grip; it is not as victorious or influential as it used to be. Christ has risen; and soon death will hold no one! Christ's victory over death is so rarely explained, but it is glorious. Now we can understand why the statement, "**The last enemy that will be destroyed is death**" (verse 26) comes *after* the fact that each one shall be raised in his own order. It is a wonderful revelation.

THE EVENTS DESCRIBED IN THE BOOK OF REVELATION

Chapters 6 through to 18 of the Book of Revelation describe the horrors of the Tribulation. Then, in chapter 19, we glimpse the Second Advent of Christ and the glorious victory accompanying Christ's return. Then we come to the Millennium.

The Millennium (Revelation 20:1-6)

"**Then I [John] saw an angel coming down from heaven, having the key to the bottomless pit and a great chain in his hand**" (Revelation 20:1). The bottomless pit is sometimes called the great 'Abyss'. It is the place where Satan is going to be locked up. It is the devil's jail. A great chain is going to bind him up—and it is strong enough to hold him, so that he will have no influence during the Millennium.[1]

"**He laid hold of the dragon, that serpent of old, who is the Devil and Satan, and bound him for a thousand years**" (verse 2). The angel will chain up Satan for 1000 years. That is why this period is called "The Millennium". Satan is called "that serpent of old"—a reference to his appearance in the Garden of Eden (see Genesis chapter 3). He has been around for a long time; but his days are definitely numbered!

"**And he** [the angel] **cast him into the bottomless pit, and shut him up, and set a seal on him...**" (verse 3a). Satan will be shut in, implying a lid will be put on the bottomless pit. No one will be able to hear his cries! They used to put a seal on a pit or dungeon, to make sure that the prisoner inside had not escaped. I am sure that, every day, the seal will be checked to ensure that Satan is still in there; and of course he will be!

If the Rapture were to occur next year, then Satan would be bound just seven years after that. Therefore, we are talking here about an event that might be just seven or eight years away from today, or perhaps 10 or 20 years from now. Whenever it is, it will be soon! No wonder Satan is getting anxious; he knows what's going to happen. He's going to be thrown into the bottomless pit and chained up, and a tight lid will be put over him. Then, he is going to spend 1000 years all by himself, shut up in solitary confinement. He will no longer be able to use the earth as his plaything.

"**So that he should deceive the nations no more till the thousand years were finished**" (verse 3b). This tells us that Satan *is* currently deceiving the nations. They *are* truly deceived. The day may come when the governments of our nations forbid us from talking about Hell or talking about judgment, because they will say it is psychologically harmful for people to think about such things! But they are deceived. The very people who might pass such laws will themselves end up in death and Hades, then before the great white throne and, finally, in the eternal lake of fire.

---

[1] More details about the Millennium, and what it will be like on the earth at that time, are given in Basic Bible Studies 60-61, entitled "The Millennium" and Special Topic Studies 7-10 entitled "The Millennial Issue".

THE GREAT WHITE THRONE

"**But after these things he must be released for a little while**" (verse 3c). For a short while, at the end of the Millennium, Satan will be let out, as we shall see.

The First Resurrection

"**And I saw thrones, and they sat on them, and judgment was committed to them. And I saw the souls of those who had been beheaded for their witness to Jesus and for the word of God, who had not worshipped the beast or his image, and had not received his mark on their foreheads or on their hands. And they lived and reigned with Christ for a thousand years**" (verse 4). This refers to the Tribulational martyrs. They are resurrected at the beginning of the Millennium and they then live and reign with Christ during the Millennium. They did not receive the mark of the Beast—the identification mark or seal of the Beast's religious organization that will be established during the Tribulation. Rather, these saints stuck closely to the Lord during those terrible years and, as a result, they were tortured and killed. But now they are raised, as part of C Company, and they live and reign with Christ for 1000 years!

"**But the rest of the dead did not live again until the thousand years were finished. This is the first resurrection**" (verse 5). The first sentence here in verse 5 could be put in brackets. It describes what shall happen to the rest of the dead. Verse 4, the second part of verse 5 and verse 6 go together; it is obvious as you read on. The first resurrection can be defined as the resurrection of all believers before the Millennium. (The second resurrection is the resurrection of all unbelievers, which will not take place until after the Millennium. However, John mentions it here to fill in what is going to happen to the rest of the dead.)

"**Blessed and holy is he who has part in the first resurrection. Over such the second death has no power...**" (verse 6a). Amen! The second death is the name given to eternal judgment in the lake of fire. It is not physical death, which is the first death. Believers will not experience the second death, "**but they shall be priests of God and of Christ, and shall reign with Him a thousand years**" (verse 6b). Hallelujah!

If you are a believer you will not be thrown into the lake of fire. The Word of God says so; and it cannot be broken. The second death will have no effect upon you. Praise God! This is the gospel message in the Book of Revelation. To be included in this first resurrection, believe on the Lord Jesus Christ and be saved! What does it cost you but your pride? If you put your trust in Him, the second death will have no power over you. But the converse is also true: if you do not believe, the second death awaits you.

Satan is Loosed at the End of the Millennium (Revelation 20:7-10)

We now jump 1000 years to the end of the Millennium: **"Now when the thousand years have expired, Satan will be released from his prison and will go out to deceive the nations which are in the four corners of the earth, Gog and Magog, to gather them together to battle, whose number is as the sand of the sea. They went up on the breadth of the earth and surrounded the camp of the saints and the beloved city. And fire came down from God out of heaven and devoured them"** (verse 7-9). I am not going to go through this in detail here.[2] The "saints" here are those who are believers at the end of the Millennium. The "beloved city" is Jerusalem.

"And the devil, who deceived them, was cast into the lake of fire and brimstone where the beast and the false prophet are. And they will be tormented day and night for ever and ever" (verse 10). When we dealt with the judgment of Satan, we identified his three falls. Here is the main scripture describing Satan's third fall—his final judgment. At the end of the Millennium, Satan will be released for a short time, to go out and deceive the nations for a final time. Then, he will be thrown into the lake of fire forever.

The Beast and the False Prophet will have been in the lake of fire for 1000 years already. They are going to be cast in there before the Millennium (see Revelation 19:20). Now we come to the great white throne.

Final Judgment at the Great White Throne (Revelation 20:11-15)

Resurrection is permanent; and unbelievers will go to be with the devil in the lake of fire, to be tormented day and night forever and ever. There is no escape. I know this offends our human minds, but the Bible is a greater authority than our human minds. Let us recognize this. In fact, we can get nowhere with this subject unless we accept the reality that the Bible indeed is the inspired Word of God. God means what He says, and it is not for us to question the Bible as far as these things are concerned. We do so at our peril. God's Word surpasses all human reasoning and comprehension.

---

[2]Satan's final rebellion is described in more detail in Basic Bible Study 61, which explains the reasons why God will release him for a short while and what it will prove.

Here we come finally to our main passage. This is not fantasy. It is not just a story. It really will be like this. **"Then I saw a great white throne and Him who sat on it, from whose face the earth and the heaven fled away. And there was found no place for them"** (verse 11). At the end of the Millennium, the earth and heaven—that is, the whole universe—will pass away and be destroyed, by fire. This will make way for a new heaven and a new earth (Revelation 21:1).

It seems as if there will be some type of nuclear process, and the earth and heaven will simply melt away: "**...the heavens will pass away with a great noise, and the elements will melt with fervent heat; both the earth and the works that are in it will be burned up....all these things will be dissolved....the heavens, being on fire, will be dissolved, and the elements will melt with fervent heat**" (see 2 Peter 3:10b-12).

Isaiah described this as like a scroll being rolled up. He couldn't describe it in any other way: "**All the host of heaven shall be dissolved, and the heavens shall be rolled up like a scroll; all their host shall fall down as the leaf falls from the vine, and as fruit falling from a fig tree**" (Isaiah 34:4). If you have seen pictures of an atomic bomb exploding, the cloud looks as if it rolls up into itself. Such a nuclear phenomenon could be similar to what Isaiah described. This verse also implies that the stars will plummet down through the sky. We do not know how God will do these things, but it will be a spectacular event of such enormous magnitude that we can scarcely imagine it.

This is Jesus being revealed as He truly is, in all power and glory. When He comes at the end of the Millennium, in the awesome power and great glory that are His, the earth and the whole universe will have to disappear 'in a flash of smoke'.[3] That is how powerful Jesus really is. (Isn't it therefore good to know that He is on your side, if you are a believer!) Earth and heaven shall have to flee away from the face of Jesus, but there is nowhere for them to go. Why? Because Jesus is omnipresent! When the earth and heaven are destroyed, they will probably be added to the lake of fire.

The Second Resurrection

Now we come to the resurrection of unbelievers—of D Company. "**And I saw the dead, small and great, standing before God**" (Revelation 20:12a). I think the way that this is put is tragic. If John had said the "great

---

[3] Just as all things were created through Jesus, the Son of God (John 1:3, Colossians 1:16), so He will bring this present universe to an end (Hebrews 1:10-12).

and small", we could immediately say, "It doesn't matter how great you are: whether you're a king or lord, it doesn't matter; you're going to stand there!" But the small are put first here. Some people think that, because they are insignificant, because they have not done any harm to anyone, but have just lived a quiet life, they are going to be all right on the day of judgment. But they are deceived. Living a quiet life will not make you acceptable to God. I have heard it said that perfect love is not the only thing that casts out fear: ignorance and apathy do so also. But these are not an excuse. Salvation comes only through one Man, the Lord Jesus Christ. Therefore, whether you live in a palace or a bed-sit, whether you are the noisiest person or the most shy and introverted person, you need the Lord Jesus. You need His salvation; you need His grace. The small and the great will stand together before God.

"And books were opened. And another book was opened, which is the book of life. And the dead were judged according to their works, by the things which were written in the books" (verse 12b). These people's sins *were* taken by Jesus on the Cross. Jesus really did die for the sins of the whole world. But these people are not saved, because they never put their trust in Him for salvation.

The books contain lists of everything these people have ever done in their lives. I believe that God will look through the books, as if trying to find something that could possibly earn them salvation. He will try to find something they have done that is good enough—that matches what Christ did. But He won't find any such thing, of course. I expect that we will hear many of these people crying out, "But, Lord, I've done this!"…."But Lord, I've done that!" However, God will say, "I know. I can read it here. However, it is not good enough. Do you mean to say that you thought your own works could get you into heaven?"

The Book of Life will be opened too. It is a register of all those who have believed on the Lord Jesus Christ. It is as if God, in grace, double-checks to see if some of the unbelievers' names might be in there; but it's no good.

Can you imagine the feelings in these people's hearts? Can you imagine what is actually going to go through their minds at this point? They might say, "But I did all those good works!", yet He will reply, "All your good works are as filthy rags to Me! They are worthless as far as I am concerned. Why wouldn't you simply believe on Christ and accept His work on your behalf?" Some might argue, "But I never had the opportunity," and God will remind them, "Yes you did. Don't you remember that man who told you about Jesus? You thought he was a religious fanatic; so you dismissed his message as old-fashioned nonsense." The Lord will have to say to all those unbelievers, "You turned down the only remedy." Then, tragically, judgment will have to follow.

"The sea gave up the dead who were in it" (verse 13a). Those who died on land and at sea will all be included. There is no unbeliever who can escape this judgment. No matter how anyone died, *all* are going to be resurrected.

God knows every single human being that has ever lived. Every human bone, skull or human remain that is found on this earth belongs to someone who, one day, is going to be resurrected—either in the first resurrection or at the end of the Millennium. The earth is sometimes called "the land of the living" but, actually, it is a great cemetery. That is the truth, isn't it? Millions of people are buried on this earth, and their remains are still here, no matter how decayed. The Lord knows each one of them and they are all going to be resurrected—tragically for most of them. Judgment is inescapable.

Notice what it says next: "**...and death and Hades delivered up the dead who were in them**" (verse 13b). This refers to the final resurrection of all unbelievers. Death is finally emptied of every human soul. "**And they were judged, each one according to his works**" (verse 13c). Notice that the Lord looks at the *works* of these people, and judges them according to their *works*. However, He will have to say to each one, "It's no good! Your works are not good enough to save you."

Verse 14 is a very interesting verse: "**Then death and Hades were cast into the lake of fire. This is the second death.**" Some Christians warn unbelievers, "You are going to spend eternity in Hell!" but that is not strictly true. 'Hell' (synonymous now with 'Hades', since only unbelievers are there)[4] is only a *temporary* stopping place for the unregenerate—a temporary place. It is the eternal lake of fire that is the real danger for unbelievers.

At the end of the Millennium, when all the dead unbelievers have been raised, death and Hades are going to be cast into the lake of fire. Why? Because they will be completely empty! Death will have no one in its grip anymore; Hades will have no one in it. They will be utterly finished. Therefore, they will be thrown into the lake of fire. Do you remember how I defined the second death? It means to be cast into the lake of fire forever.

---

[4] An explanation of the terms 'Hell', 'Hades', 'Sheol' and 'Gehenna' is given in Footnote 18 in Chapter 3 of the book "Salvation" by Roger Price.

The next verse is the most tragic of them all: "**And anyone not found written in the book of life was cast into the lake of fire**" (verse 15). This means all the unregenerate ones—all the unbelievers. It is the final judgment, the Last Judgment, that results from the great white throne—the casting into the lake of fire of all unbelievers throughout history. It is surely coming.

The verse says literally, "And if anyone was found not having been written in the book of life..."; and the Greek implies that the condition is fulfilled. The ones judged will be those not found written in the Book of Life. This confirms that those judged at the great white throne will be the unregenerate. D Company consists entirely of unbelievers. This judgment will have no effect upon those included in the first resurrection. Therefore, if you are a believer, do not be afraid of this event!

Conclusion: the Urgency of Trusting in Christ

Many have said that Hell, eternal judgment and the lake of fire are just theories—the product of the apostle Paul's warped imagination. But I want to make this point: Paul actually had relatively little to say about Hell, about judgment, and about the lake of fire. The person who spoke about these things more than anyone else was the Lord Jesus Christ Himself. He was the One who reiterated time and again that judgment was coming upon unbelievers—and not just temporal judgment, but *eternal* judgment. He said again and again that there will be weeping and gnashing of teeth, that there will be everlasting fire, and that those who will not believe on Him stand condemned already.

We certainly should accept and trust the words of the Lord Jesus on this. He is the One who truly knows and understands the full horror of it. He's the *only* one, in fact. If anyone ever says to you, "The lake of fire is just Paul's doctrine," then point out that the Lord Jesus said much more about it than anyone else. That is how important an issue it is.

God does not want any person to end up in the lake of fire forever. That is why Christ died for everyone.[5] He "**desires all men to be saved and to come to the knowledge of the truth**" (see 1 Timothy 2:4). He wants everyone to be saved. The lake of fire is not designed for the human race. Jesus said it is "**prepared for the devil and his angels**" (Matthew 25:41).

---

[5] God sent Jesus Christ to be the saviour of all men (see 1 Timothy 4:10 and 2 Peter 2:1).

God has given the remedy. If you choose to ignore the remedy then it is 'on your own head'. The remedy is simple. The remedy is easy. But it has to be humbly accepted. The tragedy of all tragedies is that, when the devil goes to the lake of fire, he is going to drag many people with him.

Jesus defined how we belong to one of two families on this earth: the family of God or the family of the devil. Each family has a different eternal destiny. Jesus said to some of the Pharisees, **"You are of your father the devil"** (see John 8:44a). After the devil is cast into the lake of fire, every unbeliever who belongs to his family will follow him there.

That is the reality. It is urgent. It is so important. This is going to affect our relatives, our neighbours and our friends. This final judgment, the most awful and terrible judgment, is the judgment that will be meted out at the great white throne.

The alternative to the lake of fire is everlasting life with Christ, who loves us so much! The door is not closed yet. The opportunity to repent and believe on Christ is still available to everyone. Let us repeat the good news once more: **"Believe on the Lord Jesus Christ, and you will be saved"** (Acts 16:31b).

I am going to end with two passages from John chapter 3. Forgive me for my repetition, but the gospel message is urgent.

"For God so loved the world that He gave His only begotten Son, that whoever believes in Him should not perish but have everlasting life. For God did not send His Son into the world to condemn the world, but that the world through Him might be saved. He who believes in Him is not condemned; but he who does not believe is condemned already, because he has not believed in the name of the only begotten Son of God" (John 3:16-18).

"He who believes in the Son has everlasting life; and he who does not believe the Son shall not see life, but the wrath of God abides on him" (John 3:36).

You may feel secure now; but if you have not yet believed on Christ, the wrath of God abides upon you. However, your experience now cannot be compared with the fearful prospect ahead.

May we as Christians, as the Lord's servants, as God's beloved children, decide that this world is not for us. It is perishing; it is dying; it is fading away. May we give ourselves wholly to the Lord—entirely for His service. We have a message for the world and it is such an important one. It requires our dedication: 100 per cent, not 99 per cent. May we ask every day for the Lord to fill us with His power, with His Holy Spirit, that we might be effective witnesses for Him in a world where people are in desperate need, lost and going to a lost eternity.

May God bless you all. Amen.

Appendix
Examples of visible demonstrations that God used in the Old Testament

God gave many visible signs in the Old Testament to illustrate what He was saying through His spokesmen, the prophets. Here, we will consider just four. There are many more.

1. Zechariah

Zechariah chapter 11 describes a number of visible demonstrations that Zechariah gave while he was teaching, to warn the people. "**So I fed the flock for slaughter, in particular the poor of the flock. I took for myself two staffs: the one I called Beauty, and the other I called Bonds; and I fed the flock**" (verse 7). Zechariah thus named two staffs—that is, two long pieces of wood. Perhaps he wrote or engraved the names on their sides. These staffs represented important things to Judah at the time.

"**And I took my staff, Beauty, and cut it in two, that I might break the covenant which I had made with all the peoples**" (verse 10). This first staff was called "Beauty" (or "Pleasantness") and it represented something important. Zechariah got hold of the staff and, in front of the people, he cut it in half—and the people knew what it meant. It was a practical demonstration.

Further on, in verse 14, Zechariah said, "**Then I cut in two my other staff, Bonds, that I might break the brotherhood between Judah and Israel.**" The second staff was called "Bonds" (or "Bound Together"). God was going to break any alliance between Judah and Israel. The staff represented such unity, so Zechariah demonstrated what God was saying by breaking it.

This is just one example. Important teaching was being given by Zechariah; but he also gave a visual representation, to help make his point and to help the people remember the message.

2. Ezekiel

Ezekiel gave many visible demonstrations too. In chapter 5 of the Book of Ezekiel alone we find several. We shall just look at the first two verses.

APPENDIX

In verse 1, the LORD said, **"And you, son of man, take a sharp sword, take it as a barber's razor, and pass it over your head and your beard; then take balances to weigh and divide the hair."** Ezekiel had to shave off all his hair and his beard, in front of all the people—because he was going to demonstrate something. Then he had to weigh the hair and divide it into three equal piles.

"You shall burn with fire one-third in the midst of the city, when the days of the siege are finished..." (verse 2a). Ezekiel thus had to walk into the centre of the city. You can imagine the crowd following him, saying, "Guess what? Ezekiel's just shaved all his hair off!" The people would be fascinated. It was a perfect opportunity for God to give a clear message to them. Ezekiel had to take one-third of his hair and, at an appointed time, in the midst of the city, set fire to it. **"...Then you shall take one-third and strike around it with the sword, and one-third you shall scatter in the wind: I will draw out a sword after them"** (verse 2b).

What did this represent? Ezekiel's hair represented the people of the city. God was saying that a third were going to die as a result of pestilence and famine within the city, another third were going to die by the sword, and the other third were going to be scattered (see verse 12).

It was a warning. God's message behind it was, "Repent, or else this is going to happen to you!" And if you read the rest of the chapter, that is what Ezekiel went on to explain. The object lesson came first; then the explanation and warning came directly after.

3. Jeremiah and Hananiah

In Jeremiah chapter 28 we find Jeremiah speaking to the priests and people in the Temple in Jerusalem, bearing a yoke on his neck (see verses 5, 10). God had told him previously to make bonds and yokes as a visual aid to accompany his message (Jeremiah 27:2). The yoke Jeremiah bore probably consisted of a wooden beam across the shoulders. As you can imagine, such a sight would collect a crowd, and it provided a ready-made congregation! Jeremiah was faithful. He always preached God's messages. But why was he doing this? What was he saying? He was saying, "You people think you're free; but you're soon going to be shackled to Nebuchadnezzar, King of Babylon! He's going to come and take the city!"

However, in Jeremiah chapter 28 we also find a *false* prophet called Hananiah. **"Then Hananiah the prophet took the yoke off the prophet Jeremiah's neck and broke it. And Hananiah spoke in the presence of all the people, saying, "Thus says the Lord, 'Even so I will break the** yoke of Nebuchadnezzar king of Babylon from the neck of all nations within the space of two full years.' " And the prophet Jeremiah went his way**" (verses 10-11). What was Hananiah saying? He was effectively saying, "You're talking rubbish, Jeremiah! It is not going to happen! Nebuchadnezzar will be defeated within two years." Hananiah was a false, lying prophet. However, all the people, of course, chose to believe him. People usually go after good news. But his message was not true.

"**Then the word of the LORD came to Jeremiah, after Hananiah the prophet had broken the yoke from the neck of the prophet Jeremiah, saying, "Go and tell Hananiah, saying, 'Thus says the LORD: "You have broken the yokes of wood, but you have made in their place yokes of iron" ' "**" (verses 12-13). God was saying, "You won't be able to break those yokes, Hananiah!"

"**' 'For thus says the LORD of hosts, the God of Israel: "I have put a yoke of iron on the neck of all these nations, that they may serve Nebuchadnezzar king of Babylon; and they shall serve him. I have given him the beasts of the field also." ' " Then the prophet Jeremiah said to Hananiah the prophet, "Hear now, Hananiah, the LORD has not sent you, but you make this people trust in a lie. Therefore thus says the LORD: 'Behold, I will cast you from the face of the earth. This year you shall die, because you have taught rebellion against the LORD' "** (verses 14-16).

The word of the Lord came to pass. "**So Hananiah the prophet died the same year in the seventh month**" (verse 17).

4. Jeremiah and Seraiah

Our final example is also in the Book of Jeremiah, in chapter 51. "**So Jeremiah wrote in a book all the evil that would come upon Babylon, all these words that are written against Babylon. And Jeremiah said to Seraiah, "When you arrive in Babylon and see it, and read all these words, then you shall say, 'O LORD, You have spoken against this place to cut it off, so that none shall remain in it, neither man nor beast, but it shall be desolate for ever.' Now it shall be, when you have finished reading this book, that you shall tie a stone to it and throw it out into the Euphrates. Then you shall say, 'Thus Babylon shall sink and not rise from the catastrophe that I will bring upon her. And they shall be weary' " "** (verses 60-64a).

Seraiah was a Judean prince who served as quartermaster. He went with King Zedekiah to Babylon during the fourth year of the king's reign

APPENDIX

(Jeremiah 51:59). Jeremiah told him to go into Babylon and read out what he had written about Babylon in a book (possibly a scroll)—probably the whole of Jeremiah chapters 50 and 51. Then Seraiah had to tie a stone to it and hurl it out into the River Euphrates, which ran right through Babylon. As the people watched it go bubbling down, never to be seen again, Seraiah would say, "That's exactly what's going to happen to this city." That was the object lesson.

BIBLIOGRAPHY

The following books were used as references during compilation of these studies in written form:

'The Zondervan Pictorial Encyclopedia of the Bible' (in 5 volumes), General Editor M.C. Tenney (Zondervan, 1980).

'The NKJV Greek English Interlinear New Testament' (Thomas Nelson Publishers, USA, 1994).

'Strong's Exhaustive Concordance' (Baker Book House, USA, 1981).

'New American Standard Exhaustive Concordance' (Holman, USA, 1981).

'The History of the World in Christian Perspective', L. Hicks—Editor (A Beka Book Publications, USA, 1990).

'World History and Cultures—in Christian Perspective', George T. Thompson, Laurel Elizabeth Hicks, assisted by Michael R. Lowman (A Beka Book Publications, USA, 1982).

'Israel and the Nations', F.F. Bruce, revised by D.F. Payne (Paternoster Press, 1997).

'The Five Books of Moses' (The Schocken Bible: Volume I), translated by Everett Fox (Schocken Books Inc., USA, 1995).

'The Complete Jewish Bible', translated by David H. Stern (Jewish New Testament Publications, Inc., USA, 1998).

'The Luck of Nineveh', Arnold C. Brackman (Eyre Methuen Ltd., UK, 1980).

'Cleopatra—From History to Legend', Edith Flamarion (Thames and Hudson, New Horizons series, 1997).

'Jonah: Bible Study Commentary', John H. Walton (Lamplighter Books, Zondervan Publishing House, USA, 1982).

'That Incredible Book... The Bible', Dr. Clifford A. Wilson (Pacific Christian Ministries, Australia, 1993).

'The Bible was Right After All', Dr. Clifford A. Wilson (Pacific Christian Ministries, Australia, 1993).

Other Books by Roger Price (in print)

'*Salvation*', Basic Bible Studies Course, Series 1
'*In the Beginning*'
(both available from CCF Tapes).

'*Explaining What Happens After Death*' (Sovereign World).

LIST OF TAPES

BIBLE STUDY TAPES BY ROGER PRICE

All the studies in the Basic Bible Studies course, as well as many others, can be obtained on audio cassette from:

CCF Tapes,
30 Crescent Road,
Bognor Regis,
W. Sussex,
PO21 1QG,
England.

Please send for a free catalogue.

BASIC BIBLE STUDIES course

Series 1 - SALVATION

BBS 1. Introduction (to the whole course)
BBS 2. The Barrier
BBS 3. The Virgin Birth
BBS 4. Redemption
BBS 5. Atonement and Expiation
BBS 6. Why be born again?
BBS 7. Propitiation
BBS 8. The Unforgivable Sin
BBS 9-11. Eternal Security (Parts 1-3)
BBS 12. 1 John 1v9
BBS 13. Romans 8v28
BBS 14. The Rich Young Ruler

Series 2 - JUDGMENTS

Grace before Judgment
BBS 15. Jesus the Judge
BBS 16. The Age of Methuselah
BBS 17. Jonah

The Judgment of Satan
BBS 18. The Three Falls

The Judgment of Jesus
BBS 19. Crooked Counsel
BBS 20. When Calvary Blossomed

The Judgment of Believers
BBS 21. Self-Judgment or Chastening?
BBS 22. The Reasons for Discipline

The Judgment of Believers' Works
BBS 23. Palaces or Mud Huts?

Judgment of Israel and the Nations
BBS 24. The Five Cycles of Discipline
BBS 25. Horns and Carpenters
BBS 26. The Baptism of Fire
BBS 27. The Wise and Foolish Virgins

Judgment of Unbelievers
BBS 28. The Great White Throne

Series 3 - FULFILLED PROPHECY

BBS 29. The Critics' Dilemma
BBS 30. Faith and Hope
BBS 31. False Prophecy
BBS 32. Literal or Not?
BBS 33-34. Specific Fulfilments of
          Prophecy (Parts 1-2)
BBS 35-36. The Fall of Babylon
          (Parts 1-2)
BBS 37. The Four Monsters of Daniel
BBS 38. The Prophecy of Noah
BBS 39. The Run-up to The Messiah
BBS 40. The Pedigree of The Messiah
BBS 41. Signs of The Messiah
BBS 42. The Suffering Servant

Series 4 - UNFULFILLED PROPHECY

BBS 43. The Tower of Babel
BBS 44. The Abrahamic Covenant
BBS 45. Does Israel Have a Future?
BBS 46. What really happened at
        Pentecost
BBS 47. The Mystery of The Church
BBS 48. Will the Church Go Through
        the Tribulation?
BBS 49. Daniel's Seventy Weeks
BBS 50. The Rapture of the Church
BBS 51. The Monster Stirs
BBS 52. Seals, Trumpets and Vials
BBS 53. The Beast
BBS 54. The Satanic Trinity
BBS 55. The Woman Clothed With
      the Sun

LIST OF TAPES

BBS 56. Evangelism in The Tribulation
BBS 57. The Run-up to Armageddon
BBS 58. The Second Advent of
    Jesus Christ
BBS 59. Does Russia Have a Future?
BBS 60-61. The Millennium (Parts 1 & 2)
BBS 62. The Eternal State
BBS 63. The Fulfilment of God's Plan

Series 5 - THE CHARACTER OF GOD

BBS 64. Does God Exist?
BBS 65. God - Who is He?
BBS 66-68. The Trinity (Parts 1-3)
BBS 69. God's Sovereignty
BBS 70. God's Holiness
BBS 71. God's Omniscience
BBS 72. God's Omnipotence
BBS 73. God's Omnipresence
BBS 74. God is Eternal
BBS 75. God is Love
BBS 76. God Never Changes
BBS 77. God - Faithful and True

Series 6 - THE WORD OF GOD

BBS 78. What We Believe about the Bible
BBS 79. Every Word that Proceeds from
    the Mouth of God
BBS 80. Men and Texts
BBS 81. The Canon of Scripture
BBS 82. Problem Passages
BBS 83. How to Study the Bible Yourself

BBS 84-86. Dispensations (Parts 1-3)
(N.B. BBS 87-91 were not recorded.)

Series 7 - ESSENTIALS FOR
    GROWTH

The Baptism of the Holy Spirit
BBS 92. Principles outlined
BBS 93. Acts Onwards

The Gifts of the Holy Spirit
BBS 94-95. Moving in the Gifts of the Spirit
    (Parts 1-2)
BBS 96. Prophecy: God's Word or Mine?

Spiritual Breathing
BBS 97. The Mechanics of Prayer
BBS 98. Prayers of Faith

Spiritual Nourishment
BBS 99. Eating the Word
    (and Christian Meditation)

Spiritual Exercise
BBS 100. Walking in the Spirit
BBS 101. Forgiveness
BBS 102. Functioning in the Church
    (including the '37 Things')

Applying the Blood
BBS 103. Applying the Blood
BBS 104. Fasting

SPECIAL TOPIC STUDIES

These tapes are designed to complement the Basic Bible Studies course and provide extra material on many points. Whilst not actually forming part of the basic series, some nevertheless contain revelations of fundamental truths which affect every area of our lives.

STS 1-2. Divorce (and Remarriage)

STS 3-6. Respect and Authority;
    Anarchy and Rebellion

STS 7-10. *The Millennial Issue*
    Parts 1-2 - The Three Main Views
    Parts 3-4 - The Premillennial View

STS 11-15. *Victorious Christian Living*
    Part 1 - The Glorified Man
    Part 2 - The Devil Under Our Feet
    Part 3 - Victory Over Demons
    Part 4 - Pulling Down the
        Strongholds
    Part 5 - Operation Footstool

STS 16-17. The Natural Family
STS 18-19. The Spiritual Family
STS 20. Single Status
STS 21-22. Can a Christian Have a Demon?

STS 23-27. *The Blood of the New Covenant*
    Part 1 - The Life is in the Blood
    Part 2 - A God of Covenants
    Part 3 - The Torn Veil
    Part 4 - The New Covenant
    Part 5 - The Trail of His Blood

STS 28-30. Should Women Wear Hats
    in Church?

The Kingdom of God
STS 31-32. The Kingdom of God
STS 33. Pressing into the Kingdom

LIST OF TAPES

STS 34-37. *King Jesus*
    Part 1 - Our God Reigns
    Part 2 - Born to be King
    Part 3 - The Enthronement of Jesus
    Part 4 - King for Ever

STS 38. Who Were the Wise Men?
STS 39. What Happens When a Persons Dies?
STS 40. The Rights of the Firstborn

STS 41-45. Chronology
(4 talks on 5 C90 tapes, including 9 charts)

STS 46-47. Baptism
STS 48. Who Are We in Christ?
STS 49-50. The Power of God Within Us
STS 51-52. Thou Shalt Not steal
STS 53. Growing Up in God
STS 54-55. Fatalism
STS 56-57. The Anatomy of Chaos
STS 58-59. Capital Punishment

STS 60-62. *The Doctrine of War*
    Part 1 - The Fall is Real
    Part 2 - Was Jesus a Pacifist?
    Part 3 - The Rules of Warfare

STS 63-66. *Dominion*
    Part 1 - God's Call for Dominion
    Part 2 - The Grapes of Eschol
    Part 3 - Death to the Canaanites
    Part 4 - The Valley of Achor

STS 67-69. *'Singles Conference' Studies*
    Part 1 - God's Purpose for Your Life
    Part 2 - God's Partner for Your Life
    Part 3 - Wisdom - The Perfect Partner For Any Life

STS 70. Father Loves You
STS 71. The Cup of Jesus
STS 72. Stand Fast in the Liberty

STS 73-74. *'Liberty Conference' Studies*
    Part 1 - Liberty for God's Chosen Generation
    Part 2 - The Law of Liberty

STS 75-78. *Sonship*
    Part 1 - The Family of God
    Part 2 - Like Father, Like Son
    Part 3 - Preparing God's Sons
    Part 4 - The Royal Inheritance

STS 79. The Fragrance of Jesus
STS 80. Moving on With God

STS 81-82. *'Religion or Reality?' Conference*
    Part 1 - Beware Religion
    Part 2 - Facing up to Reality

STS 83. The Best Years of Your Life (Retirement)
STS 84. Sexuality (for adults only!)
STS 85. The Seal of God

STS 86-88. *The Temple*
    Part 1 - God With Us
    Part 2 - Jesus Christ: The Real Temple
    Part 3 - A Temple of Living Stones

STS 89-90. The Giants of Genesis 6 (and Vegetarianism)
STS 91-92. The Truth About Israel
STS 93. The Sin of Fear and Worry
STS 94-95. Guidance
STS 96-97. Alive in Christ

STS 98-99. *Numerology*
    Part 1 - Numbers in the Bible
    Part 2 - Spiritual Arithmetic

STS 100. Poison in Your Mouth (The Tongue)

STS 101-105. *The Healthy Christian*
    Part 1 - The Healthy Christian
    Part 2 - The Healthy Body
    Part 3 - The Healthy Spirit
    Part 4 - The Healthy Soul
    Part 5 - The Healthy Conscience

STS 106-107. *Hail to the Coming King*
    Part 1 - The Approaching Day
    Part 2 - The Bride of Christ

STS 108-109. *The Highway of Holiness*
    Part 1 - Unoccupied Highways
    Part 2 - Be Ye Perfect

STS 110. God's Faithfulness to Israel
STS 111-112. Spiritual Warfare
STS 113. Worship
STS 114. The Body of Christ
STS 115. Beacons or Smudgepots?
STS 116. Chewing the Cud
STS 117. The Physical God
STS 118. The Fatherhood of God
STS 119. Open Channels for God
STS 120. Spiritual Inertia

STS 121-123. *A Fresh Look at Salvation*
    Part 1 - Why We Need Salvation
    Part 2 - Jesus, the Pioneer of our Salvation
    Part 3 - Jesus, the answer

STS 124-125. *Studies in Hebrews 6:1*
    Part 1 - The Resurrection of the Dead
    Part 2 - Eternal Judgment

STS 126. Creation vs Evolution

LIST OF TAPES

STS 127. Training the Heart
STS 128. Steps towards Maturity
STS 129. Roger's Testimony
STS 130. The Second World War
STS 131-134. *How to Believe What You Believe*
    Part 1 - The Problem
    Part 2 - Getting into the Word
    Part 3 - Living in the Word
    Part 4 - Believing God Every Day
STS 135-136. *Hearing and Understanding God's Word*
    Part 1 - Hearing and Understanding It
    Part 2 - How to be Open to It

STS 137. Angels
STS 138. No Crying Allowed
STS 139. Israel and the Church
STS 140. Depression
STS 141. Christian Maturity
STS 142. Feed My Sheep
STS 143. Conditions of Revival
STS 144-145. I Will Build My Church
STS 146-147. Humble Yourselves
STS 148. Inequality
STS 149. Forgiveness

FELLOWSHIP LIFE STUDIES

This course covers the most important aspects of fellowship life. Roger establishes the aims and develops them before covering the vital principles of authority and order. Body Ministry, how to deal with the unruly and how to look after the poor and needy are among the most important concepts dealt with.

FLS 1. Fellowship (Koinonia)
FLS 2. Commune or Community?
FLS 3. The Poor You Have Always With You
FLS 4. The Real Poor
FLS 5. Aims and Vision
FLS 6. Praise and Thanksgiving
FLS 7. Making Melody in Your Heart
FLS 8. The Acid Test of Our Love
FLS 9-10. Body Ministry (Parts 1 and 2)
FLS 11. One Another
FLS 12. Local Area Groups

FLS 13. Evangelism
FLS 14. Doing Good in the World
FLS 15. Dwelling Together in Peace
FLS 16. Eldership
FLS 17. Submission
FLS 18. Membership and Troublemakers
FLS 19. Leadership (and Covering)
FLS 20. Deacons
FLS 21. Other Ministries
FLS 22-23. Giving (Parts 1 and 2)
FLS 24. Times of Testing

Leadership Training Course

TC 1. Part 1 - The Essentials of Leadership
TC 2. Part 2 - The Four Dimensions of Leadership
TC 3. Part 3 - Responsibilities to the Flock
TC 4. Part 4 - Living Sacrifices

Eldership Training Course

TC 5. Part 1 - The Structure of Authority
TC 6. Part 2 - The Qualities of an Elder
TC 7. Part 3 - Preach the Word
TC 8. Part 4 - Perfecting the Saints